The W

MW00882270

THE WALK APPLIED:
Living the New Creation Life as a Citizen of God's Kingdom in a Secular World

Copyright © 2018
By Rev. Dr. N. Patrick Marica
All rights reserved
ISBN: 978-1797471907

www.godlytraining.org
gtm@godlytraining.org

FOCUS FORWARD
PUBLISHING

i

The Walk Applied

THE WALK APPLIED:
Living the New Creation Life as a Citizen of God's Kingdom in a Secular World

www.godlytraining.org
gtm@godlytraining.org

The Walk Applied

The Walk Applied

TABLE OF CONTENTS

The Walk Applied

PREFACE

"…If it's the last thing I do on earth, I'm going to find out why
God put me here in the first place!"
Paul-Henri Thiry

"…I keep asking that the God of our Lord Jesus Christ,
the glorious Father, may give you the
Spirit of wisdom and revelation,
so that you may know him better…" (Eph 1:17)

The church accepts change slowly – almost glacially if you will.
This reticence to change is a good thing, especially when it comes
to the Word of God. We want to be sure that we "divide" the Word
properly in "Spirit and in Truth." When a new concept appears in
the Christian ecosystem, it must be examined thoroughly. Those
who introduce a new take on God's word must expect that it will be
put under the Biblical microscope so that believers can be sure that
it is congruent with the absolute truth of God's word.

The new and exciting approach of "The Walk Applied" brings to
the Christian milieu a perspective that is rarely addressed: What
does it mean to be a "Spiritual Being" operating in the Natural?
What does it mean for me to be a "new creation in Christ"? What's
my real identity as a Christian? I'm going to make an outrageous
claim – that the Walk Applied is the "Real Deal" – a heady claim,
that! Egotistical and conceited? No, not at all. It is just that the Walk
Applied elucidates numerous topics related to the Christian Identity
in a way the vast majority of Christians have never heard before. Is
it rock-solid biblical? I say emphatically: "YES!"

The Walk Applied

The time for a truly unique and different rock solid biblical approach is certainly here. We live in urgent times that call for urgent measures that are totally founded in the absolute truth of God's word. Every year, thousands upon thousands leave God's churches for various reasons.

The need for renewal and revival is well beyond desperation. We must respond. God commands us to. Jesus commissioned us to do it. People are lost and dying and going to hell for an eternity. It is nowhere near enough anymore to have people mumble the answer to 3 questions and give them a pat on the head and tell them to find a church and read their Bible and pray. Jesus discipled 11 men into a truly authentic, life-changing relationship with Him, "teaching them to obey everything I have commanded you". That is what we are called to do. It has to be the "real deal" or else we've just wasted our time and theirs.

I do not wish to belabor further the billions of gallons of ink and the countless trees that have been spent bemoaning the state of the church today. The good news is that revival is taking place around the world. God's word is working as always when people's hearts are willing to be opened to the sweet call of our Heavenly Father.

There is surely little doubt that the Church is under merciless attack. There are many who question the ability of the church to survive the onslaught coming from so many different quarters. The question is not if the church will survive. It is Jesus' church, not ours, and "... greater is He that is in me than he that is in the world." The real question is: How many Christians will survive the tsunami of secularism and humanism? We are called by God to be making disciples, yet, by virtually all accounts, more and more in our ever-increasing secular society are seeing the church as irrelevant. According to Barna, some 82% of Americans claim they are Christian, but only one-third of that 82% believe that Satan is a real being. Which Bible are they reading – when they read it at all?

The Walk Applied

In his book, *Why Christian Kids Leave the Faith*, Tom Bissett gives four reasons why the church isn't working that I find most compelling. Bisset believes that people have troubling, unanswered questions about their faith. Many think the Gospel just isn't answering these tough questions of life. In other words, their Christian "faith" just isn't delivering. The peace, joy, meaning and happiness that Christian faith has promised – well, where is it? What happened? Bisset points out that if their faith in this "God thing" isn't working, then the otherworldly things in their lives are becoming more important than their faith. People slowly drift away, preoccupied with business, pleasure, material ambitions, personal problems or other hard realities that are simply part of living. After all, our worldly pleasure and pursuits seem like they bring us happiness, don't they? At least, they work some of the time! Bisset tells us that if a person's faith isn't working and they can't learn to trust it, then they can never actually own it. These people can't bring themselves to trust God! How can someone make truly authentic faith choices in their lives, if they don't trust in the Heavenly Father?

To reiterate, the modern Church in the West is experiencing great tumult. The various Christian denominations argue over doctrine, which Bible to use, baptism, and any number of other ecumenical battlegrounds. The claim from here is that fewer and fewer so-called Christians are truly being discipled or mentored into a true, living, breathing walk with Jesus Christ. A walk that truly delivers as advertised. Walk into almost any Christian bookstore or peruse a Christian bookstore site. Hundreds of books on Discipleship line the bookshelves, but the vast majority repeat the same line over and over: Here's what you DO. Isaiah's stern warning haunts us:

"So then, the word of the LORD to them will become: Do this, do that, a rule for this, a rule for that; a little here, a little there—so that as they go they will fall backward; they will be injured and snared and captured...." (Isaiah 28:13)

The Walk Applied

Rarely do we find an exposition on how this "Jesus thing" operates from the "top down." What's this "sonship" thing all about? What does it mean to be adopted? What does it mean to be a citizen of the Kingdom? We constantly talk about what we do to approach Jesus from the "ground up." Without a solid understanding of how the Kingdom works - a concept which is explained in great detail in both Testaments as we shall see - how can we ever truly understand how to approach Jesus in the way that the Father intended?

One of the themes of this volume is that that a significant percentage believe wrong things about His Kingdom and how it operates in the natural. That said, there are many in the pews who do believe in Jesus and the Gospel He espoused. Yet, while numerous blessed and profound sermons that exhibit awesome exegesis of His Word, the pure "spiritual stuff" is hitting a virtually impenetrable wall of idolatry, doctrinal confusion, and, well, downright disbelief. The preaching of God's Word in many cases falls to the floor, only to be blown away like chaff in many cases. God's Word does not return void, of course, for "those who have ears to hear." Tragically, many are not receiving His Word because they do not have "ears to hear". The result? Christians who aren't more like Jesus by the time they hit Olive Garden for lunch. Christians who are more confused, discouraged and frustrated at 12:30 than at 10:15. Christians who energetically proclaim "...the sermon was awesome!" but cannot remember a single line, much less the title. Christians who express frustration over the Old Testament because "it doesn't tell me what to do."

THE "REAL DEAL"

I speak with Christians all the time who have grown disillusioned and disconnected. They're tired of "Church as usual"! Time and time again they tell me they want the "REAL DEAL." Indeed, there is a growing chorus of voices – especially among the young: "there's gotta to be a better way!" The modern Christian milieu has become a raucous cacophony of competing theories, suggestions,

The Walk Applied

confusing doctrines, numerous Christian ideologies and countless screaming voices that express a profound and sad dissatisfaction. There has to be a better way.

The sensible and different voice of "the Walk Applied" has been written to describe that better way. Indeed, it will be all too tempting to ignore or discard what follows and utter under your breath. "I've heard it all before" or "There's nothing new under the sun" or "I've never even heard of this guy before" or perhaps "how could this possibly be any different?" I am going to ask you to give it one more shot. And yes, I promise you, it is profoundly different.

Welcome to the "Real Deal."

Note: In a book like this, some repetition is unavoidable. Various passages of scripture have applicability in more than one place, so I repeat them as needed. Also, there are certain sections of text that make reading the book much easier if repeated as needed. The reader will also notice there are copious scripture references. That is by design. Because many of the themes addressed in the book are new and different, it seems prudent to present as much scripture as possible. To my knowledge, many of the concepts and ideas presented herein are original with this book. I would appreciate hearing from those who have written along the same lines.

The Walk Applied

ABOUT THE AUTHOR

God called me into His service in 1993 – about 18 months after I was saved. It started simply enough. There we were: 5 men meeting in an accountability group. I had no clue what was to come.

Over the past 25 years, I have had the enormous honor and privilege of ministering successfully to well over 100 hurting Christian men and couples. God has led me down an amazing path that I could not have imagined all those years ago.

I was blessed to be able to receive my MA in Marriage and Family Therapy from Liberty University in 2011. I was awarded my D.Min. in 2018. I have been the Director of Godly Training Ministries since 1993.

Please feel free to contact me at www.godlytraining.org or email me at gtm@godlytraining.org

DEDICATION

It is my sincere prayer that this book leads you into the scriptures like a good Berean from the Book of Acts. I pray that this book blesses you with a better understanding of God's Spiritual Kingdom and how He designed it to work here in the natural realm. I pray further that what I written revolutionizes your walk with Jesus Christ and brings you into an amazing intimacy with Jesus that you never dared imagine that you might have.

This book is dedicated to my family, those who God has sent to me to help, restore, and invest in, and the many Godly teachers that God has sent me.

xiii

The Walk Applied

CHAPTER 1:
THE FALL & THE FLESH

The Walk Applied

The Walk Applied

CHAPTER 1
THE FALL & THE FLESH
WHY THE BRIDE OF CHRIST?

Jesus desires His bride (His church) to share an eternal and intimate relationship with Him (Isa 62:5, Rev 19:7-9, Rev 21:2). Scripture doesn't tell us why or how the notion of the bride came about, but it does tell us that Jesus will indeed rejoice over His church (those who are saved constitute His church) as His bride. Scripture reveals that there are two fundamental conditions that the bride must meet: The bride must be declared perfectly righteous, and the bride must be faithful.

When we experience salvation whereby we come to know and accept Jesus as our Lord and Savior, we are then declared perfect and righteous. Matthew 5:48 says *"Be perfect as your Father in Heaven is perfect"*. To be saved means that righteousness is imputed to us and we are judged to be perfect. Thus, the first of the two conditions are met via salvation.

The second condition for the bride is faithfulness. Scripture confirms in several places that the bride must be faithful (Ps 37:28; Ps 97:10; Pro 2:8). Isaiah 1:26 says: *"I will restore your judges as in days of old, your counselors as at the beginning. Afterward, you will be called the City of Righteousness, the Faithful City."* Psalm 101:6 tells us *"...My eyes will be on the faithful in the land, that they may dwell with me; he whose walk is blameless will minister to me."*

To demonstrate faithfulness, however, is not nearly as straightforward as salvation. However, faithfulness is not imputed into us; faithfulness must be demonstrated:

"but the one who stands firm to the end will be saved" (Matt 24:13)

3

The Walk Applied

"You will be hated by everyone because of me, but the one who stands firm to the end will be saved." (Matt 10:22)

In other words, those who are faithful to the end are the ones who are saved. Now, in order for the bride to prove faithful, you must have an environment for the bride to prove to be faithful. In other words, there must be an environment that allows for free will and choice. There has to be a place and time to choose between God and something else. To demonstrate faithfulness, God must be chosen from at least one other alternative.

FREE WILL & GOD'S SOVEREIGNTY

God granted us a free will so we could choose who our spiritual authority will be. God is Love. Love never demands; love offers you a choice. If you tragically choose to come under the power and control the "prince of this world" (John 12:31), a hellish eternity ultimately awaits you. Choose to sincerely submit God's authority and heaven is yours as is the privilege of being Jesus' bride. We are free to turn our back and walk away from God if we so choose. Free will and the seductive power of choice presents an overwhelming urge to know what we do not know. Choice manifests a most alluring option to have what we do not: "...*the woman saw that the fruit... was desirable for gaining wisdom* (Gen 3:6)".

THE FALL

We need to understand the reason why the Fall was necessary and why God allowed it. Genesis 3:4 and 3:22 tell us that Adam and Eve did not know the difference between good and evil:

"For God knows that when you eat from it your eyes will be opened, and you will be like God, knowing good and evil." (Gen 3:4)

4

The Walk Applied

"And the Lord God said, "The man has now become like one of us, knowing good and evil." (Gen 3:22)

We might also infer that Adam and Eve did not know what death was. Think about it: Lucifer, the angels, and Adam and Eve all lived in God's presence. How would they have known what death and evil was? God had told them what death and evil were, but how could they have appreciated it? Eve's response to the serpent's prompt indicates that they had been told they would die. Yet, they chose to rebel against Godly authority. Adam and Eve, Lucifer, and 1/3 of the angels chose to rebel, even though they were in the direct presence of God. How could they possibly do that?

Free will means that we are free to choose. To have the capacity to choose God and deny Satan (or vice versa), Adam, Eve, and the rest of humanity needs to have a legitimate choice made available. God needed to create an environment such that a legitimate opportunity to choose between God and Satan in order to allow for us to be able to choose between God and Satan. We are allowed the choice to accept or deny God as sovereign authority. God, in His glorious wisdom, never forces Himself upon us. On the one hand, we can believe in God and submit to Godly authority out of love. On the other hand, we can come under Satan's power and control. To choose Satanic power and control is rebellion against God. There is no gray area. We can either choose the sovereignty of God or the "Prince of this World." Note that God is always in total and complete command of all things. God has merely allowed Satan temporary power over the planet.

Scripture tells us that God is Love. God would never dictate to us that we must love Him - we must be allowed to make that choice. In order to be able to truly choose to submit to Godly authority, we need to know what it is like to exist outside of Godly authority. We must understand the difference between good and evil. To understand good, we must understand evil. We need to have

The Walk Applied

experiential knowledge of evil. Since God is the sole origin of anything that is good or worthwhile, there are horrific consequences for not choosing to submit to God's loving authority.

It had to be demonstrated that God was and is our only hope. God's requires that we be faithful to Him and Him alone; there cannot and is not be another besides Him. To reiterate: God, in His unlimited wisdom, allows us to experience evil because we need to have experiential knowledge of evil. We need to experience evil, so we understand what God protects us from.

We recall that *"war broke out in Heaven"* (Rev 12:7). Lucifer, a third of the angels, and Adam and Eve all chose to come out of Godly authority, even though they were in the direct presence of a sovereign God. God will not tolerate rebellion or disobedience in His Heaven, unless He allows it. (Job indicates that Satan is allowed to be in the presence of the throne). Otherwise, sin is not allowed in Heaven.

Let us pause for a moment to clarify as needed. The suggestion that we can choose to come out of Godly authority and consequently come under satanic authority can be troublesome. For some, the notion can connote that Satan has authority where God does not (thus implying that God is somehow not sovereign). While this concept will be explored more fully later, perhaps it's better to see it as "the intermediate rule of Satan." God is certainly always in complete control, and He is absolutely sovereign. However, the Bible tells us no less than three times specifically that Satan is "…the Prince of this world." If authority were not an either/or proposition, then we would not have to be redeemed, or we would be without hope. (We will examine the authority/submission mechanism in much greater detail later.) To put it another way, it is imperative that we must *be like God, knowing good and evil."* (Gen 3:5) Indeed, Satan's statement was, in fact, true: "*For God knows that when you eat of it, your eyes will be opened, and you will be*

6

The Walk Applied

like God, knowing good and evil." (Gen 3:5) Genesis 3:22 says: *"the LORD God said, "The man has now become like one of us, knowing [the difference between] good and evil."* Certainly, this outcome was foreseen by God. Lucifer, Adam and Eve, as well as one-third of the angels did not have experiential knowledge of evil.

THE ANGELS

The angels, since they were also in the perfect presence of God, knew nothing of evil and death. Like Adam and Eve, and us, they had to be shown what death and evil were. Dr. Timothy Johnson was known to many television viewers as the longtime Chief Medical Correspondent for ABC News. He is also an ordained pastor, and the author of *"Finding God in the Questions: A Personal Journey"*. He once opined that he thought "we are a demonstration project for the angels" when asked why God created us. This sentiment makes a lot of sense, especially when you consider the scriptures given below. These passages support Dr. Johnson's contention:

"For it seems to me that God has put us apostles on display at the end of the procession, like those condemned to die in the arena. We have been made a spectacle to the whole universe, to angels as well as to human beings." (1 Cor 4:9)

"A man ought not to cover his head, since he is the image and glory of God; but woman is the glory of man. For man did not come from woman, but woman from man; neither was man created for woman, but woman for man. It is for this reason that a woman ought to have authority over her own head, because of the angels." (1 Cor 11:7-12)

"Therefore, since we are surrounded by such a great cloud of witnesses, let us throw off everything that hinders and the sin that so easily entangles. And let us run with perseverance the race

7

The Walk Applied

marked out for us, fixing our eyes on Jesus, the pioneer and perfecter of faith. For the joy set before him he endured the cross, scorning its shame, and sat down at the right hand of the throne of God. Consider him who endured such opposition from sinners, so that you will not grow weary and lose heart."
(Heb 12:1-3)

AUTHORITY VS. POWER

The fundamental battle is all about whose authority you choose to come under. We can decide to come under God's sovereign authority, or we can choose to come under Satan's power and control (again, the Bible mentions that Satan is the prince of this world in 3 separate passages). The implication of who you choose to submit to has profound consequences. To be under God's sovereign authority will bring peace, love, hope, blessing and clarity. To be under Satan's power and control will bring chaos, confusion, depression, and hopelessness.

Perhaps a better way to look at this distinction between Satan and God would be to express it as the difference between authority and power. The word "authority" comes from the Latin word "augere"-for "author", which means to "create the conditions for growth". When we attach the suffix "-ity" (meaning 'the ongoing state of"), we see that the word authority means the continual state of creating the conditions for growth.

It is most profound to realize that one of the continuing commands given in the Bible is to go forth and bear fruit for the Kingdom. Without the bearing of fruit from growth, there is only stagnation and death. According to Dictionary.com, one of the definitions of the "power" is "the possession of control or command over others."

The crucial difference here in these concepts is that authority comes about by choice of those who elect to submit; control via power

8

The Walk Applied

comes about by manipulation, fear, coercion or intimidation, among others. God asks us to submit to Him out of love; Satan tries to exert power and control. For example, Satan manipulated Adam and Eve in the garden. Yes, both succumbed to manipulative temptation, and both fell under the power (read: command and control) of Satan, thus necessitating the need for redemption. The expression of command and control (power) ultimately results in stagnation and death.

It is also important to understand that our existence in the natural cannot and will not work. Fundamentally, what God is showing us is that, unless we willingly and lovingly submit to his authority, this existence is simply not tenable. In God's great wisdom, He understood that it must be demonstrated and proved that it is only through Him that we can have peace. Any other way simply cannot and will not work. It is only by submission to God's authority, his grace and his goodness, that we can exist in peace.

CONSEQUENCES OF THE FALL

When Adam and Eve made their fatal choice to fall, we saw profound consequences to their choices:

- Death as a spiritual being (Gen 2:17)
- Banishment from the garden (Gen 3:22-23)
- They now knew the difference between good and evil
        (Gen 3:5; Gen 3:22)
- Fear, shame, and guilt made them afraid (Gen 3:8)
- Blame also entered the picture (Gen 3:12-13)
- They also realized that they were naked.(Gen 3:7)
- They now saw themselves negatively, as opposed to positively
        (Gen 2:25; Gen 3:7)
- They covered themselves because of shame and guilt (Gen 3:7)
- Both feared being rejected by the other because of judgment
        (Gen 3:7)

9

The Walk Applied

So, for the first time we see judgment: the action of putting ourselves in spiritual authority over another. If there was no fear of judgement then there would be no need for covering. Adam and Eve now had a radically different belief system. Their behavior after the fall was profoundly different than it was before the fall. They now saw the world significantly differently than they did before, and consequently, they acted quite differently.

THE FOUNDATIONAL LAYER
OF THE SINFUL FLESH

Consider the state of mind of Adam & Eve when they were exiled from the garden. The garden was the only home they had ever known; every need had been fully supplied. Now, they would have to fend for themselves. The onrush of emotions must have been overwhelming. The Genesis account has a distinct feel to it in that the execution of God's judgment was swift. It seems highly likely that within a matter of minutes what was once their home was now forever denied them. Besides the guilt, the regret, and the shame, there must have been an ominous dread: who will take care of us? We can guess that security – or the lack of it – was a primary consideration in their makeup, as it is in ours. These elements of guilt, shame, and security bring us to the foundational layer of the dynamic of the sinful, natural flesh. In a sensational sermon delivered by Tim Keller of Redeemer Presbyterian Church of New York, he expounds upon the relationship of guilt, shame, and the fall:

"Genesis tells us we were created in the image of God. We know we fell. We know deep inside that there is something wrong with us. Guilt describes our conviction that we know we did the wrong thing. We know we owe Him because of what we did. Guilt is specific – we can point to it and say "yes, I did it," or "no, I didn't do it." Shame is different than guilt. Shame is that feeling of regret we feel

The Walk Applied

when we realize the horror of what we've done. Shame is like smoke – we can't pin it down, you can't erase it. Despite our salvation, we still sense our guilt and shame over what we have done. While guilt may have been resolved in some who have truly accepted that Jesus did die and paid the price and resolved our guilt, it's very rare that we find someone who has resolved the shame issue".

SECURITY

The Walk Applied postulates that our drive for safety and security is a foundational, innate, and intrinsic need. When we believe that we have little or no sense of safety, our response can be very visceral and primal.

WORSHIP

We define worship as the active relationship that exists between us and what we believe provides our security. Rick Warren writes in the Purpose Driven Life that we are "hard-wired to worship." In other words, God has implanted within us an innate need to seek our security in something outside of ourselves that we perceive as being superior to ourselves. Further, we recognize that we are vulnerable and that we acknowledge that we are indeed in great need of protection. Indeed, the profound idea is that we recognize our smallness and that we need something or somebody more powerful than us to protect us.

A NEW UNDERSTANDING OF THE SINFUL FLESH

Ask Christians what "the flesh" is, and you'll get a wide variety of answers. Many would no doubt answer something like "the flesh is our propensity to sin" or "do the wrong things." In light of the above discussion, let us explore a new and completely different context on the flesh.

11

The Walk Applied

THE CURSE: WHY ME?

The Bible teaches that every single human being that has ever occupied this planet is born under a curse. Many object to this. "Why me? I didn't do anything! I'm not responsible for what they did! I didn't ask to be born!" But we must accept the reality that God sets the rules, and they are not negotiable. We only have one existence that is available to us; this natural existence is what have.

God, in His infinite wisdom, allowed us the enormous privilege of the capability to choose or deny Him. He could have destroyed Adam and Eve and been done with it. But that was not the plan. God's response was to allow us an idolatrous belief system that undergirds and forms the foundation of our sin issues. The two idolatry systems - Rebellion Idolatry and Need Idolatry systems are intrinsic and innate. We cannot "remove" them; they are deeply embedded such that only Jesus can resolve the problem.

THE SINFUL FLESH: THE FOUNDATION

The foundation of the natural belief system has four roots:

GUILT: The inner, gnawing paranoia because we know we have offended God.
SHAME: Our deep-seated regret that we offended God; The deep root of why we feel that something "is wrong with us."
INSECURITY: Since we have been separated from God, who will take care of us?
IDOLATRY: False worship: Our innate need to seek that which will bring us security. Idolatry is manifested when we:
  - Worship anything other than God
  - Worship what we believe is security
  - Worship what brings us pleasure

The Walk Applied

THE BELIEF SYSTEMS OF IDOLATRY:
NEED IDOLATRY & REBELLION IDOLATRY

Adam and Eve chose to rebel and disobey God. They willingly and knowingly came out of Godly Authority, and, as a result, came under intermediate Satanic control. God, in His infinite wisdom, allowed us the enormous privilege to choose or deny Him. He also graciously granted consequences for our sinful choice. Instead of simply destroying us, God's response was to allow us an idolatrous belief system that undergirds the foundation of our sin issues.

There are two such belief systems: Rebellion Idolatry and Need Idolatry. We will see that these two systems are so ingrained in us that only Jesus can resolve our idolatry problems. We will live in a sinful flesh for the duration of our natural lives.

REBELLION IDOLATRY IDOLS	NEED IDOLATRY IDOLS
PRIDE	PROVISION
PERFORMANCE	HOME
SECURITY	ACCEPTANCE/INTIMACY
FACADE	IDENTITY
PLEASURE	KNOWLEDGE
ENTITLEMENT	PURPOSE

REBELLION IDOLATRY:
THE DELUSION OF CONTROL
PRIDE: I AM THE AUTHORITY; I CONTROL ME
FALSE BELIEFS:
- I am the authority; I am above God
- I must be the "Judge" over others so I can take power over them.
    I cannot allow others to be in power over me.
- Free will and choice give me the "right" to reject
    Godly authority as I see fit.
- It is perfectly permissible to come out of Godly authority

13

The Walk Applied

Adam and Eve chose to disobey. They exhibited pride, defined here as the belief that it is permissible to come out of Godly authority. By implication, submission to intermediate satanic control must follow, which we'll see later leads to the chaotic.

Pride idolatry has enormous implications for our worldview and our deep-seated internal belief systems. Primarily, it means that we believe that we are above God. It means we believe that we are the authority figure in our lives. The inference for us is that we will believe that we not only have permission to come out of Godly authority; we will also believe that the seductive power of choice gives us the right to come out of Godly authority when we think it is in our best interest to do so; thus. we are above God. Pride idolatry establishes within us the sinful belief that we MUST do whatever we need to do to have power over others. I MUST be the "judge". To the fullest extent possible, I cannot allow anyone to be in power over me; I cannot allow others to judge me. The foundational false belief with pride is "I am in control". The core belief here is that if I am the "judge", I can control you; I am superior to you.

FAÇADE:
I MUST PRESENT AN IMAGE OF MYSELF
SO THAT OTHERS CANNOT JUDGE ME

FALSE BELIEFS:
- I can control what others think by the way
    I cover and present myself.
- I can control how others perceive me

Adam and Eve covered themselves after the fall. They were avoiding judgment by one another. We attempt to "project an image" of ourselves in accordance to what we perceive will put us in power over others. Façade is self-deceiving in that it depends upon our perception of how others perceive us. In effect, this belief

The Walk Applied

allows others to control us in that we are really submitting to others. Façade is the false belief that "prevents us" from being judged. Façade, in our own mind, establishes us as the power. It deludes us into thinking that we are actually judging others, since in our own minds we then become the "power".

SECURITY
HUMAN INSTITUTIONS PROTECT ME

FALSE BELIEFS:
- Human institutions protect me.
- I can control what happens to me.

Security is the false belief that our safety lies in human institutions. Security may be seen in the perceived protection afforded by government or financial institutions. It's not difficult to find people who believe that their security is in their jobs or their retirement accounts or that the government protects them or that some other human institution can be counted on. Yet, virtually every human institution fails on a daily basis in one way or another. Every day we hear numerous different complaints: "We need a different president!" "Kick 'em all out of Congress…". "We need to pass a law so that this will never happen again". "How dare they lay me off!" Natural and man-made disasters plague our existence continually. Criminal activity is a fact of life. We read about horrific child abuse every day. The list goes on and on. The awful and sobering reality is that we live in a sin-ridden world whereby we are threatened in numerous ways every day, yet we operate under the delusion that we are somehow insulated to one degree or another.

Another way that we play out the false belief of security is manifested in the differences that we observe in how women and men express their aspirations in life. Women can be very competitive when it comes to the perceived success of their

15

husbands and their kids. For many women, security can be seen as the protection of the husband within the institution of marriage. For many men, security is achievement within human institutions or talent or skill or advancement within organizations. Men can certainly express their urge to compete via their wealth, position, and status. Let us note that both sexes are equally guilty when it comes to competitive behavior; neither gender has a monopoly. Competition can be a fine thing - there is typically nothing wrong with the drive to excel – but we surely need to ask the basic question: what's my motivation?

A SPECIAL CASE: GENESIS 3:16

A special case is Gen 3:16: *"To the woman he said, ...your desire will be for your husband, and he will rule over you."*, the contention here is that God is allowing the belief to be instilled in Eve that she will depend upon sinful men for her security instead of looking to the Living God for her security. She will also contend with the duality of not only seeing her husband as her security, while trying to usurp his authority in marriage because of her sinful desire to judge. She will want to "mold" him into her idea of security. The husband will also contend with power and control issues as he deals with judgment and achievement. Since the husband operates out of performance, he will very likely try to control her as he asserts himself as "the leader". He may indeed "judge" her by misunderstanding her need for security as invasive. Facade enters the picture when we consider that men may overly desire a "trophy" wife. Women may overly desire the triple 6's: six pack abs, a six-figure salary and six feet tall.

The Walk Applied

PERFORMANCE:
THE BETTER I PERFORM,
THE LESS PEOPLE CAN JUDGE ME

FALSE BELIEFS:
- I can control my "position" in the community
  by how well I "perform".
- I can control the conditions by which I enter God's house.

Adam's predicament was all too apparent after the fall. Now he would be responsible for supporting Eve and their children. He would somehow have to provide shelter and work to obtain food and clothing. He now bore the responsibility for his own survival as well as others. In other words, he would have to perform in order for them to live. It would not be enough for him to merely meet his own standards; there were now others who had to be considered as well. Was there enough? Would Eve be satisfied? Were the children warm enough? Performance is defined to be the core belief that the better I perform within the context of human institutions, not only will I be "successful", thus becoming "more secure", but the "higher I rise", the less likely it is that someone can "judge me". This belief will drive most men to exert power and control in many areas of their life. Certainly, women are not immune; they will exert competitive tendencies with other women as well as with their children. They will also idolize performance in their husbands as the key to their own security.

Performance idolatry is rooted in what Keller discusses in his aforementioned sermon. Keller emphasizes that "since we were made in the image of God, we know deep inside that we betrayed God". Keller further explains that "our fleshly guilt and shame establish within us the idea that we [innately] know we owe God". Performance Idolatry says that we will "payback" what we "owe" and show "how good" we are through our deeds and actions. Thus,

17

The Walk Applied

others or God will "owe me" and my deeds will establish my righteousness & authority over others.

The foundational error with Performance Idolatry is that it's a theology of works. If you could somehow work your way into heaven, that would nullify the cross. The New Testament is very clear and specific on this point. Would Jesus ever do what He did if we could earn our way to Heaven? The covenant of Salvation is based on faith, not works. Indeed, Isaiah points out that our works mean nothing. No level of performance can satisfy God's covenantal conditions; performance is never a factor.

God has established one standard by which all can enter God's house. The false belief for performance is that I can control the conditions by which I enter God's house. This fraudulent idea is tantamount to saying that you should let me in your house because I think you should. The idea that no level of performance can satisfy the entrance requirement is a very powerful notion. Indeed, why did God purpose, plan and execute the process in such a way? Think about it. Do you readily allow people in your house that you don't trust?

If performance was the standard, what would be good enough? What would be the standard? Suppose you and I went to the movies. Suppose further that your ticket cost $5, and mine cost $1. Surely, you would want a justification as to why I got in for less money. Almost certainly you would expect that justification to make sense to you, not the theatre owner. Further, even though the theater owner leased the movie from the studio and paid for the equipment and the building and paid the employees' salaries and has every right to charge whatever price he wants, you would still very likely howl in protest that the price difference was unfair!

The Walk Applied

PLEASURE:
GOD WON'T MAKE ME "HAPPY" SO
I HAVE TO MAKE MYSELF "HAPPY"

FALSE BELIEFS:
- The temporary escape from the sinful chaotic and my shame
- The creation of false intimacy and acceptance whereby I do not have to reveal the "real me"

According to Romans chapter1, pleasure involves a scenario whereby the refusal to worship God - e.g. idolatry - results in perversion and chaos. To relieve anxiety and chaos and attempt to reach a state of peace (even though we know it will always be temporary), we will seek pleasure. Romans reports that we will substitute intimate pleasure (sex) to meet our need for intimacy. When pleasure is substituted for intimacy, we can emotionally "hide" and we don't have to reveal ourselves. We can avoid being "judged" in this way; this is in line with the façade structure of belief. According to Romans, there will be virtually no limit to our depravity. The core false belief of pleasure is that "If God won't make me happy, then I have the right to make myself happy." This false belief reflects a profound lack of trust in God.

Pleasure is often associated with sin. Sin does encompass illicit activities that do indeed bring a very temporary pleasure and peace. Sometimes, we seemingly "get away with it". Many times, however, sin brings consequences that can be significant and profound. That impulsive action that was seemingly so minor can turn into a lifetime of misery.

In Romans, Paul tells us that we will seek illicit pleasures as a direct result of our unbelief and failure to worship Him. Paul tells us that many of those who live the unsaved life will turn to depravity. In other words, there will be no recognition of moral principles, any

19

option is open. Paul's extensive list serves to emphasize the gross immorality of unrestricted pleasure.

ENTITLEMENT:
I AM "ABOVE" YOU, SO I
DESERVE WHAT YOU HAVE

FALSE BELIEFS:
- I should have what you have because I am "above" you, and I am entitled to judge you.
- What right do you have to have something I don't?

Since I am "above" you, I deserve what you have. When Eve gave into the temptation to indulge, the rationale of entitlement is what pushed her over the edge. The tempter's prompt caused Eve to reason that since God could have the fruit, Eve should be able to as well. Why should anything be held back from anyone? Entitlement is what allowed Eve to process and accept the proposition that she could, in fact, agree to come out of Godly authority despite her clear knowledge that "she would die". That is to say, when Eve looked at the fruit, something stirred within her (as well as Adam) that "spoke" to her and "said": "Well, it looks ok and it looks like it will benefit me. What's the harm? Eve rationalized because of this belief "If God has it, why can't I?" It can also be construed that she believed she did not need God to meet her needs or wants, in light of the fact that she believed that the fruit would give her something that God would not.

The core false belief of entitlement is that "I'm above you so I should have what you have". I should at least have the same as everyone else. This creates confusion and chaos because entitlement says that I must have more than you have and what I have must be better than what you have. Obviously, there is a logical inconsistency here. It's physically impossible for everyone to have the same as everyone else. Only God can create a system whereby all are truly equal.

The Walk Applied

NEED IDOLATRY: "FALSE WORSHIP"

We all have needs and wants. Regardless of how we aspire to occupy our place on this planet – be it an outlandish, lavish lifestyle or the most basic, ascetic existence – we still have the basics that must be met. How will these basic life requirements be met for each and every one of us? The contention here is that we idolize 6 basic and foundational human needs. Need Idolatry in the context of a sinful, driven flesh can be summarized in one question: Do we seek God to satisfy them, or do we seek our own way?

Need idolatry occurs when we make our legitimate human needs our idols. The Bible implies six fundamental human needs: Purpose, Provision, Home, Intimacy and Acceptance, Knowledge and Identity.

PURPOSE

FALSE PURPOSE BELIEF:
"I'm free to believe whatever I like. There is no God, so I'm not accountable to anyone. Thus, my purpose and mission are whatever I want it to be if I even want to have one." If my purpose is more "noble" than yours, or if I achieve more than you do, I can judge you."

Adam and Eve were to rule over the other living creatures, subdue the earth, and work the garden (Gen 1:27-28). Purpose idolatry occurs when we see our reason for being anything other than our purpose in Christ. We see this idolatry in the modern day all the time. The root of the purpose idol is "I'm free to believe whatever I like. Since there is no God, so I'm not accountable to anyone. Thus, my purpose and mission are whatever I want it to be if I even want to have one. Thus, if my purpose is "better" than yours as I see it, or if I "achieve" more than you do, I can judge you."

21

The Walk Applied

God provides our eternal purpose through the personal and effectual calling He has placed on our lives. We will discuss the notion of the call later. For now, understand that God wants to put you where he has for His purposes and His reasons. As you walk with Jesus and sincerely seek him and turn your life over to Him, He will fill you with purpose and peace. Never underestimate your call regardless of how you may perceive it in earthly secular terms. The definition of success in God's economy is how well did you walk the path He wanted you to walk – regardless of your station. In Acts 8, Phillip was miraculously given access to the treasurer of Egypt for the purposes of converting the Egyptian official. Phillip should never have been able to approach such a powerful man – much less actually spend time with the third highest ranking official in the most powerful country in the world at that time. Yet, Phillip followed his call and was given a personal appointment through the miraculous works of God. Because of that meeting, the evangelization of Africa began.

Few will be given such a privilege as Phillip. But what matters is that you are faithful to God's call – day by day, year by year. Indeed, we must never forget that the walk with Jesus IS the object. Earthly success is not the object. Faithfulness to the His personal effectual call on your life in addition to your ongoing relationship to Him is what counts.

PROVISION

FALSE PROVISION BELIEF:
"I have more than you, so I'm superior to you, thus, I can judge you. What I have is better, so I'm better. Since I have more than enough, I don't need God. The more I accumulate, the more secure I am".

We all need provision: Light, food, water, air, rest, pleasure, shelter, clothing, etc. Adam and Eve needed the same things. Provision idolatry occurs when we see anyone but God as our true source for

22

our human needs. Jesus highlighted this type of idolatry in the Sermon on the Mount. The core belief of this idol is "I have more than you, so I'm superior to you, thus, I can judge you. What I have is better, so I'm better. Since I have more than enough, I don't need God. The more I accumulate, the more secure I am".

HOME (SECURITY)

FALSE HOME BELIEF:
"Human institutions protect me. If I am strong enough, I can protect myself. thus, I don't need god. If I can protect myself, I'm superior to you; thus, I can judge you."

Home is a fundamental human need; it is the physical expression of security. Genesis describes the location and boundaries of the garden; if Adam was to "go and subdue", he certainly needed to know where to return. Adam and Eve surely saw the Garden as home. He certainly understood establishing a separate location (home) for a newly married couple (Gen 2:10-14; 24). Home idolatry is implicit in the emotional link that we have between shelter, land and how we perceive our security as rooted in our homes and families. This idolatry is especially evident after natural tragedies. Home represents an innate and intrinsic need to have a space that we recognize as our own. We feel safe in an area that we recognize has our unique boundaries vis-à-vis others. A violation of "our space" can be very traumatic.

The central belief of home idolatry is "Human institutions protect me. Since I'm strong enough, I can protect myself. Thus, I don't need God. Thus, I am superior to you; therefore, I can judge you."

ACCEPTANCE AND INTIMACY

FALSE ACCEPTANCE BELIEF:

23

The Walk Applied

"I cannot let anyone see the real me, otherwise, they can judge me. I can achieve intimacy via sex, or by projecting the right façade. I can control my family and how the community sees me via power, coercion, manipulation, and façade. Since I can achieve acceptance in these ways, I don't need God."

Adam needed companionship, acceptance, and intimacy (Gen 2:18-25). Genesis 2:24-25 implies that Adam foresaw the need for family and the need for community as well. To be sure, acceptance idolatry can be observed readily today. The core belief is: I can achieve intimacy via sex, or by projecting the right façade. I cannot let anyone see the real me, otherwise, they can judge me. I can control my family and how the community sees me via coercion, manipulation, and façade. Since I can achieve intimacy and acceptance these ways, I don't need God.

KNOWLEDGE

FALSE KNOWLEDGE BELIEF:
"Knowledge is king. We can figure out what we need to know. We are evolving to a "higher level", thus, we don't need God. If I know more than you, or if I can create the facade that I know more, then I'm superior to you and I can judge you."

Adam knew how to communicate. What language did he speak? Where did he acquire a language? How did he know what to name the animals? How did he know what a biological father and mother were? Where did he get his conception of a wife? These cultural concepts indicate Adam had absorbed far more than a rudimentary knowledge of his surroundings. He likely understood technology; he was responsible for the care of the garden. Indeed, there seems no contesting the notion that "rational man" sees science, knowledge, and technology as "the answer" to our problems. To be sure, knowledge and our natural God-given curiosity regarding our temporal environment has become an idol.

24

The Walk Applied

The foundational belief is that knowledge is king. We can figure out what we need to know. We are always evolving to a "higher level", thus, we don't need God. If I know more than you, or if I can create the facade that I know more than you, then I am superior to you, so I can judge you."

IDENTITY

FALSE IDENTITY BELIEF:
"My identity is found in how I relate to others and human institutions. My foundational understanding of how I fit in this world – my worldview - and how I relate to others is found in my idols: performance, façade, security, etc. I believe that what is important and true is found in the natural."

Adam needed an identity; he needed to know who he was in relation to others. He needed a name that would set him apart. He needed to understand where he was in an authority and submission structure with others. Identity idolatry is nothing new. Seeing our identity as anything other than new creations in Christ is idolatrous. Yet, in the modern day we commonly see the quest to "know who we are". The central belief of Identity is found in how I relate to others and human institutions. In other words, my foundational understanding of how I fit in this world and how I relate to others is found in three idols: performance, façade and security. I believe that what is important and true is found in the natural.

WE ARE IDOLATORS

These idolatry belief systems were given to us such that they are interwoven into the deepest fabric of our being. Sinful belief systems compromise what we know as the flesh, and they govern our fleshly behavior. It's important that we understand the twelve idols as presented here represent a worst-case scenario. For

25

The Walk Applied

example, not everyone feels they are completely entitled as presented here. Certainly, there are many who recognize that there is more than just knowledge. However, it is also axiomatic that all of humanity is plagued by a relentless and overwhelming sinful flesh, and that we all deal with all twelve traits of the idolatrous flesh to one extent or another.

A critical distinction worth mentioning here is that we tend to see ourselves as sinners, but not idolaters. We like to view ourselves as good, decent people who occasionally sin do the wrong thing. We recoil at the thought that we might actually be – dare we say it? – idolaters. It rarely, if ever, enters our realm of comprehension. "That's what they used to do in the Old Testament! I'm nothing like that. I don't worship statues or sacrifice my kids!"

The truth is, however, is that we are all guilty of idolatry as we've discussed in the preceding paragraphs. We are all in rebellion against God to one degree or another even though we may be saved. This existence is not about how well we can stop sinning or being a decent human being. It's about seeking a living breathing relationship with Jesus and following the path He has set for each and every one of us.

THE SYMPTOMS OF IDOLATRY:
JUDGMENT & SELF-SEEKING

Romans and James tells us how idolatry has devastating and profound consequences. Romans 2:1 and 2:8 gives the main symptoms of idolatry: judgment and self-seeking. Romans 2:2 tells us that we all pass judgment. In other words, we attempt to take spiritual authority over one another. Romans 2:8 describes "self-seeking" (from the Greek "eritheia" translated "chaos"), which describes how we do things out of selfish interest such that we foment chaos. (Rom 2:6-9) tells us that self-seekers reject truth and follow evil. Four things await self-seekers: wrath, anger, trouble &

The Walk Applied

distress. Romans 1 gives us a crucial link between idolatry, beliefs and actions, which we summarize here:

"God's eternal power and divine nature are obvious; men have no excuse. We don't recognize him as supreme despite the obvious evidence (read: we are out of His authority!) Thus, our thinking (belief) has become futile; our foolish hearts have become dark (belief) and we worship idols (belief). Therefore, we: bought into the lie (belief); we worship idols (belief); we revel in sinful desires (belief); and we are turned over to depraved minds (belief). The result: we do perverse things (actions)." ...they have become filled with every kind of wickedness, evil, greed and depravity. They are full of envy, murder, strife, deceit and malice. They are gossips, slanderers, god-haters, insolent, arrogant and boastful; they invent ways of doing evil; they disobey their parents; they are senseless, faithless, heartless, ruthless. Although they know God's righteous decree that those who do such things deserve death, they not only continue to do these very things but also approve of those who practice them. Therefore, we have no excuse..." (Rom 1:20 - 2:3).

The passage goes on to describe that we also see the destructive actions of judgment. Judgment – the taking of spiritual authority over others – is only allowed by God and those who He chooses! James expresses the same sentiment:

"...But if you harbor bitter envy and selfish ambition in your hearts...For where you have envy and selfish ambition, there you find disorder and every evil practice. What causes fights and quarrels among you? Don't they come from your desires that battle within you? You want something but don't get it. You kill and covet, but you cannot have what you want. You quarrel and fight. You do not have, because you do not ask God. When you ask, you do not receive, because you ask with wrong motives..." (James 3:13-16; 4:1-4).

The Walk Applied

Is it any surprise to find out that self-seeking and selfish ambition are described by the same Greek word: eritheia? Indeed, what are the results of eritheia? Disorder and every evil practice! We have more examples of eritheia:

"... I fear that there may be quarreling, jealousy, outbursts of anger, factions, slander, gossip, arrogance and disorder." (2 Cor 12:20)

"The acts of the sinful nature are obvious: sexual immorality, impurity and debauchery; idolatry and witchcraft; hatred, discord, jealousy, fits of rage, selfish ambition, dissensions, and factions." (Gal 5:19-20).
James also addresses the topic of judgment:

"...Anyone who speaks against his brother or judges him speaks against the law and judges it. When you judge the law, you are not keeping it, but sitting in judgment on it. There is only one Lawgiver and Judge, the one who is able to save and destroy. But you—who are you to judge your neighbor?" (James 4:11-12)

The emphasis is clear: we are not to judge! Taking on spiritual authority that is not yours leads only to eritheia: chaos!

EXPECTATIONS: A FORM OF JUDGEMENT

Expectations are a form of judgment. We all have expectations to one degree or another depending on the situation. Many of these are legitimate and proper. Spouses have a legitimate expectation that they will be faithful to one another. If we use our credit card to make a purchase, we have an expectation that it will be handled without identity theft resulting. Parents typically expect that children will obey. Teachers have an expectation that students will do their homework. Drivers expect that the vehicles behind them will also stop at the red light. Realistically, however, none of these expectations is justified.

28

The Walk Applied

Truly, all we should ever expect from sinful people around us is sinful behavior. Granted, the vast majority of dealings we have with others go smoothly and pleasantly. Indeed, the Bible teaches us that we are sinners to the core, and that there is almost no limit to what we are capable of. While we may believe that most will honor our expectations of others, we have no authentic basis for those expectations. In the same vein, we live in an overwhelmingly sinful, fallen world whereby tragedy happens all the time. Natural disasters, disease, epidemics, crime, war, accidents, economic maladies – just to mention a few - are often significant and profound events in people's lives. Many times, they bring about life-altering trauma, and people's lives are never the same. Our hopes and dreams - our expectations - our judgments - of what we think are lives are supposed to be can be shattered in an instant. In some cases, we may face a lifelong condition that will demand suffering and quite possibly drain our emotional reserves and test us to limits we never thought we had. Grief, anger, resentment, despair, sadness, bitterness – all of these and more can describe our emotions when our lives are interrupted drastically and tragically. To be sure, these emotions are normal and to be expected. After all, harmful stuff is not supposed to happen to us! Tragedies happen others!

Nowhere does God guarantee that our lives will be free of tragedy and suffering. The Word tells us that we will experience suffering in our lives. The Bible teaches us that he will walk with us while we endure our cup of suffering. Thus, we can see how our expectations - our judgments - of our sinful world can exacerbate how we internalize trauma and tragedy in a profound and deep way.

SYMPTOMS OF JUDGEMENT & SELF-SEEKING

Judgment and self-seeking are symptomatic of the flesh. Anything that smacks of power and/or promotion of self (especially at the expense of others) typically finds its roots in judgment or self-

The Walk Applied

seeking. After all, both are merely extensions of Satan's main thrust: power and control over others. The following list is a good representation of how Judgment and self-seeking are manifested. As you peruse the list, you may wish to contemplate how and why each one is indicative of judgment and self-seeking.

Control	Manipulation	Intimidation
Instill Fear	Unreasonable suspicion	Jealousy
Temper	Frequent complaining	Avoidance
Jealousy	Excessive Anger	Frequent outbursts
Criticism	Resentment	Bitterness
Lying	Etc.	

THE NATURAL WORLDVIEW SYSTEM

PRIDE: FREE WILL: IT'S OK TO COME OUT OF GODLY AUTHORITY I _MUST_ BE IN AUTHORITY; I _MUST_ BE THE "JUDGE" LEADS TO GUILT – SHAME – PARANOIA - THE CURSE

REBELLION IDOLATRY: THE "DELUSION OF CONTROL":
FAÇADE: I CAN CONTROL WHAT OTHERS THINK ABOUT ME
PERFORMANCE: LESS BAD THINGS I DO + MORE GOOD THINGS = MAKE ME A "BETTER PERSON" THEN YOU
ENTITLEMENT: I SHOULD HAVE WHAT YOU HAVE BECAUSE I'M "BETTER"
SECURITY: I CAN CONTROL WHAT HAPPENS TO ME
PLEASURE: TEMPORARY RESOLUTION OF ANXIETY (LACK OF PEACE)

NEED IDOLATRY: "FALSE WORSHIP":
THE "MORE" OR "BETTER" I "HAVE" OR "AM";
THE MORE I CAN "JUDGE" YOU:
PROVISION – PURPOSE - INTIMACY
HOME (SECURITY) – KNOWLEDGE - IDENTITY

The Walk Applied

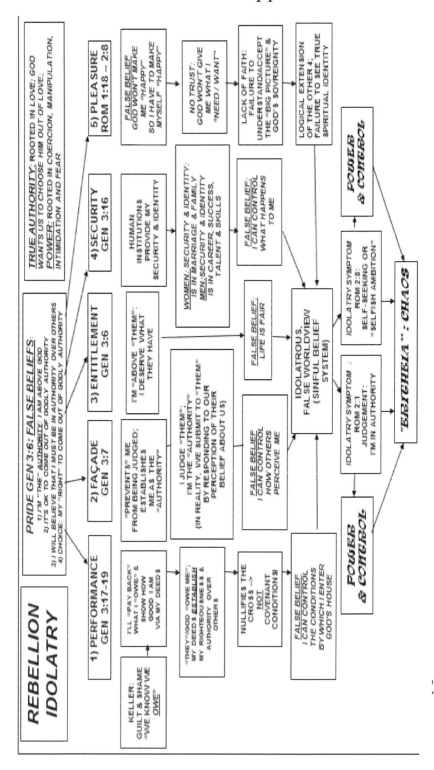

The Walk Applied

NEED IDOLATRY

PROVISION:
LIGHT, FOOD, WATER, AIR, REST, PLEASURE, SHELTER, CLOTHING

FALSE PROVISION BELIEF: "I HAVE MORE THAN YOU, SO I'M SUPERIOR TO YOU. THUS, I CAN JUDGE YOU. WHAT I HAVE IS BETTER, SO I'M BETTER. SINCE I HAVE MORE THAN ENOUGH, I DON'T NEED GOD. THE MORE I ACCUMULATE, THE MORE SECURE I AM"

HOME:
BOUNDARIES, SAFETY

FALSE HOME BELIEF: "HUMAN INSTITUTIONS PROTECT ME. IF I AM STRONG ENOUGH, I CAN PROTECT MYSELF. THUS, I DON'T NEED GOD. IF I CAN PROTECT MYSELF, I'M SUPERIOR TO YOU; THUS, I CAN JUDGE YOU.

ACCEPTANCE:
INTIMACY, FAMILY, COMMUNITY

FALSE ACCEPTANCE BELIEF: "I CAN ACHIEVE INTIMACY VIA SEX, OR BY PROJECTING THE RIGHT FAÇADE. I CANNOT LET ANYONE SEE THE REAL ME, OTHERWISE, THEY CAN JUDGE ME. I CAN CONTROL MY FAMILY AND HOW THE COMMUNITY SEES ME VIA POWER, COERCION, MANIPULATION, AND FAÇADE. SINCE I CAN ACHIEVE INTIMACY THESE WAYS, I DON'T NEED GOD

IDENTITY:
NAME, AN AUTHORITY STRUCTURE, VALUES, CULTURE

FALSE IDENTITY BELIEF: "MY IDENTITY IS FOUND IN HOW I RELATE TO OTHERS AND HUMAN INSTITUTIONS. MY IDEA OF HOW I FIT IN THIS WORLD AND HOW I RELATE TO OTHERS IS FOUND IN THREE IDOLS: PERFORMANCE, FAÇADE AND SECURITY. I BELIEVE THAT WHAT IS IMPORTANT AND TRUE IS FOUND IN THE NATURAL

KNOWLEDGE:
LANGUAGE, COMMUNICATION, INFORMATION, TECHNOLOGY

FALSE KNOWLEDGE BELIEF: "KNOWLEDGE IS KING. WE CAN FIGURE OUT WHAT WE NEED TO KNOW. WE ARE EVOLVING TO A "HIGHER LEVEL". THUS, WE DON'T NEED GOD. IF I KNOW MORE THAN YOU, OR IF I CAN CREATE THE BELIEF THAT I KNOW MORE, THEN I'M SUPERIOR TO YOU: THUS, I CAN JUDGE YOU"

PURPOSE:
BE FRUITFUL, SUBDUE & RULE THE EARTH, TEND THE GARDEN

FALSE PURPOSE & MISSION BELIEF: "I'M FREE TO BELIEVE WHATEVER I LIKE. THERE IS NO GOD, SO I'M NOT ACCOUNTABLE TO ANYONE. THUS, MY PURPOSE AND MISSION ARE WHATEVER I WANT IT TO BE. IF I EVEN WANT TO HAVE ONE." IF MY PURPOSE IS MORE "NOBLE" THAN YOURS, OR IF I ACHIEVE MORE THAN YOU DO, I CAN JUDGE YOU"

FILTERED THROUGH THE 6 ROOT IDOLS:
PRIDE
REBELLION
PERFORMANC
FAÇADE
SECURITY
ENTITLEMENT
PLEASURE
AND THE 2 IDOLATRY SYMPTOMS:
SELF-SEEKING
JUDGEMENT:
ESTABLISH THE ILLUSION OF POWER AND CONTROL

The Walk Applied

THE ORPHANED SPIRIT:
"WRATH ANGER TROUBLE AND DISTRESS"

The Orphaned Spirit phenomena typically occurs when you believe that you were abandoned, betrayed, rejected or deeply hurt by your spiritual authority (usually your biological parents). Those who have an orphaned spirit have been known to describe their experience as a profound deprivation of acceptance and intimacy. There is almost always a feeling of helplessness; there can be an overwhelming sense of insecurity. Paranoia can be observed because there is the sense that security is for all intent and purposes totally and completely absent. In many cases, there is a pronounced and tragic sense of violation. It goes without saying some may feel horribly victimized - helpless and powerless playthings who were objects of some gross malevolent evil. There is no denying that the vast majority of these cases do have good reason for their hurt, anger, rage, and bitterness. They did not ask to be born; yet they were subjected to an environment that was outrageous sinful and unspeakable things may have been foisted on them.

Of course, the Orphaned Sprit does not just occur in a family setting. Trauma that precipitates the Orphaned Spirit can come from any number of sources: tragedy, attack, and war are but a few. Any number of emotional abuses that may bring on the Orphaned Sprit include bullying, humiliation, criticism, being demeaned or dismissed, being belittled, contempt by others – just to name a few. The same symptoms enumerated in the prior paragraph can certainly apply here as well.

Those who deal with an Orphaned Spirit can tend to hold on to their overwhelming anger and hurt for years and even decades. Tragically, many go to their grave after holding on to the enormous bitterness that made life a living hell. People who choose to live this way typically experience massive depression; many finally commit suicide to escape the overwhelming anguish.

The Walk Applied

There is no escaping that we live in a sinful, depraved world whereby there is virtually no limit to the evil and depravity. The Bible tells us as much. Jeremiah has stunning news for us: *""The human heart is the most deceitful of all things, and desperately wicked.*" Unfortunately, our families, relatives, friends, and acquaintances - all of our "people circles" - are not excluded. Jeremiah's statement tells us that all of us are dark-hearted sinners who are capable of anything we can think of despite our fervent pleas and fantasies that insist that we are surrounded by good and decent people. And many times, we are involved with people who truly loving and treat us well.

But let us recall our discussion of expectations. As we discussed earlier, the only thing we can realistically expect out of anyone is sinful behavior. We can hope and pray that things turn out nicely, but the stark truth is very often the opposite. Sometimes, the people closest to us - the ones who we expect will treat us lovingly and honorably - simply do not, and deeply hurt and violate the ones they are supposed to love.

When we are young, often we believe parents and adults are "perfect". Since we perceive them to be perfect, if they hurt us, the problem must somehow be us. We must have done something to have this done to us. Therefore, we can tend believe that something must be wrong with us. We see this lots of times when parents are divorced. The kids are perfectly innocent, but many children feel they are the problem. This awful, unneeded guilt and shame can persist for years and even decades. The other side of the coin are those individuals who somehow innately recognize very early on at even the youngest of ages that they have done nothing wrong and their abuser is terribly wrong in foisting their antics on their young defenseless victims. In any case, the end result for the poor soul on the receiving end of abuse and torment will almost always be the same: resentment, fear, anger, hatred, etc.

The Walk Applied

Yet, that does not mesh with another fundamental belief that we should not be mistreated. We have a natural belief: they shouldn't do that! They are supposed to be our security! We want protection and love from those who are supposed to protect us. The innate fight or flight response also kicks in. Many times, we simply can't escape; we are trapped.

Our discussion should not be construed to be limited to the immediate family. The extended family can certainly be complicit as well as the community at large. Unmitigated, all of these influences can breed ever growing anger, resentment and bitterness over the years and decades. The heart, over time, can turn to emotional stone, and forgiveness may become virtually impossible.

Yet, we are not only called to forgive, we are called to forgive the unforgivable. God tells us that we must forgive, or He will not forgive us. Despite how difficult it may be, true forgiveness is something we must bring ourselves to do. If we do not forgive, we will likely never achieve a state of true peace.

Many who deal with an Orphaned Spirit will find that they are contributing to their suffering, as hard as that might be to accept. Many recoil at that statement and understandably so. After all, "How dare they do that?!?!" Romans Chapter 2:8-9 tells us that because of our unmet expectations - a form of judgment - we "are self-seeking and [we] reject the truth and follow evil... [The result is] wrath and anger... trouble and distress for every human being who does evil.

The Walk Applied

The Orphaned Spirit is a complex topic and a few paragraphs do not give the proper respect to its importance. However, we can comment here on a couple of topics where the notion of the Orphaned Spirit is applicable.

PTSD ("Post Traumatic Stress Disorder")

PTSD has been typically associated with the military and those who have been in combat. The horrific violence, the sights, sounds and smells of action are unimaginable by those who have never experienced the horrors of war. The terrible memories are without question unforgettable and nightmarish. The litany of symptoms and behaviors for veterans who suffer from PTSD is lengthy and heart-breaking.

But PTSD is certainly not limited to veterans of combat. The list of those who might display symptoms of PTSD is lengthy: Victims of abuse. Crime victims. Rape. Accident victims. Incest victims. Those who have experienced tragedy of almost any kind can certainly expect to exhibit symptoms of PTSD to one degree or another. The heartbreak is brutal and palpable in many cases.

A common trait that's often observed with PTSD is the absence of feeling safe and feeling extremely vulnerable. The violation, the fear, the betrayal, the devastation, the enormous emotional pain and anxiety, etc., all contribute to overwhelming feelings of helplessness, loneliness and fear. The result can be very traumatic instances of anger, self-harm and very violent behaviors, just to name a few. Nightmares are common. The contention from here is that PTSD and the Orphaned Spirit are very much alike. The difference: The Orphaned spirit is associated with the spiritual and theological while PTSD is the preferred term in therapeutic circles.

The Walk Applied

CHAPTER 2:
THE HEART
BELIEF SYSTEM

The Walk Applied

The Walk Applied

CHAPTER 2:
THE HEART BELIEF SYSTEM

We now turn our attention to the Heart Belief System ("The Heart"). The heart belief system is our new belief system that God uses over time to supplant the flesh as part of the salvation conversion experience. We will see that the heart gives us a completely new identity. 2 Cor 5:17 is a wonderfully ponderous passage:

"...If anyone is in Christ, the new creation has come: The old has gone, the new is here!"

When we comply with the salvation covenant, we are born again – that is to say, saved. The implications for our lives are enormous. We have a new lineage. We can now commune in the Spiritual realm. We are declared citizens of a His Kingdom. We are newly adopted into God's family. We are forgiven for every single one of our sins: past, present, and future. Finally, our Spirit has been raised to life as part of the second birth that Jesus taught Nicodemus about.

THE HEART:
THE NEW BELIEF SYSTEM OF THE SAVED

Paul tells us in the New Testament that only those whose Spirit has been raised and brought to Spiritual life can comprehend the Spiritual. Unfortunately, the Heart belief system is not integrated quickly into our psyche or ethos. We still live with a sinful, driven and relentless flesh that, by God's perfect design, compels us to seek Jesus and commune with Jesus every single second of every waking day. The Heart belief system, over our lifetime, slowly but surely replaces the sinful Flesh as we walk with Jesus in an intimate and personal relationship with Him. The reality is that we will only fully shed the sinful flesh when we pass from this natural existence into the Spiritual realm where those who are saved will enjoy full fellowship with Jesus and heavenly Father.

41

The Walk Applied

THE HEART
BELIEF SYSTEM
CONSTRUCTS:

THE ASSURANCE CONSTRUCT
replaces
REBELLION IDOLATRY

This idol:	Is replaced by:
PRIDE	HUMILITY
PERFORMANCE	SONSHIP
FAÇADE	ACCEPTANCE
SECURITY	STEWARDHIP
ENTITLEMENT	ADOPTION
PLEASURE	PEACE

THE GUARANTEE CONSTRUCT
replaces
NEED IDOLATRY

This idol:	Is replaced by:
PROVISION	GUARANTEE OF PROVISION
HOME	SECURITY
IDENTITY	SPIRITUAL IDENTITY
ACCEPTANCE & INTIMACY	ADOPTION
KNOWLEDGE	WISDOM
PURPOSE	CALLING

The Walk Applied

THE ASSURANCE CONSTRUCT

HUMILITY replaces PRIDE

Humility teaches us that God is absolutely sovereign in all things. Over time, we learn to become humble servants. Indeed, humility ultimately brings us a palpable undercurrent of serenity and joy no matter what the circumstances. Humility is understood to be an intentional act of loving submission because we acknowledge that His will is sovereign in all things.

SONSHIP replaces PERFORMANCE

We have been adopted into the family of God with all the rights and privileges that being in the family of God brings with it. Redemption means we have been literally "purchased back" from Satan's power. Our "title deed" has passed from Satan back to God. We will never be rejected because of what we do or don't do. In His Word, God clearly proclaims the He will never leave us, nor will He forsake us. Jesus' death and resurrection paid the awful price that needed to be paid for sin. We are adopted sons and citizens of God's Kingdom.

ACCEPTANCE replaces FACADE

There is no longer any need to show a façade. We are fully accepted as we are, despite our deplorable sinful condition. That's why it is important to understand that we are His adopted children fully and totally. We are citizens of God's country. We have sealed with the deposit of the Holy Spirit. Our sins have been fully paid for, past, present and future. All has been taken care of!

The Walk Applied

STEWARDSHIP replaces SECURITY

The notion of stewardship means that we own nothing, and that we are fully dependent on God to faithfully provide for each and every need that we have when we need it. God is always faithful, and His word tells us that he will never leave us and he will never fail us. We could easily substitute the word custodian for stewardship. God wants us to use what he provides us with in a Godly way. We are managers of all the good things He wants to give us. When we are faithful to His calling on our lives, we can be sure that He will take loving care of us according to His purpose, plan, and will.

ADOPTION replaces ENTITLEMENT

We talked earlier about how Eve believed she was entitled to what God told our original parents they could not have. You will recall that false belief underlying entitlement is that we are all entitled to the same things in equal amounts – a notion that defies logic and simply cannot be. In actuality, entitlement would really mean that I should have more than you because my fleshly idolatry would have me believe that because I am better than you, I should have more than you. In return, you would staunchly believe that you should have more than me because – well certainly, you are better than me! Quite a mess!

Adoption does away with any notion of entitlement, because when we are adopted, we have full legal rights as an heir to the Kingdom. You and I would have everything God wants us to have to the fullest. As adopted sons, we operate under the doctrine of sonship. That means that we are treated the same as legally adopted sons. In Biblical times, to be an adopted son meant that you were treated exactly the same as any other biological heir. It also meant that your past- no matter what you did – was for all intent and purposes erased. Your status was completely changed as of the day you were

44

The Walk Applied

adopted. And that's how God looks at us starting with the moment we are saved. Our sins – past present and future – have all been covered by the blood of Jesus, no exception! We are fully loved and fully accepted - no matter what our condition or what we have done. There is no sin or offense that is so bad that it cannot be forgiven. The only exception is if we do not believe. That would mean we are truly not saved!

PEACE replaces PLEASURE

To be saved means you should be walking in peace. Obviously, this does not always happen. Christians have the same problems as anyone else. To be a Christian does not mean you won't have the same worries as those who are not saved. It is indeed sad that many who profess to be followers of Jesus simply do not act like it, and lead lifestyles that are not exemplary of their new status in Christ. Tragically, there are also many who profess to be saved, but truly, they are not. More to the point, Romans 2 describes a lifestyle of hedonism and outright immorality. These awful depictions of a relentless pursuit of pleasure should never happen with a true Christian. There should be exhibited a peaceful and moral life, that reflects a life that is anything but chaotic.

All that said, for the true Christian, there should be an underlying sense of serenity and peace, even in the toughest of situations and the worst of tragedy. When all is said and done, a true Christian has the sense that it's all going to turn out ok, despite the circumstances. The true Christian understands that he is eternal, and that ultimately, he will spend eternity with Christ. There should be an undercurrent of serenity and joy.

We certainly don't want to discount those who are most certainly saved but have not yet learned how to be in peace. Christians are at various stages in their walk with Christ, and God clearly knows the state of each and every person. So, it's easy to misinterpret the

The Walk Applied

motives and actions of a Christian and where they are in their walk. Through struggles and trials, as the Christian walks out the walk, he comes to understand that God is ever faithful, and He is true to His word.

THE GUARANTEE CONSTRUCT

THE GUARANTEE OF PROVISION replaces PROVISION

God is faithful to provide for every need we have - and some, if not all, of our wants. In the Sermon on the Mount, Jesus emphasizes that God is very aware of our every need and is anxious to meet our every need. This is where your faith comes in.

In the overall context of the Bible and how it applies to our lives, we must never forget what it means to have a relationship with God. A significant part of serving our creator God is that He has a purpose plan and will for our lives and submitting to God's plan for our life is a substantial part of our relationship with Him. When we pursue our calling, we can expect that God will meet our every need.

This is not to say that our lives will be "peaches and cream". Suffering to one degree or another is part of the equation – Jesus tells us that. For some, that calling – that path – will be dangerous and could involve significant risk. Read Foxe's Book of Martyrs (or any other book about martyrs, for that matter) – it is full of stories of men and women who suffered and died for God's Kingdom. Like Jesus, and as Paul tells us in Romans 8:17:

Now if we are children, then we are heirs—heirs of God and co-heirs with Christ, if indeed we share in his sufferings in order that we may also share in his glory. I consider that our present sufferings are not worth comparing with the glory that will be revealed in us.

In other words, Jesus suffered just like us (actually, far greater than any of us can ever expect to!)

46

The Walk Applied

SECURITY replaces HOME

The natural need/idol of home is merely the physical manifestation of what we know as security. There is a fundamental drive in all of us for shelter. Certainly, this includes far more than just protection from the elements. It seems intuitive that the drive for what we know or desire as "HOME" is a very complex, invested deep emotional amalgam of protection, family, intimacy, comfort and love. When we enter our "HOME", there is usually an emotion that is unlike anything else that reflects something that's almost primal. No doubt, the notion of "HOME" reflects a certain something that seems far more than the sum of the parts. Conversely, when that notion of 'HOME' is violated by natural disaster or at the hands of others - accidentally or violently – there's usually profound feelings of violation, betrayal and insecurity as well as fear, anxiety and any number of other emotions. A house is a structure, but a "HOME" is something far more.

SPIRITUAL IDENTITY replaces IDENTITY

The Bible lays out a vison of what it means to be a new creation in Christ – a vision that is so exciting and overwhelming that nothing in the natural can even begin to compare with it. We were bought and paid for via the death and suffering of the Son of God. In other words, we have been deemed priceless; our value is inestimable. We are fully accepted and loved, and nothing can change that. We have been adopted and made citizens of His spiritual kingdom. We each have been declared and judged perfect via the promise covenant. We each have been given a grand purpose and a mighty calling that is fulfilling beyond anything we might accomplish in the natural for earthly purposes. And we will spend eternity in the company of the Living God. Nothing on earth can compare to that, or even approach it.

The Walk Applied

ADOPTION REPLACES INTIMACY & ACCEPTANCE

We all want to be accepted by those around us, and it represents a very powerful urge in our faith. Indeed, there is nothing inherently wrong with seeking intimacy and acceptance. God encourages these qualities in our life, and He brings people into our life that can satisfy this legitimate need. But we can never forget that Christ is "the way, the truth and the life." It is in a true spiritual relationship that we experience full acceptance, intimacy, and love. It is in the safe harbor of Christ that we can find the full peace of someone who supports us and never reject us. Hebrews tells us:

"Keep your lives free from the love of money and be content with what you have, because God has said, "Never will I leave you; never will I forsake you." So we say with confidence, "The Lord is my helper; I will not be afraid. What can man do to me?" (Heb 13:5-6)

WISDOM REPLACES KNOWLEDGE

In our rational society, knowledge is king. We want to believe that we can somehow, we can figure out everything we need to know. Since we are "evolving" to ever higher levels, we don't need God. This false belief belies the truth that "knowledge puffs up" and that without love, knowledge is worthless. Make no mistake knowledge is indeed valuable in the right context. Galatians reports that God wants us to increase in knowledge. Yet, Proverbs 3:15 plainly tells us that wisdom is vastly superior to mere knowledge: *"She is more precious than rubies; nothing you desire can compare with her."*

48

The Walk Applied

CALLING REPLACES PURPOSE

In God, we have a purpose, plan and will that bring us a fulfillment that far exceeds any natural purpose. It is true that there are many noble and worthwhile purposes here in the natural, it seems intuitive that God has an eternal purpose that applies to each and every one of us. Jeremiah has a very ponderous message for us:

"This is what the LORD says: "Stand at the crossroads and look; ask for the ancient paths, ask where the good way is, and walk in it, and you will find rest for your souls." (Jer 6:16)

"...let us run with perseverance the race marked out for us." (Heb 12:1)

"I will instruct you and teach you in the way you should go" (Ps 32:8)

As we'll discuss later, we are eternal creatures living an eternal existence and we will have to face an almighty God who sent us here to seek and obey His will. What is of primary import to God in our relationship with Him is that we walk the path He has set aside for us. The question that God will ask of us is: "Did you follow the path I set aside for you? Good question, that!

49

The Walk Applied

CHAPTER 3
SALVATION

The Walk Applied

The Walk Applied

CHAPTER 3
SALVATION

We have discussed that those who are saved are the bride of Christ. We know Jesus is coming back for his bride. We may not be able to fully comprehend what it means to be the bride and the bible does not tell us why Jesus wants a bride. We do know that to be the Bride of Christ, we must be saved.

To be saved, we must acknowledge some elemental propositions of the Salvation Covenant. First, we agree that we are sinners who are separated from God because of our sin. Second, we recognize that Jesus was indeed God in the flesh who lived the perfect life and redeemed us by paying the only acceptable price for our sin – a price that we could never pay. Third, we concur that we must submit our lives wholly to the one true living creator God of the Universe.

When we come into agreement with God, we fulfill our end of the great Promise Covenant that God offers to us, and we are then re-born. Our spirit is then raised from the dead, and we are then judged perfect and righteous because we have complied with what God has asked us. The Promise Covenant guarantees us eternal life in Heaven, fellowship with our Heavenly Father and Jesus as the Bride of Christ, payment for our sins and much more. Another way of stating God's conditions for salvation and the heaven are as follows:

1) We must be declared perfect (Matt 5:48). Because of the fall and the subsequent curse, humans are inherently sinful; therefore, the only way to achieve perfect righteousness is to be declared so by God. Matthew 5:48 tells us that we must "*be perfect as our Father in heaven is perfect*". Coming into agreement with God's salvation covenant is the only way we can be declared perfect. Our works mean nothing as far as righteousness is concerned.

The Walk Applied

2) Submission to God's authority as the One True Sovereign Creator God of all things thru faith in Jesus Christ.

3) We must firmly believe that Jesus was God in the flesh who suffered and died on the cross and rose from the dead as the payment for all of mankind's sins; past present and future.

4) We fully acknowledge that we are sinners who are separated from God because of our sinfulness. This is not just some minor, offhand admission of our sin and our guilt. In our sinful condition, God views us as actually being in rebellion against Him! That's why in Romans 2 He talks about His great wrath against those who do not believe in Him.

Salvation is the act of entering into a legally binding covenant relationship with God. Simply put, a covenant is a legal, binding agreement on both sides. Salvation is God's offer to us to be accepted under his terms, and his terms only. He does not have to offer us salvation; He does so solely at his discretion, and completely under his conditions. We do not have to accept his offer. Should we choose to decline, then we are choosing to live without him in the eternal realm. Not accepting his continuing offer also means that we live under Satan's authority for the duration of our natural lives. The offer is of salvation is available virtually through our lifetime.

Another way of looking at salvation is by seeing it as "settlement". We acknowledge that we have come out of agreement with God (we repent). We further acknowledge God's sovereign authority over us. Indeed, we come into agreement with God by speaking and believing that agreement. Further we accept the Jesus death on the cross as the sole, atoning act for sin. God reciprocates with justification, by declaring us righteous and perfect. Since the price for sin was paid by Jesus death on the cross, we can accept the

The Walk Applied

imputing and declaration of righteousness unto us. This is what allows us to commune with Him, and qualifies us for heaven.

Many Christians fail to recognize that God's great offer to us is, in fact, a legal and binding transaction. It is not somehow conditional on what we do after the fact. When we come into agreement with God's great promise covenant, salvation is signed, sealed and delivered. Paul lets us know for certain that it is a legal guarantee! We are sealed with God's seal!

"Now it is God who makes both us and you stand firm in Christ. He anointed us, set his seal of ownership on us, and put his Spirit in our hearts as a deposit, guaranteeing what is to come."
(2 Cor 1:21-22)

For many, however, salvation can become a "covenant of works". Christians can easily find themselves believing that now they have to "do good things" or "stop doing bad things". It is a trap that even the most seasoned Christian can find themselves entwined in. Unfortunately, what it can mean for some is that if they do the following five things, they are more Godly people:

- Pray
- Read my bible
- Go to church
- Stop doing "bad" things
- Do more "good" things

Without question, these are worthwhile pursuits. The issue becomes quite problematic, however, when a works and performance orientation become the basis of our submissive relationship with Christ. Christ died and rose again so that we might have an ongoing, intimate relationship with him, not to see how well we could stop sinning!

The Walk Applied

The bottom line of our participation in the promise covenant of salvation is that we maintain a living, breathing, intimate, submissive relationship with Jesus on a daily basis. Unfortunately, for many Christians, working this spiritual relationship out on a daily basis such that it has a significant practical impact remains a mystery. Later, we will address the question of "How do you do this Jesus thing, anyway?"

A CRUCIAL DISTINCTION

A very subtle but profound distinction that needs to be made regarding salvation is that the criteria for getting into Heaven is NOT salvation. What gets you into Heaven is that your spirit is alive. Now, the absolute pre-requisite for your spirit to be alive is that you must be saved – you must be born again. We understand that only life can be present in Heaven, not death. Thus, what actually gets you into Heaven is that your Spirit is alive.

REPENTANCE: THE PRIMARY INGREDIENT

Repentance means to <u>sincerely</u> commit to turn away from idolatry. To repent means to "change direction". You acknowledge that you are making a solemn life-changing pledge to turn to God to worship Him and Him alone.

A problem for many is that they mis-interpret what true repentance is. They tend to think that if you commit the same sin again, you "didn't really mean what you said" or you "didn't do it right". Both of these views are nonsense. When you truly repent, you are stating to God that you want to shed your fleshly belief system and take on your new Godly belief system that has already been installed in you by virtue of the fact that the Spirit has taken up residence in you. Only you and the Lord can examine your true motives, however. If you said a prayer of repentance to make it sound good, you need to confess your sin. That said, you may have a weak area in your life

The Walk Applied

– like many addicts, for example – that will take time and work to resolve. I have worked with a number of individuals who have had a challenging time resolving sin areas in their lives. They uttered prayers of repentance as sincerely as any I've heard. Each time they fell, we'd utter prayers of repentance together. Ultimately, they would be healed.

A simple prayer of repentance tells God that you reject the idolatry in your life, and that you want to take on whatever the Sprit has for you. Simple, direct, and to the point. No fanfare or wailing or theatrics. Then ask God to lead you along Godly paths that He has in store for you!

YOU CANNOT "LOSE YOUR SALVATION"

A topic of lively debate in the church is whether or not one can "lose" their salvation. Our position here is that salvation is a binding covenant that says that once you come to saving knowledge of Jesus Christ, you are always saved. This belief is usually stated "once saved, always saved". Many in the church concur with that statement; others disagree. We believe that Scripture lays it out in no uncertain terms that we can know for an absolute fact that we are saved:

"I write these things to you who believe in the name of the Son of God so that you may know that you have eternal life" (1 John 5:13)

"...set his seal of ownership on us, and put his Spirit in our hearts as a deposit, guaranteeing what is to come." (2 Cor 1:22)

"Now the one who has fashioned us for this very purpose is God, who has given us the Spirit as a deposit, guaranteeing what is to come." (2 Cor 5:5)

The Walk Applied

"...who is a deposit guaranteeing our inheritance until the redemption of those who are God's possession—to the praise of his glory.' (Eph 1:14)

In addition to the scriptures above, there is nothing in the Bible that specifically lays out how we would lose our salvation. Given the extraordinary significance of being born again, one might surmise that God would surely specify the conditions under which one might lose their salvation.

Indeed, the implication that we can lose our salvation or walk away from salvation presents significant scriptural problems. The logical implication is that you could conceivably have multiple "salvation experiences". That would mean that you could have multiple spiritual "births" and "deaths". That position strains biblical credibility to say the least. Multiple adoptions and multiple "Godly citizenships" simply cannot be, according to scripture. The Bible talks specifically about two births and one death – never multiple births and deaths. In John 3:5-7, Jesus explains all this to Nicodemus:

"Jesus answered, "Very truly I tell you, no one can enter the kingdom of God unless they are born of water and the Spirit. Flesh gives birth to flesh, but the Spirit gives birth to spirit. You should not be surprised at my saying, 'You must be born again.'

Romans 6 emphasizes that there can only be one death!

"Now if we died with Christ, we believe that we will also live with him. For we know that since Christ was raised from the dead, he cannot die again; death no longer has mastery over him. The death he died, he died to sin once for all; but the life he lives, he lives to God. In the same way, count yourselves dead to sin but alive to God in Christ Jesus." (Rom 6:8-11)

The Walk Applied

YOU ARE ALIVE BECAUSE
THE SPIRIT INHABITS YOU

Amazingly enough, scripture clearly proclaims that you are alive because of the Spirits inhabitation. The Spirit takes up residence in you and brings you to life at the instant of salvation. We'll see how Tim Keller talks about this concept very shortly. Note the following passages:

"I have been crucified with Christ and I no longer live, but Christ lives in me. The life I now live in the body, I live by faith in the Son of God, who loved me and gave himself for me." (Gal 2:20)

"Set your minds on things above, not on earthly things. For you died, and your life is now hidden with Christ in God." (Col 3:2-3)

"For we know that if the earthly tent we live in is destroyed, ... For while we are in this tent" (2 Cor 5:2,4)

"So from now on we regard no one from a worldly point of view..." (2 Cor 5:16-17)

"Now if we have died with Christ, we believe that we shall also live with Him..." (Rom 6:8)

We reiterate: the amazing truth is that you are now alive because God's Holy Spirit keeps you alive. If you could lose your salvation, that would mean that the Spirit would leave you and you would die – what would then raise you instantaneously again? And even if you were somehow to remain alive, how many times would the Spirit "re-inhabit" you? There's nothing in scripture that support this idea.

59

The Walk Applied

There are those who will tragically proclaim that they no longer believe. We would maintain that for those who walk away from the faith that they never were saved to begin with. They usually mean they "want to try this Jesus thing out" to see if they will benefit in one way or another. When it does not work out to their satisfaction – what they think should happen, they will usually walk away. Perhaps they had a personal issue that they expected God to take away or resolve and God didn't "perform" in the way they expected.

Another sad situation is when a person proclaims to be saved but is never discipled properly. This should never happen, but it happens far too often. Remember, Jesus told us to make disciples, not just get them saved.

SALVATION "CORALLARIES": KNOWING FOR A FACT THAT I AM SAVED

The promise covenant of salvation has enormous impact for our lives. We will cover the most significant salvation "corollaries" here. To clarify, these are not required in order to be saved, but they are significant indicators that you have, in fact, been saved. These "salvation corollaries" can help guide those who question whether or not they are truly saved. If you read the next few paragraphs and find that you are lacking in most of them, then perhaps it is time to check in with God. If you are truly saved you really should be experiencing at least 5 of these to one degree or another. Some may have issues with #6 due to their history of disappointment in various churches.

We note here that there are various doctrinal truths like the Trinity and the resurrection (among others) that Christians need to accept as God's truth. The following list is dedicated to the internal motivations that really should be present in your heart.

The Walk Applied

You should have a fundamental desire to know and serve God.

One aspect of true salvation is that at some point, there should be an abiding, fundamental desire to simply know God and have a desire to serve Him. If you proclaim that you have decided that He is truly the One True Living Sovereign Creator God, don't you want to know Him? It simply doesn't make sense that if you have truly come to believe that God Himself loves you, how could you simply ignore Him? To not foundational motivation to be drawn to Him should really cause you to examine yourself.

You should have a fundamental desire to have an intimate personal relationship with "Abba Father".

God is emphatic that He desires for us to have a deeply personal and intimate relationship with him. He makes it clear in His word that He accepts us exactly as we are: completely and without reservation. He made us in His image (Gen. 1) and He loves us far more than we can ask or even begin to imagine. In fact, the phrase "Abba Father" in the Bible actually means "Daddy"! God wants us to see Him as a warm, loving, protective father who loves us and accepts us exactly as we are. He has implanted within us an abiding desire to relate to him in an intimate way, and salvation "wakes up" that desire. Thus, there should be a distinct and deep desire to get to know Him, relate to Him and indeed love him.

The belief that the Bible is God's inerrant Word of truth.

Christians believe that the Bible is God's revelation to mankind about Himself, the spiritual realm and what he wants us to know about our existence. We believe firmly that God's word is the basis of all truth, and that it sets forth, unadulterated truth. Since it is God's truth revealed to us, it instructs us and changes us as we read it and integrate it. Don't make the mistake of thinking you cannot question His word! Christians question His word all the time, and

The Walk Applied

He encourages us to do so. That said, if you do not recognize God's word as the basis of truth, it's very likely time to examine your relationship with God.

The desire to bear lasting personal & corporate fruit.

Evidence of our relationship with God should be the notion that we want to do what His Word directs us to. That means we want to "bear lasting fruit" – in Biblical terms, we want to be about the business of building His Kingdom by being a "people changer". We ourselves should want to change. We should be about the business of helping others change, as well. In other words, there should be a fundamental leading to do "Godly things". If that drive isn't there in some way shape or form, you should consider getting together with God.

You died to the flesh.

We just covered this in great detail, but the profound truth in this concept is something that many Christians fail to appreciate. So, it's worth reinforcing. We'll go about it in a separate way this time. Paul, in his letter to the Colossians, makes the stunning assertion that when we accept Christ, we actually die:

"Since, then, you have been raised with Christ, set your hearts on things above, where Christ is, seated at the right hand of God. Set your minds on things above, not on earthly things. For you died, and your life is now hidden with Christ in God. When Christ, who is your life, appears, then you also will appear with him in glory." (Col 3:3)

The Walk Applied

Jesus apparently died on the cross only after he gave up His spirit:

"And when Jesus had cried out again...he gave up his spirit." (Matt 27:50)

In Romans, Paul goes to great lengths to contend that this is much more than any figurative language. Paul wants us to understand that he is talking about an actual death – just as if we had "flat-lined" on the operating table:

"We were therefore buried with him through baptism into death in order that, just as Christ was raised from the dead through the glory of the Father, we too may live a new life. For if we have been united with him in a death like his, we will certainly also be united with him in a resurrection like his. For we know that our old self was crucified with him so that the body ruled by sin might be done away with, that we should no longer be slaves to sin because anyone who has died has been set free from sin. <u>Now if we died with Christ, we believe that we will also live with him.</u> For we know that since Christ was raised from the dead, he cannot die again; death no longer has mastery over him. The death he died, he died to sin once for all; but the life he lives, he lives to God. <u>In the same way, count yourselves dead to sin but alive to God in Christ Jesus."</u>
(Rom 6:4-11).

Keller contends that we actually do die, but the Spirit takes up residence in us instantaneously and actually keeps us alive. Romans 8 supports Keller's amazing conclusion in no uncertain terms:

"But you are not in the flesh but in the Spirit, if indeed the Spirit of God dwells in you. Now if anyone does not have the Spirit of Christ, he is not His. And if Christ is in you, the body dead because of sin, but the Spirit is life because of righteousness. But if the Spirit of Him who raised Jesus from the dead dwells in you, He who raised

63

The Walk Applied

Christ from the dead will also give life to your mortal bodies through His Spirit who dwells in you. " (Rom 8:9-11)

Once again, this idea may be shocking and not just a little outlandish to some. Yet, His Word is confirming what Keller concludes: When we come to know Christ, we physically die. The Holy Spirit then takes up residence in us in a way we cannot understand and actually keeps us alive. Truly astounding!

The desire to congregate with God's people.

There is little doubt that God wants his people to congregate and worship corporately on the Sabbath. Isaiah 58 talks about what it means to honor the Sabbath:

"If you keep your feet from breaking the Sabbath and from doing as you please on my holy day, if you call the Sabbath a delight and the Lord's holy day honorable, and if you honor it by not going your own way and not doing as you please or speaking idle words, then you will find your joy in the Lord, and I will cause you to ride in triumph on the heights of the land and to feast on the inheritance of your father Jacob. "For the mouth of the Lord has spoken.
(Isa 58:9-10).

This is not the place for an exposition of the Sabbath and what it all means. Yet, the idea of honoring the Sabbath is certainly critical in God's thinking. It is most unfortunate when we hear of people who decide not to attend Sunday services on a regular consistent basis, for this is certainly not God's will. Indeed, the clear contention of God's word: Be an active part of a congregation and find a place to serve as God intends you to.

The Walk Applied

LEGAL IMPLICATIONS OF SALVATION

As noted earlier, salvation is a legal transaction initiated by God. Let's examine some of the "legal implications" of the Promise Covenant of Salvation.

ATONEMENT

Jesus death on the cross and His subsequent resurrection three days later constitute a very profound concept known as the Atonement. In simplest terms it means that Jesus paid the price for sin - mine, yours, all of humanity - for all eternity. God Himself says in His Word that the only acceptable payment for mankind's collective sin would be a perfect sinless blood sacrifice. The Bible says that the wages of sin are death. Thus, Jesus, the Father's Son became God in the flesh (via the birth from a virgin – a human impossibility) by taking on human form. He lived the perfect, sinless life that was required to be the perfect and acceptable payment for sin. Jesus took it upon himself to accept a brutal and agonizing death by crucifixion. In so doing, He paid the awful price for sin that we could never pay. His resurrection three days later was the victory over death and gave the ultimate proof (although there are many others recorded in the Bible) the Jesus was in fact, God in the flesh.

REDEMPTION

You have been redeemed - literally, you have been bought and paid for. Jesus paid for you with the currency of his blood being shed via his torturous death on the cross. In essence, the "title deed" to you passed from the "prince of this world" to our Heavenly Father. The Father, because He is the Creator God, reserves the right to claim us as His very own because he made each and every one of us. However, He asks that we choose to come under His authority. God does not demand that we love him. This is a choice we must

The Walk Applied

make. God is Love and love does demand or require that we love in return. We have a free will to choose God or reject him.

JUSTIFICATION

An integral part of salvation is that upon your agreement with the Promise Covenant, you are now declared justified. This means that you have been judged perfectly righteous by God. Since Jesus paid the required price for sin, and you accepted the offer of Salvation that means that your sins are covered by the Blood of Jesus. In the eyes of God, you have been declared perfect – indeed, just as if you HAD NEVER SINNED. This is a difficult doctrine for many to absorb because we don't stop sinning. After all, we are idolaters who sin by nature. The difference here is our understanding of God's "rules". The price of all of humanity's sin was the shedding of blood by the perfect offering – which could only be fulfilled by Jesus. Once Jesus accomplished his horrific task, sin was paid for forever. The awful price was paid in full. With the offering of the promise covenant and your acceptance of the covenant, God judges that your personal sin has now been accounted for - past, present and future. Thus, your sin no longer counts against you. Will you sin again? Of course. Many who are saved may even experience regression - some significantly so. There are no hard and fast rules about how your individual experience will work out with Jesus. What is asked of you, though, is that you are faithful as you walk the road with Jesus. We will cover this in greater detail later.

REGENERATION:
YOUR SPIRIT IS RAISED FROM THE DEAD

The notion of regeneration can be a difficult concept to absorb. To be "regenerated" means that your "Spirit-Man" has been raised to life the instant you are saved. Let's try to simplify, shall we?

The Walk Applied

It is the opinion of the large majority of Christians that we human beings are actually made up of 3 "parts" if you will: Body, Soul, and Spirit. First, we all occupy a natural body – our flesh and blood, bones, muscles, nerves, skin, brain, etc. and the various organs that we all have. Sometimes referred to as our flesh, our natural body can be viewed as our "container" that allows us to participate in the physical world that we know and see every day. Second, we all possess a soul. You can liken it to the "modem" that connects you to the Heavenly realm. It's what allows the flesh to communicate between the spirit man and the Heavenly realm. Third, we all have what is called the "Spirit Man". When we are saved, our Spirit man is brought to life as God's Holy Spirit takes up spiritual residence in us. The Holy Spirit is actually God's spirit – the third member of the trinity – who comes to live in us. As Jesus tells us, the Spirit is the one leads us into all truth.

BAPTISM: A RITE OF PASSAGE

Jesus commanded us to be baptized; He wanted us to make a public declaration of salvation. Baptism symbolizes the resurrection of your spirit as well as your public demonstration of your private commitment to God. Baptism is also a rite of passage that should have a palpable, emotional impact on you. In Biblical times, the act changed how others perceived you, and it changed you in how you perceived yourself. In our times, it should certainly change how we see ourselves. Baptism is not required to be saved, and it is most unfortunate that most see it as little more than ceremonial in our day and age.

SANCTIFICATION

To be sanctified means that you are now set aside for God's use. The Bible tells us that we have been purchased (redeemed, as we discussed earlier) by God, and He now owns us. Among other things, it also means that you are a priest in His kingdom. You also

The Walk Applied

now have a calling on your life. You can now understand the spiritual. Before, you only knew the natural and its ways. Now, as you walk the path with Jesus, you will learn over time how to "live the spiritual".

SALVATION & GOOD WORKS:
WHY "WORKS WON'T WORK"

Most Christians understand that our salvation walk with Jesus differs radically from religion in that faith in Jesus is based on what Jesus did. Religion is based on what we do. Sadly, many Christians believe that because they are "basically pretty good" and "they have never done anything really bad" they deserve to go to Heaven. In other words, they believe that their works justify them. There are 5 reasons why works simply won't work. We can thank the late D. James Kennedy – a wonderful man of God - for the following exposition of why "works don't work".

GOOD WORKS ARE ARBITRARY

If works were the standard, what would decide the standard of goodness? The golden rule? The 10 commandments? Would we just do our best? There would have to be a different yardstick for each and every person. How unfair would that be? Imagine if you and I went to the movies together, and they charged me $5, and they charged you $10. You would howl in protest and demand to know why you were charged more than me!

GOOD WORKS LACK ASSURANCE

Turning the argument around, we can see that good works lack assurance. Again, what's the standard? What's the yardstick? What's the measure? To reiterate, you would literally have to have a different standard for just about everyone. The Bible clearly states the requirements of the Salvation covenant so that we can know for

The Walk Applied

a fact that we are saved. It leaves no doubt as to whether or not you are saved or not. You never need to worry if you had "scored enough points".

GOOD WORKS ASK GOD TO APPROVE OF EVIL

By covenant, we are declared perfect. What makes us evil is shed. What gets us into heaven is that our spirit is alive. There can be no sin or evil in heaven. Therefore, there can be no evil or sin allowed into heaven. Salvation by works would mean that God would have to approve of sin and evil in Heaven, which cannot be.

GOOD WORKS CONTRADICT THE BIBLE

The Bible declares that we are saved by faith, not works. Any system of works is by definition arbitrary and capricious. A system of works is dependent on us and what we do. The Bible tells us that Christ did all the heavy lifting: all we have to do is believe. Salvation is dependent on what Jesus and what he has already done, not by any set of works.

WHAT'S MORE FAIR?

An arbitrary standard or one that is the same for everyone? Many espouse the notion that if you're a "good" person, you'll go to heaven. However, that just doesn't hold up when we examine what that really means.

HELL & ETERNAL SEPARATION FROM GOD

The Bible clearly teaches that if we are not saved we will experience eternal separation from God in a place (Hell) where God Himself has elected not to dwell in. Agree with it or not, God has decreed that Hell is the consequence for not being saved. Hell is well-documented in the Scriptures and Jesus himself declared that there

The Walk Applied

is a Hell. There are many excellent articles on the reality of Hell as a place whereby there is eternal separation from God. Two articles in particular can be found at the following links:

https://www.gotquestions.org/who-will-go-to-hell.html
http://www1.cbn.com/questions/hell-real-place

A pertinent question to pose here is: why doesn't God just "vaporize" us when we die if we are not going to Heaven? To many of us, it seems entirely "unfair" that just because we don't make the right choice when we are alive that we are eternally condemned! After all, what kind of a loving and just God would condemn people to an eternity of torture? Eternal condemnation seems terribly harsh. Ponderous questions, indeed.

We have to remember that God is perfect and Sovereign over all. He sets the rules, and His rules and commands are always just and right, no matter how it may appear to us or how much we may disagree. Another realization is that nowhere in Scripture do we find where God obliterates any of his spiritual creations. (Genesis 3 where reportedly Adam and Eve's spirits died is perhaps the sole exception; it is far more likely that their spirits "left" them). The profound significance of this statement is not to be underestimated and is a key to understanding the whole notion of Hell and why God allows it. God will not destroy his spiritual creations because he has total respect for life in the spiritual realm. He allows them to choose where they will spend eternity.

We recall that those who were in heaven or in the presence of God chose to fall. The Bible tells us that Satan, Adam and Eve, and a full one third of the angels made a conscious decision to rebel and come out of Godly Authority. So, even though they were in the presence of God, they still chose to come out of Godly Authority. They exercised free will to do so, as we all can. Thus, His requirement is that we must believe and submit out of faith. God

70

The Walk Applied

has decreed that we must be perfect as He is perfect (Matt 5:48). God has stated clearly in His word the way to be declared perfect, and He gives us solid assurances as well. (1 John 5:14-15).

God asks but one thing: Total and sincere allegiance to Him as the one true living forever God of the universe. God will not allow rebellion in His heaven. You would not allow rebellion in your own home, so why should He?

The Walk Applied

CHAPTER 4
THE NEW CREATION

The Walk Applied

The Walk Applied

CHAPTER 4
THE SPIRITUAL IDENTITY:
THE NEW CREATION

What does it mean to be a Christian? In today's society, ask anyone who defines themselves to be a Christian, and you'll likely get many different answers. The Bible teaches us that to be a Christian is to be a born-again believer who maintains an ongoing faithful relationship with our Lord and Savior Jesus. Some might simply say they are a follower of Jesus Christ. But what does that mean to us on a practical, day to day, basis? How do we translate that to something that's really meaningful? Is it a concept we can express in a few words such that it will take on real meaning for us? Let's start by looking at the "Christian identity". In Christian circles, it won't take very long before you start hearing terminology such as "your Christian identity" or "your identity is found in Jesus" or "your spiritual Identity".

THE IMAGE OF GOD: "IMAGO DEI"

Recall that we were made in the image of God: The "Imago Dei":

"So God created mankind in his own image, in the image of God he created them; male and female he created them." (Gen 1:27)

The phrase "male and female he created them" is crucial here. It's maintained that both male and female are "separate" images of God. Only when we are united together under the marital covenant are we a complete image of God. Otherwise, why would He tell us that the two have become one? Given the complex differences between a man and a woman, it makes sense that each gender has some qualities of God, but not all. A perplexing scripture is Mark 10:

75

The Walk Applied

"A man ... is the image and glory of God; but woman is the glory of man. For man did not come from woman, but woman from man neither was man created for woman, but woman for man. Nevertheless, in the Lord woman is not independent of man, nor is man independent of woman. For as woman came from man, so also man is born of woman. But everything comes from God. " (Mark 10:6-9)

This scripture, even though it differentiates between Man and Woman, still supports the idea that together, we get a complete image of God. The passage points out that even though the sexes are different, they are inextricably tied. Because the woman came after the man, she is to the glory of man because she came from the man. Yet, the scripture makes it plain that we are both of one another.

The significance of being made in the image of God is a profound notion. It's the reason why we "sense" there's a spiritual realm outside of us. It's why we just "know" there's something else that's beyond what we see. Even as children, we feared the dark after Mom or Dad turned out the lights. Many of us just "knew" there was that awful monster under bed or in the closet – who couldn't get to us as long as we were under the covers!

THE MAKING OF ADAM AND EVE

It is profound to note that Adam and Eve were not created by speaking them into existence where nothing existed prior. Instead, they were both made from pre-existing materials – still something only God could do. Adam came from dust, and Eve was fashioned from Adam's rib – a bone. Now, the question becomes why did God do that? By making Adam and Eve from different substances no one could ever say that they were somehow different from the rest of humanity. Indeed, Adam and eve were just like us: they were formed from pre-existing material under a process that only God

76

The Walk Applied

could do. Paul makes a startling statement in his second letter to the Corinthians:

"So from now on we regard no one from a worldly point of view. Though we once regarded Christ in this way, we do so no longer. Therefore, if anyone is in Christ, he is a new creation; the old has gone, the new has come!" (2 Cor 5:16-17)

Paul tells us that if anyone is in Christ, he is a new creation. Remember, when we were saved, we experienced a second, spiritual birth; we were brought to life as spiritual creatures thru a spiritual birth. The act of being saved brought us to life as spiritual creatures as well as physical, natural creature! As Paul further elaborates in 1st Corinthians:

"... it is sown a natural body, it is raised a spiritual body. If there is a natural body, there is also a spiritual body.... The spiritual did not come first, but the natural, and after that the spiritual."
(1 Cor 15:44-46)

Does this seem hard to accept? For some, it might be. God is a spiritual being who lives in the spiritual realm. Angels are spiritual beings. Heaven is in the spiritual realm. For you to be able to commune with God, you must be brought to life as a spiritual being. In our natural bodies, we cannot commune with the spiritual realm. Since you still participate in the natural realm, you must retain your natural, physical body. So, as a Christian, you'll start to think of your existence as not only a natural, physical existence – what you've come to know since you were birthed by your natural mother – but also as a spiritual existence. Understanding what it means to have a spiritual existence will have huge implications for you and how you learn to live your life! Eph 4:22-24 reads:

"You were taught, with regard to your former way of life, to put off your old self, which is being corrupted by its deceitful desires; to be

The Walk Applied

made new in the attitude of your minds; and to put on the new self, created to be like God in true righteousness and holiness. "

Paul tells us to put off the old self and put on the new self. The passage tells us that we were created to be like God in true righteousness and holiness. Paul also tells us we are made new in the attitude of your minds. To have a new attitude is to begin to see things differently than you ever have before. Again, living as a spiritual creature means that over the course of the rest of your life, you'll learn how to think and act differently than you did prior to your salvation. Your belief system will change.

Let's examine additional verses. You may want to try to express in your own words what you think they mean. If you don't understand, don't worry about it; ask your mentor (or your pastor or another experienced Christian) to help you understand.

"Do not lie to each other, since you have taken off your old self with its practices and have put on the new self, which is being renewed in knowledge in the image of its Creator. " (Col 3:9)

"So we fix our eyes not on what is seen, but on what is unseen. For what is seen is temporary, but what is unseen is eternal. "
(2 Cor 4:18)

"...Take hold of the eternal life to which you were called when you made your good confession in the presence of many witnesses. "
(1 Tim 6:12)

"Do not conform any longer to the pattern of this world, but be transformed by the renewing of your mind. " (Rom 12:2)

"And we, who with unveiled faces all reflect the Lord's glory, are being transformed into his likeness with ever-increasing glory, which comes from the Lord, who is the Spirit. " (2 Cor 3:18)

The Walk Applied

Once again, we revisit the mystery of how the Spirit actually keeps us alive so as to emphasize the import of this concept. Passages in the New Testament teach us that we are now actually alive because of the inhabitation of Holy Spirit in us. Tim Keller, Pastor of Redeemer Presbyterian Church in New York City, has taught that we actually physically die – just that same as if we "flat-lined" on the operating table. In the next instant, the Holy Spirit enters us and revives us so quickly that we never even notice what has happened.

"Since, then, you have been raised with Christ, set your hearts on things above, where Christ is seated at the right hand of God. Set your minds on things above, not on earthly things. For you died, and your life is now hidden with Christ in God. When Christ, who is your life, appears, then you also will appear with him in glory." (Col 3:1-4)

"But if Christ is in you, your body is dead because of sin, yet your spirit is alive because of righteousness. And if the Spirit of him who raised Jesus from the dead is living in you, he who raised Christ from the dead will also give life to your mortal bodies through his Spirit, who lives in you." (Rom 8:10-11)

"I have been crucified with Christ and I no longer live, but Christ lives in me. The life I now live in the body, I live by faith in the Son of God, who loved me and gave himself for me." (Gal 2:20)

"Here is a trustworthy saying: If we died with him, we will also live with him" (2 Tim 2:11)

Matthew and John both refer to Jesus death on the cross in a rather strange way. They tell us that Jesus gave His Spirit, instead of saying that He died.

The Walk Applied

"And when Jesus had cried out again in a loud voice, he gave up his spirit" (Matt 27:50)

"When he had received the drink, Jesus said, "It is finished." With that, he bowed his head and gave up his spirit." (John 19:30)

Let's write a working definition of the Christian Identity:

**You are a spiritual creature living a spiritual existence
placed in the natural realm according to
God's purpose, plan, and will
to bear fruit that will last for the kingdom**

You are a spiritual creature: As we just discussed, there are 2 types of existences: the natural and the spiritual, which co-exist at the same time. You are still a natural creature negotiating the natural, but it's critical that you understand that you are also a spiritual being as well.

Living a spiritual existence: We're going to cover this in much greater detail later but understand that what you do in the natural realm affects the spiritual realm and vice versa. The relationship of these two realms may make no sense at all to you right now (that's ok! – it takes a while to get this concept down!!). As we get into the operation of the spiritual realm we're going to find that the spiritual realm controls the natural realm. Thus, it's critical to understand that you utilize "spiritual tools" to accomplish your Godly purpose here in the natural. Probably all very confusing, but it will make sense later – just hold on!

Placed in the natural realm: Even though we have been born again as a spiritual being, we've been left here in the natural. As we'll see later, it's our job to negotiate the natural as a spiritual being.

The Walk Applied

According to God's purpose, plan and will: God has a great purpose and plan for everyone – including you! It may not be apparent to you now, but God's word tells us that we all have a purpose!

To bear fruit that will last for the kingdom: The command has never changed we're to go bear fruit that will last for the Kingdom. More on that later.

We've begun to understand that you are a spiritual creature as well as natural creature and the implications for us. What does that mean for our lives? As a born-again follower of Jesus Christ, the ramifications for you and how you live your life are indeed major. Perhaps most important is what you will come to believe about your life. You may not understand (or believe) the following about yourselves, but as you pursue your relationship with Christ, God will bring you the point whereby you intimately believe what follows about your life. Indeed, you will be changed in ways you never thought possible! Remember all of the following attributes are justified in scripture.

THE SPIRITUAL BEING LIVING A SPIRITUAL EXISTENCE IN THE NATURAL IS:

ADOPTED
> You have been legally adopted into the family of God
> You are in the bloodline of Abraham

RIGHTEOUS
> You have been justified; God has declared you righteous
> and imputed righteousness to you

SANCTIFIED
> God has set you apart as holy for His use
> to accomplish His mission

The Walk Applied

ETERNAL
    You are eternal
    Death is nothing more than a change of form
    The natural life is preparation for the spiritual realm
VALUABLE
    You are a pearl of great price worth dying for
    You are fully loved and fully accepted
    You cannot be separated from the love of God
ANNOINTED
    You are anointed and appointed to go
    You have everything you need to complete your mission
VICTORIOUS
    You are more than a conqueror
    You are an overcomer by definition
PEACEFUL
    You are at peace because you intimately know and believe:
    God is completely in command of every aspect of your life
    You see God's hand in every circumstance
SURRENDERED
    Your life is completely surrendered to the Lord
    You genuinely want to fully come under God's authority
    You have pledged your life to complete a Godly mission
LAYS DOWN HIS LIFE FOR THE LORD
    Offers his life so as to bear much fruit that will last
    Seeks God's will for all the major decisions in his life
    Desires that Christ will increase and that you will decrease
AN ACTIVE BLESSER OF ALL WHO ENCOUNTER HIM
    He continually blesses all who he meets
    He never curses anyone
A PEOPLE CHANGER
    People are changed because they know you.
    People are drawn to you because you are salt and light.

The Walk Applied

OUR HERITAGE

- We are legally adopted into the bloodline of Abraham
- The heroes of Hebrews 11 are our forefathers spiritually and legally: We are their descendants in every sense of the word.

THE MISSION

- Submit to God's authority out of love
- Passionately commune with God
- Passionately seek the wisdom of God
- Bear lasting corporate fruit for the kingdom:
  - Be a "People Changer" and make disciples
  - Restore the hurting
  - Changing others simply because they know you
- Bear lasting personal fruit
- Rip down the principalities of Satan

THE VISION

- Learn thru your ongoing, continuous relationship with Jesus to negotiate the natural realm as a spiritual creature living a spiritual existence. We are here to be trained:
  - To prepare us for heaven
  - Prepare for heavenly tasks that God has set aside for us

Paul Billheimer, in his book, "Destined For The Throne", says this about our existence here:

"It is God's way of giving the church on-the-job-training... this world is a laboratory in which those destined for the throne are learning...as an apprenticeship for an eternity of reigning with Christ...what foes will be left to overcome in the eternal ages, we do not know... Therefore, from all eternity, all that precedes the marriage supper of the lamb is preliminary and preparatory. Only

83

The Walk Applied

thereafter will God's program for the eternal ages begin to unfold.... up and until then, the entire universe under the Son's regulation and control is being manipulated by God for one purpose – to prepare and train the bride"

" ...train yourself to be godly. For physical training is of some value, but godliness has value for all things, holding promise for both the present life and the life to come. This is a trustworthy saying that deserves full acceptance." (1 Tim 4:7-9)

A crucial realization is that when we come to understand that we are eternal, we grasp that our death is nothing more than a change of form! This natural life is merely the first phase of our existence. This natural realm is the training ground for our eventual eternal existence. When we start thinking of ourselves as eternal, the context of our thinking changes dramatically!

THE PROCESS IS THE KEY;
THE DAILY WALK WITH JESUS IS THE OBJECT

God has a purpose, plan, will, and a way for each and every one of us. God knows both our beginning and where He wants us in the end. We don't know the end, so we follow Him. It's up to us to trust Him. Remember: *"Jesus answered, "I am the way and the truth and the life."* (John 14:6)

The Bible gives numerous passages that make it abundantly clear what it means to know that our identity is in Christ. Below are a number of these scriptures. These give ample proof that your perception of yourself should be totally different than how you may have seen yourself prior to being saved. Indeed, your heart should leap for joy as you ponder what the Bible says about you and you new identity in Christ.

The Walk Applied

1 Cor 3:16	God's temple where the spirit of God dwells
1 Cor 6:17	United with the Lord
1 Cor 6:19-20	Purchased and owned by God
1 John 4:4	From God and have overcome the devil
1 John 5:11-12	Living an eternal life through the son
1 John 5:18	Born of God; no evil thing can harm me
1 Pet 2:24	Healed by his wounds
1 Pet 5:1	Going to share in the glory to be revealed
2 Cor 1:20-22	Anointed & sealed by God
2 Cor 10:4	Empowered to demolish evil strongholds
2 Cor 10:5	Taking captive every thought
2 Cor 4:18	Fixing my eyes on the unseen
2 Cor 5:7	Walking by faith
2 Cor 5:17	A new creation
2 Cor 5:21	The righteousness of God
2 Cor 6:1	God's co-worker
2 Pet 1:4	Participating in the divine nature
2 Tim 1:7	The possessor of a spirit of power, love
Acts 1:8	Christ's personal witness
Col 1:13	Delivered from the dominion of darkness
Col 1:14	Forgiven
Col 2:13	Alive in Christ & forgiven
Due 28:6	Blessed coming and blessed going
Due 28:13	The head and not the tail
Eph 1:1	A saint
Eph 1:3	Blessed with all spiritual blessings
Eph 1:5	Adopted as God's child
Eph 2:6	Seated with Christ in the heavenly realm
Eph 2:8	Saved by grace thru faith
Eph 2:10	God's workmanship
Eph 2:18	Given direct access to God
Eph 3:12	Able to approach God with freedom
Eph 5:1	An imitator of Jesus

The Walk Applied

Eph 6:10	Strong in the Lord
Gal 3:13	Redeemed from the curse of the law
Gal 3:13-14	Receiving the blessings given to Abraham
Heb 4:16	Able to find grace and mercy in time of need
John 1:12	God's child
John 15:15	Christ's friend
John 15:16	Chosen and appointed to bear fruit
Luke 10:19	Exercising my authority over the enemy
Matt 5:13	The salt of the earth
Matt 5:14	The light of the world
Phi 1:6	The good work begun will be perfected
Phi 3:20	A citizen of heaven
Phi 4:13	Capable of doing everything thru Christ
Phi 4:19	Getting all my needs met thru his glorious riches
Ps 91:11	Guarded in all my ways by his angels
Ps 107:2	Redeemed from the hand of the enemy
Rom 5:1	Justified through faith
Rom 8:1	Free forever from condemnation
Rom 8:16	A child of God
Rom 8:17	God's heir
Rom 8:28	Assured that all things work for good
Rom 8:31f	Free from condemnation
Rom 8:37	More than a conqueror
Rom 8:39-40	Inseparable from the love of God
Rom 12:2	Being transformed by the renewing of my mind

THE SPIRITUAL IDENTITY: PERSONALITY TRAITS

We'll now examine different personality traits that the New Testament tells us what we should aspire to exhibit as new creations in Christ as part of our spiritual identity. This listing comes from 2 main sources: what are commonly referred to as the Beatitudes in the Sermon on the Mount (Matthew 5) and Galatians 5. We'll start with the Beatitudes:

The Walk Applied

POOR IN SPIRIT: We acknowledge our spiritual bankruptcy. We confess our unworthiness and utter dependence on God.

MOURNS FOR THE LOST: We mourn over not only the condition of the lost, but to mourn over the suffering of God's people.

MEEK: We're free from malice and a vengeful spirit.

HUNGER AND THIRST FOR RIGHTEOUSNESS: We hunger and thirst that we may be righteous (wholly sold out to God's will from the heart). Unrighteousness should grieve us and makes us homesick for the new heaven and earth.

MERCIFUL: We embraces forgiveness for the guilty and compassion for the suffering and needy. We acknowledge to others that we are sinners; we have compassion on others, for they are sinners, as well.

PURE IN HEART: We aspire to have true inner moral purity. We should be single minded and have an undivided heart. The "pure in heart" are those who are utterly sincere in their walk with Jesus.

PEACEMAKER: We seek reconciliation with others. Disciples of Jesus delight to make peace wherever possible. We, as heirs of the kingdom, who are meek and poor in spirit, express loving righteousness. We are merciful, so we are especially equipped for peacemaking. In so doing, we reflect Our heavenly Father's character.

The Walk Applied

THE FRUIT OF THE SPIRIT: GALATIANS 5

A fundamental aspect of a truly intimate relationship with Jesus means we will change over time. Sanctification tells us that as we pursue Jesus, we will begin to look more like Jesus in thought and deed. In his letter to the Galatians, Paul details 9 areas we will develop in over time. Paul's caution to us is that we not try to hurry the Sprit's work in us; instead, he tells us to "keep in step with the Spirit", and not try to work around or get ahead of the Spirit. The Holy Spirit's job is to lead us into all truth: he knows best how and when to develop us as the Father sees fit.

Loving, Joyful, Peaceful: Christian habits of mind.
Patient, Kind, Good: Christian social virtues.
Faithful, Gentle, Self-Controlled: Christian traits of the Heart.

PERSECUTION & SUFFERING

It will be quickly apparent as you step forward as a true follower of Jesus Christ, there will be many who will not take kindly to your new status. Jesus flatly stated that there will be those who will hate you for what you believe. Jesus made it abundantly clear that we can certainly expect the following: We will be persecuted, insulted, slandered and libeled. Unbelievers will try to humiliate and embarrass you. There will come times when proclaiming you Christianity will make you call on your deepest emotional reserves as well as crying out to Jesus. It's all part of the overall Christian experience. God promises to never abandon us, indeed. Let us never forget that we will spend eternity in Heaven, and as Paul tells us, our "momentary suffering" is nothing compared to our inheritance in Jesus. We have an astounding and amazing hope in Jesus, and that will never change. Our hope is in Jesus, and that has to be our context. Jesus told us that trouble is part of our life here. All of us will (not may) experience physical and/or emotional suffering. Jesus warned us in no uncertain terms:

The Walk Applied

"I have told you these things, so that in me you may have peace. In this world you will have trouble. But take heart! I have overcome the world." (John 16:33)

Examine more closely what Jesus says. He does not promise to relieve our suffering or emotional distress in this passage. Jesus wants us to know that our comfort will come from His victory. He wants us to understand there will be <u>context</u> to our plight when we enter into challenging times. In other words, we will have purpose and perspective to our suffering. We may not understand the circumstances and our distress may seem unbearable. Yet we have our hope through our faith in Jesus. It's all temporary; a time is coming when all will be resolved. Indeed, *"I can do all things through Christ who strengthens me"* (Phil 4:13).

SONSHIP & SPIRITUAL ADOPTION

Adoption and Sonship are two very under-emphasized Biblical concepts in Christianity. These topics are among the most powerful notions in the entire Bible. To dismiss sonship is to dismiss a very fundamental part of the Christian experience. If you don't understand adoption and sonship, it's very easy to miss the whole purpose of the Natural Christian existence. Understanding what they mean for us as Christians can truly transform your relationship with Christ.

(NOTE: The vast majority of this topic comes from a sermon delivered by Tim Keller of Redeemer Presbyterian Church in New York City.)

In order to begin to understand the extraordinary significance and impact of what adoption and sonship is all about, let's get some context on what Paul is talking about in the New Testament.

The Walk Applied

The Word tells us that we are legally adopted as sons and daughters of the living King. We are all sons of God through faith in Jesus Christ. Yes, you have been declared a child of God. This also means you have been given full rights as an heir. Sonship is our adoption by God that makes us a full, legal heir with complete, total love and acceptance. We accept this as what we will trust and believe in. It means that we have been declared sons already. It's not achieved; it's not earned; it's not a wage. Sonship is freely granted and given because this is the way God wants it.

Let's look at it another way via a few syllogisms:

When you believed in Christ
> You were declared righteous
>> And you became a Son
> or

If you believe in Christ as the Son of God
> Then you are declared righteous
>> And you become a Son
> or

To be declared righteous
> And become a son
>> You must believe in Christ

Paul is describing salvation here, not just the mere act of believing in Christ and getting your ticket to heaven. When you do believe you automatically become a Son as a consequence of the covenant. You are now a legal heir in the line of Abraham. God covenanted to make us all come under the seed of Abraham and he accomplishes this thru the mechanism of adoption. This gives you a new family heritage – an entire new legacy. The ancient heroes of Hebrews 11 are now declared your ancestors in every sense of the word! Let's look at some scriptures:

The Walk Applied

"Yet to all who received him, to those who believed in his name, he gave the right to become children of God - children born not of natural descent, nor of human decision or a husband's will, but born of God." (John1:12-13)

"...You received the Spirit of sonship. And by him we cry, "Abba, Father." The Spirit himself testifies with our spirit that we are God's children. Now if we are children, then we are heirs - heirs of God and co-heirs with Christ, if indeed we share in his sufferings in order that we may also share in his glory." (Rom 8:15-17)

"You are all sons of God through faith in Christ Jesus, for all of you who were baptized into Christ have clothed yourselves with Christ. ... If you belong to Christ, then you are Abraham's seed, and heirs according to the promise." (Gal 3:26-29)

"... as the heir is a child, he is no different from a slave, although he owns the whole estate. He is subject to guardians and trustees until the time set by his father. ... God sent his Son, born of a woman, born under law, to redeem those under law, that we might receive the full rights of sons. Because you are sons, God sent the Spirit of his Son into our hearts, the Spirit who calls out, "Abba, Father." So you are no longer a slave, but a son; and since you are a son, God has made you also an heir." (Gal 4:1-7)

"And you also were included in Christ when you heard the word of truth, the gospel of your salvation. Having believed, you were marked in him with a seal, the promised Holy Spirit, who is a deposit guaranteeing our inheritance until the redemption of those who are God's possession--to the praise of his glory." (Eph 1:13-14)

The Walk Applied

PAUL: WE ARE A CHRISTIAN BEFORE WE ARE ANYTHING ELSE!

Adoption and Sonship were favorite metaphors of Paul's. For the Galatians it had a profound significance as it should for us. Let's look at Gal 3:28

"There is neither Jew nor Greek, slave nor free, male nor female, for you are all one in Christ Jesus."

Paul wasn't saying that we must lose our cultural identity or that we must somehow become "unisex" or that somehow, we have to all become virtually "identical". Paul was emphasizing that we are a Christian before we are anything else. He was pointing out that the family of God comes first and that thinking of yourself as a child of God MUST come first. For Paul, there was no debating or discussion. It's important that we don't miss the extraordinary significance of what Paul is saying. Paul's amazing assertion is nothing less than we must understand that we are a Christian before we are anything else. We are to see that the family of God comes first. We need to start thinking of ourselves as children of God, and that comes first. Indeed, we are primarily a child of God before anything else!

"And you also were included in Christ when you heard the word of truth, the gospel of your salvation. Having believed, you were marked in him with a seal, the promised Holy Spirit, who is a deposit guaranteeing our inheritance until the redemption of those who are God's possession--to the praise of his glory."
(Eph 1:13-14)

The Walk Applied

Paul was using the example of a wealthy Roman or Greek family, which is something they all would have recognized in the Greco-Roman world. Coming of age was a very well-defined process. There were 2 basic scenarios: the Greco-Roman scenario, and the Jewish scenario.

THE GRECO-ROMAN SCENARIO

According to Keller, under the Greco-Roman scenario, you sat under a tutor until 14. At that age, you could start to conduct your own affairs. However, you didn't have independence until about 25. Now, up until 14, you were considered similar to a slave, although you had ownership of the estate and all its resources. In other words, you had status! There were also scenarios whereby the wealthy person might not have a son, so; they might adopt a trusted servant or someone else they might be especially fond of.

We cannot miss the impact this had! When someone was adopted it was literally as if they never existed prior to the adoption. It was just as if they had been born into the family in the natural way. For all intents and purposes, their prior life had been wiped out. The adoptive father now took responsibility for the adopted son and took care of whatever former obligations the newly adopted son might have had. The adoptive father of course could certainly choose areas that the newly adopted son might still be responsible for. Paul does not want us to miss the extraordinary meaning this had for those listening in Biblical times, as well as the meaning it has for us. Thus, when you become God's adopted son:

93

The Walk Applied

- You have full rights as a son
- You have the intimacy of relationship
- We don't "get fired" for breaking the rules
- We have assurances of intimacy and relationship
- We have access thru prayer
- There's a boldness that comes with your new standing.
- There's a guarantee of sharing in God's glory!
- God now treats us as if we have done everything Jesus had done!

HAVE YOU ACCEPTED THE FATHER AS YOUR "SPIRITUAL DADDY"?

Let's take this exciting proposition of adoption and sonship a step further: Have you ever thought of God as your, well, Daddy?!? A phrase that we see in the Bible is "Abba Father ". It literally means "daddy!" So, Our Sprit spirit cries out for perfect intimacy from within us!! You see, God what us to accept Him as our "Daddy"! – Yes! Literally true! The question is: Have you received him as your daddy? Until you truly receive him as your true spiritual father – your Daddy, you'll never trust him! In other words, you must truly believe and accept that you have this awesome spiritual father. One of our fundamental needs is to be complete via acceptance and affirmation, which is the basis of true intimacy.

THE PRODIGAL SON

When we look at the story of the prodigal son, we see that the Father: God awaits us – not to punish us, but to rejoice in our return to Him! The perfect love, affirmation and acceptance that we so crave in the natural is readily available for us in the spiritual. We need to sincerely believe it, so we'll accept it as a completely new and unique way to live. It then follows that we must experience it so that we can learn how to live it!

The Walk Applied

We all deal with sinful people who have sinful ways. The notion of true acceptance and true intimacy while we're in the flesh has very likely been corrupted for many. There is the conviction (for a multitude of reasons) that acceptance and intimacy with others is lacking or non-existent. Depending on the level of real or perceived need, life can become a very real frantic, desperate search for acceptance and true intimacy.

A fractured/absent relationship with God is rooted in a lack of trust in God. If you don't trust God to satisfy needs and desires, you seek your own natural alternatives. You cannot be intimate with what you don't trust! If you have true intimacy, with the subsequent acceptance, you will likely be comfortable with yourself. You will be at peace! If you experience true intimacy with God, you'll also likely be very comfortable with yourself. When you trust God fully, and see Him as your true father, you will enter the rest of God!

DECLARING ABBA FATHER AS "DADDY"

I'm convinced that you need to have a specific time that you accept him as your true father. A time when you truly trusted him as your father above and beyond your salvation experience! Is this not the lesson of the prodigal son? God is waiting for you to come to him, no matter what. All you have to do is go to him, admit your overwhelming need for him and receive him as your true father. This is nothing more than accepting truth. Unless you accept your true spiritual identity as a spiritual creature living a spiritual existence here in the natural context, you will continue to live by the natural rules and strive to gain acceptance by either God or others. With God, you have complete acceptance and affirmation you just have to accept it and believe it! Thus, we pray seeking to commune with "daddy" – Abba father!

The Walk Applied

JESUS AT THE TEMPLE:
ACCEPTING HIS TRUE SPIRITUAL FATHER.

"After three days they found him in the temple courts, sitting among the teachers, listening to them and asking them questions. Everyone who heard him was amazed at his understanding and his answers. When his parents saw him, they were astonished. His mother said to him, "Son, why have you treated us like this? Your father and I have been anxiously searching for you." Why were you searching for me?" he asked. "Didn't you know I had to be in my Father's house?" But they did not understand what he was saying to them. Then he went down to Nazareth with them and was obedient to them. But his mother treasured all these things in her heart. And Jesus grew in wisdom and stature, and in favor with God and man." (Luke 2:41-52)

This very famous passage of scripture is all about recognizing Our Heavenly Father as our true Father. Jesus is making the very deliberate step of saying that His Heavenly Father is His top priority. Note that the passage indicates that Joseph and Mary did not understand what Jesus was doing. Most of us tend to think of our human relationships as primary i.e., our parents or our spouse. Here, Jesus is being very intentional. He is in no way rejecting his earthly parents: he is publicly declaring that his relationship with his Heavenly Father is paramount.

More important, Jesus wants to emphasize for us that He is publicly taking on the mantle of His Heavenly father as His true Spiritual Father. Jesus action here is a most key step and should be considered by all Christians as a vital step in the development of our relationship with Jesus. Indeed, the intentional and demonstrable acceptance of the Lord as our true Spiritual Father is a psychological step of the utmost importance. The import of this topic cannot be underestimated. We'll discuss this again later as a rite of passage.

The Walk Applied

SONSHIP & THE BLOODLINE

Understanding what the bloodline means is crucial to understanding sonship. Our bloodline has a significant impact on our lives. We have been legally adopted as God's child into the bloodline of Abraham. We can claim the heroes of Hebrews 11 as our forefathers spiritually and legally – we are their descendants in every sense of the word. This is more than a "legal" adoption! We have actually been made a "blood relative" in the spiritual bloodline of Abraham.

Your parents are your spiritual authority. Your father is the seed sower. Your mother is the seed receiver. Your parents named you. That makes them your spiritual authority. Never forget it is a very serious issue to dishonor your spiritual authority!

"Honor your father and your mother, so that you may live long in the land the LORD your God is giving you." (Exo 20:12)

"Honor your father and your mother, as the LORD your God has commanded you, so that you may live long and that it may go well with you in the land the LORD your God is giving you." (Deu 5:16)

"For God said, 'Honor your father and mother' and 'Anyone who curses his father or mother must be put to death.'" (Matt 15:4)

"For Moses said, 'Honor your father and your mother,' and, 'Anyone who curses his father or mother must be put to death'". (Mark 7:10)

We are not saying that we must put ourselves in danger by putting ourselves in absolute submission to abusive parents. We are to respect, forgive, and bless those who the Lord used to give us life. Again, it is a very serious issue to dishonor your spiritual authority. We are to respect and bless people solely by virtue of their position

97

The Walk Applied

of spiritual authority. We are to honor them because they occupy the position of spiritual authority.

WE ARE CITIZENS OF A NEW COUNTRY!

The following passages make very interesting statements:

" *...Our citizenship is in heaven.* " (Phil 3:20)

"For here we do not have a lasting city, but we are seeking the city which is to come." (Heb 13:14)

"For we know that if the earthly tent which is our house is torn down, we have a building from God, a house not made with hands, eternal in the heavens." (2 Cor 5:1)

The verses tell us that we are not only adopted, we are actually declared citizens of a new country and culture. We must learn the ways and laws of this new country and culture. In a most tangible way, it's as if we have been adopted from a country like China and now live with our new adoptive parents in America. It's a whole new way of life! As newly "naturalized citizens", we now learn to live in a "spiritual lifestyle" according to God's ways.

Please do not underestimate how powerful this notion is. The notion that we are now citizens of a new country, means we live by a separate set of laws – which God says He will write on our hearts.

BIBLICAL RITES OF PASSAGE

There are six biblical rites of passage. In our day and age, Rites of Passage have largely lost their significance, which is terribly unfortunate. In Biblical times, Rites of Passage were of the utmost psychological importance. Rites of Passage changed what you believed about yourself and changed the perception of you in the

The Walk Applied

community. It is no small consideration to note that Rites of Passage were always accompanied by a formal blessing. To not have a formal blessing would have been unthinkable – which signifies the significance of the blessing in Biblical times. We would do well to understand the overwhelming significance of the Blessing (as well as cursing, for that matter!)

CHILD -> ADULTHOOD (COMING OF AGE)

The "Mitzvah" ceremony meant that you were passing into adulthood. The word Mitzvah means "commandment" or "law". For boys, the Bar Mitzvah ceremony almost always came at 13. The Bar Mitzvah was a ceremony whereby you became "Son of the Commandment" or "Son of the Law". Girls were eligible for the Bah Mitzvah ceremony at 12 (Orthodox or Conservative Jew) or 13 (Reformed Jew). The Bah Mitzvah was a ceremony whereby you became "Daughter of the Commandment" or "Daughter of the Law". Wikipedia discusses the "Mitzvah" ceremony:

"Reaching the age of [the] Mitzvah signified becoming a full-fledged member of the Jewish community with all the rights and responsibilities that came with the ceremonies. They included moral responsibility for one's own actions; eligibility to be called to read from the Torah and lead or participate in a minyan; the right to possess personal property and to be legally married according to Jewish law; the duty to follow the 613 laws of the Torah and keep the halakha; and the capacity to testify as a witness in a Beth Din (Rabbinical court) case."

The significance of the Mitzvah lies in how seriously these ceremonies were taken. The psychological effect of these ceremonies should never be underestimated. Once you completed the ceremonies, your position as a man or woman in your local community was cemented. There was never any question about your "status". Contrast that with today, where these kinds of ceremonies are taken as something nice.

BAPTISM: PUBLIC DECLARATION
OF THE ALLEGIANCE TO CHRIST

In the Great commission, Jesus wanted us to baptize others. The public symbolism of Baptism was very profound. The symbol of being re-born is paramount, as the new believer demonstrates that he is reborn as a spiritual creature and been "raised" from the Spiritual dead. In Biblical times, the psychological change would have been unmistakable. There was little question that the baptized person saw themselves differently. Indeed, the rest of the community would certainly have viewed that individual differently. They had now publicly advertised themselves as followers of Jesus Christ, and that made all the difference.

WEDDING: PUBLIC CREATION OF
NEW AUTHORITY SUBMISSION RELATIONSHIP

We will discuss the wedding in much greater detail later in this in volume. The Bible tells us that the male ascends to the spiritual authority position - much to the consternation of some women who do not understand the true nature of the Godly authority/submission dynamic! The wife chooses to accept spiritual submission to the authority. Perhaps, the most profound aspect of this rite of passage is that another copy of the trinity is created:

"God created mankind in his own image, in the image of God He created them; male and female he created them." (Gen 1:27)

In other words, it takes a man and a woman coming together under the covenantal blessing of the Father as he creates, in effect, a new copy of the Trinity. Men and women have obvious differences, so each one individually cannot be a complete image of God. Thus, we

The Walk Applied

conclude that with the execution of the marriage covenant a new image of God's Holy Trinity is actually created.

The Rite of Passage of Marriage results in a newly married couple whose standing in the community is happily changed to no small degree – obviously! No question about it, the participants see themselves quite differently than they did before. It goes without saying that the psychological effect is more than remarkable.

LUKE 2: JESUS AT THE TEMPLE DECLARING HIS HEAVENLY FATHER TO BE HIS TRUE FATHER

Luke's chapter 2 account of Jesus as a 12-year-old who leaves his mother and father for the confines of the temple warrants further review. The reader may wish to re-read the passage again. Jesus is communicating a very important principle here via this particular rite. Jesus is making the declaration of his submission to God as His true father. Jesus is making the true submission decision to His heavenly Father over His earthly, adoptive father.

Jesus tone and action in this passage are most significant here. Jesus purposely stayed behind to go the temple but did not inform Joseph and Mary of his plans. Because this is Jesus following the Father's command ("I only do what the Father tells me to do") there is no sin here. Jesus is emphasizing in a dramatic way how important it was for Him to do what He needed to do. Finally, Mary's cryptic response: [she] "…treasured all these things in her heart" seems to clue us into a profound notion: Jesus really was the Son of God, and it was all as Gabriel had said.

The Walk Applied

THE SALVATION RITE OF PASSAGE: CREATING THE AUTHORITY/SUBMISSION RELATIONSHIP

Salvation is a promise covenant that asks for a sincere commitment on our part. We sincerely acknowledge the following three aspects of the covenant:

- I am a sinner.
- Jesus paid the price I could never pay for my sin.
- God is the one true living God who is sovereign over all.

Until we come to know Christ as our Lord and Savior, we are considered to be in rebellion against God. It's vital that we understand that the Salvation covenant creates an Authority/Submission relationship between the newly saved person and the Father. By the free will act of submission to God's authority, we honor God Himself and His ultimate sovereignty. In return, He blesses us and grafts us into His holy family, along with all the other benefits associates with Salvation.

BIRTH OF A CHILD: THE CREATION OF A NEW SUBMITTER

The birth of a child is most certainly a rite of passage for the father and the mother. They not only go from being identified as a married couple, they are now parents as well. The changes that come with having a baby are quite profound. Parents do see themselves differently, for their roles have now dramatically changed. Obviously, the impression of the new parents in their various circles have now changed as well.

102

The Walk Applied

Infant(s) can be defined to be new submitter(s) who are innately looking for an authority. They instinctively seek a protector as well as a provider. They are also looking for someone to nurture them. This all goes in line with the elements of the flesh discussed earlier. Psalm 51:6 expresses an interesting thought:

"...Yet you desired faithfulness even in the womb; you taught me wisdom in that secret place."

What could this mean? The contention from here is that the fleshly belief system is being installed from the very beginning. Infants are instinctive beings – they come "pre-wired" with needs and wants. Babies very early on seem to know things, and they learn at an amazing rate. As infants learn how to negotiate the world, their sinful flesh begins to show through. They begin to "expect" things as they develop. They cry or throw a temper tantrum when they don't get their way. Their "self-centeredness" becomes evident. They get angry and or fearful as they grow. Many will insist that these actions are merely a normal part of the growth process. Yet we pose the question: where do we get the prompts for these behaviors? Why have them at all?

Certain behaviors are necessary for any infant to survive – but the question remains: why do we have innate behaviors at all? Where did we get them from? Being angry may seem like the most natural reaction in the world when an infant does not get its way, but where did the child get the capacity to do that? Why should it? Why should we have these innate notions unless…Someone gave them to us. The Bible tells that we are made in God's image. Our "software" includes a fundamental yearning to seek and know God.

The Walk Applied

THE SANCTIFICATION PROCESS

The Bible tells us that we are sanctified when we are saved. Essentially, to be sanctified means that you have been set aside for God's use. It also means that we are to be more like Jesus. Indeed, God wants to see you become more like Jesus as you walk this life road. We call that walk the process of sanctification.

For many, sanctification remains a little understood concept. The notion of being more like Jesus can easily devolve into a sinful performance mentality. To be sure, there's no question that being more like Jesus would certainly involve less sin in in your life. Yet, it is so much more! To have a proper understanding of what sanctification really means. Let's examine a concept that can be referred to as the "sanctification progression". Simply put, I contend that there is a specific sequence that the Bible proscribes that helps us to identify where we are on the "sanctification progression".

SANCTIFICATION:
GOD'S ONGOING PROCESS OF HOLINESS

Sanctification is the process of setting us apart for his use and teaching us how to live the spiritual life. Simply put, it can be said that sanctification is the process of growing more Christ-like. It is both a one time and ongoing program. We are justified then sanctified. We have been declared righteous. Justification is granted as a free gift that we simply believe we have; we then are immersed into the ongoing process of sanctification. We've been declared righteous; now we learn how to use God's gifts as a new way to live! The spiritual being living a spiritual life in the natural knows that stopping our sin is never the object, but a by-product of our walk with Christ. We understand that performing to earn value and respect and acceptance in never the object.

The Walk Applied

THE SANCTIFICATION PROGRESSION:
THE 3 STAGES

"Therefore, if anyone is in Christ, he is a new creation; old things have passed away; behold, all things have become new." (2 Cor 5:17 NKJV)

What does it mean to be a new creation? Many Christians have a most challenging time expressing what it means to be a new creation. Indeed, Many Christians cannot put their spiritual identity into a framework that tells them how to live their daily lives. In this section, we will talk about what sanctification means, and how it impacts our spiritual identity. There are 3 specific stages to the Sanctification process:

SANCTIFICATION, STAGE 1:
A PRIEST IN THE ROYAL PRIESTHOOD

"You also, like living stones, are being built into a spiritual house to be a holy priesthood, offering spiritual sacrifices acceptable to God through Jesus Christ. ... But you are a chosen people, a royal priesthood, a holy nation, God's special possession, that you may declare the praises of him who called you out of darkness into his wonderful light." (1 Pet: 2:5 & 9)

The fact that we are members of a royal priesthood is a stunning statement. The significance of this proclamation cannot be underestimated. More simply put: It means that from the instant of salvation you have a spiritual job title! There are no exceptions; we are all declared priests in the royal priesthood. So, if we are declared priests, what are our duties? We can examine the priestly activities of the Old Testament to find our assigned tasks. We:

The Walk Applied

- Pray & praise
- Study the Word
- Intercede for one another
- Worship in spirit and in truth
- Fast
- Give sacrifices of time and money and effort
- Seek and commune with God
- Proclaim what God is doing in our lives

What this all means is that it puts our "spiritual duties" into a much larger context. As we integrate the idea that God wants us to see ourselves as priests, it gives much greater meaning to the "duties" we have. Far too often, we see them as "disciplines" or "obligations" when they are anything but onerous. A much better and far more accurate way to look at the list above is to see the list as the numerous ways we can commune with Christ. We can exercise them anywhere, anytime as we see fit.

When we recognize that we have been appointed as priests, we gain a feeling of being part of something much bigger than ourselves. Via our communion with God as priests, we are slowly changed. These "duties" – these ways of communing with Christ – are our "basic training" if you will in how we commune with Christ. They teach us how God wants us to just commune with Him. The Word changes us as the Spirit leads us into truth. In addition, we begin to see "Kairos" moments (positive and negative events in our lives that range from the very subtle to transformational that shape us and change us) as God-driven so as to make us more Godly. Over time, we are prepared for the second stage:

The Walk Applied

SANCTIFICATION, STAGE 2:
YOUR CALLING REVEALED

"This is what the Lord says: "Stand at the crossroads and look; ask for the ancient [eternal] paths, ask where the good way is, and walk in it, and you will find rest for your souls." (Jer 6:16)

"And let us run with perseverance the race marked out for us" (Heb 12:1-2)

"I will instruct you and teach you in the way you should go" *(Ps 32:8)*

"Where there is no vision, the people perish..." (Pro 29:18, KJV)

(Note: This section will be repeated when we expand on the personal and effectual call in chapter 6.)

We interpret the above passages to mean that God has an overall purpose, plan and will that is specific for you. We maintain that every single person has an individual call on their life. For some, it is a one-time call that you will have been prepared for. A good example of this is Phillip in Acts chapter 8, where he was used mightily of God. Some are called for a lifetime of service, like Paul, Moses, or Samuel. Typically, we find in the Bible that those who were called out for service wound up serving in that calling for the remainder of their lives.

Your personal call is what will give you meaning and purpose and fill you like nothing else. God will move heaven and earth to ensure you have everything you need to fulfill your calling. God will ask each and every one of us: Did you seek and follow the call?

The Walk Applied

Indeed, each person's call is as important as the next. Regardless if you have been called to be a prayer warrior and labor in obscurity, or if you have been called to be the next great Billy Graham or D. W. Moody. For a few, they will be called to be powerful men and women of God called to preach the word of God fearlessly. Others may be called to be great evangelists or erudite theologians. what is important is that you seek your calling and follow your call. No one's call is any more important than anyone else's.

For the vast majority, the personal calling can be as simple as to be a prayer warrior. Some are called to live ordinary day to day life in an extraordinary way. Many are called to be godly people in their workplace. They are apostles who demonstrate a life of Christ. People are drawn to them because others want what they have. I have a friend who believes he is called to simply be the most Godly husband and father He can possibly be.

For a few, they will be called to be powerful men and women of God called to preach the word of God fearlessly. Others may be called to be great evangelists or erudite theologians. Or just about anything else you can think of.

THE PERSONAL, EFFECTUAL CALL REVEALED: THE VEIL IS REMOVED

"...even to this day when Moses is read, a veil covers their hearts, but whenever anyone turns to the Lord, the veil is taken away." (2 Cor 3:15-16)

Moses turned and looked and saw the burning bush. He pursued it and encountered the Living God. He heard God and understood Him. The course of His life was truly changed. Moses resisted, but it was clear that his life would never be the same. To be sure, Moses was launched on an adventure he certainly never expected. There

108

The Walk Applied

are a number of instances in the scripture where we see that the veil was removed, and the personal, effectual call was revealed:

- Moses encountered God at the burning bush.
- The two men who walking to Emmaus
- Paul's encounter on the road to Damascus
- Phillip in Acts 8

As we ponder the passage above, we note some similarities:

- God engineered circumstances in their lives
- They encountered God
- They heard God speak to them
- They understood what God had to say
- They were forever changed by God
- The course of their lives was changed God

SANCTIFICATION, STAGE 3:
THE "MAN OF GOD"

"...but as for you, continue in what you have learned and have become convinced of, because you know those from whom you learned it, and how from infancy you have known the holy scriptures, which are able to make you wise for salvation through faith in Christ Jesus. All scripture is God-breathed and is useful for teaching, rebuking, correcting and training in righteousness, so that you, a man of God may be thoroughly equipped for every good work."(2Tim3:16-17)

The sanctification process ultimately prepares us for "every good work" in stage 3, where we become the "Man of God". We meet virtually every situation knowing God has our back. We are fully confident in God and how he is working in our lives. We progress to be the Man of God when we make the full submission decision. Jesus becomes the way of life, and peace & joy are a significant part

The Walk Applied

of your life. You live day-to-day while planning for the future. People are changed simply because they know you. People are either drawn to you or they turn from you because they know you're different (salt & light). Your personal call becomes your driving force, and the walking the path becomes your life plan (Jer 6:16-17). Your spiritual gifts become an integral part of your personal ethos & psyche. Work becomes our oikos: our mission field whereby God coincidentally flows provision he wants us to have.

The sanctification progression reveals your spiritual identity to you over time as you pursue Jesus. If you do not understand that you are a spiritual being living a spiritual existence placed in the natural according to God's perfect purpose plan and will to bear fruit for the kingdom then it will be most difficult to experience true peace and joy as God intended and you will not be able to understand your true calling and your true value in Jesus.

CHAPTER 5
AUTHORITY &
SUBMISSION

The Walk Applied

The Walk Applied

CHAPTER 5
AUTHORITY & SUBMISSION

The Bible reports that there is a very real spiritual struggle. Many are deceived into coming under Satan's power and control and don't even know it!

"For our struggle is not against flesh and blood, but against the rulers, against the authorities, against the powers of this dark world and against the spiritual forces of evil in the heavenly realms." *(Eph 6:12)*

"For though we live in the world, we do not wage war as the world does. The weapons we fight with are not the weapons of the world. On the contrary, they have divine power to demolish strongholds. We demolish arguments and every pretension that sets itself up against the knowledge of God, and we take captive every thought to make it obedient to Christ. And we will be ready to punish every act of disobedience, once your obedience is complete. You are looking only on the surface of things." *(2 Cor 10:3-7)*

What is this struggle all about? Apparently, Satan and God both want the same thing (later on, we'll find what each wants are polar opposites): To rule over us.

"You said in your heart, "I will ascend to heaven; I will raise my throne above the stars of God; I will sit enthroned on the mount of assembly, on the utmost heights of the sacred mountain. I will ascend above the tops of the clouds; I will make myself like the Most High." *(Isa 14:13-14)*

"It is written: "'As surely as I live,' says the Lord, 'every knee will bow before me; every tongue will confess to God." *(Rom 14:11)*

113

The Walk Applied

"...that at the name of Jesus every knee should bow, in heaven and on earth and under the earth, and every tongue confess that Jesus Christ is Lord, to the glory of God the Father." (Phil 2:10-11) "

AUTHORITY & THE NATURE OF
THE ATTACK BY SATAN

Because we tend to think in terms of performance, we typically look at sin as having "done the wrong thing". That's a true statement, and the idea that we have done the wrong thing should never be minimized. Yet, we need to be about the business of looking at our sin in an altogether different context. We need to start seeing our sin as much worse than some sort of "minimal human error". For many of us, we tend to "minimize" our sin (in accordance with our fleshly idolatry belief systems as we talked about earlier) because, after all, "I'm not that bad" or "I didn't really mean it" or any other number of rationalizations and excuses.

We need to see sin as *REBELLION* against God. This notion cannot be emphasized nearly enough. The truth is that we are sinners saved solely by God's grace. When we are saved, we are judged righteous, but we still live with a driven, relentless flesh. We still sin every day and do wrong things; we are still in rebellion each and every day. It's important to recognize that even while we worship Him and seek Him daily, we are still idolaters who sin because we are idolatrous sinners. Indeed, every time we sin, we are committing an act of rebellion against our Heavenly Father.

AUTHORITY AND SUBMISSION

Understanding the true nature of the concept of authority and submission has immeasurable implications for our lives and our daily walk with Christ. Authority and submission are established by agreement with either God or Satan. It's most important to understand that to sin is to come out of agreement with God.

114

The Walk Applied

However, as Satan will always try to seduce us via any means that he can. Satan will tempt us to seek the natural, where he's in power:

"... the prince of this world will be driven out." (John 12:31)
"... the prince of this world is coming." (John 14:30)
"... the prince of this world now stands condemned." (John 16:11)

In the Garden of Eden, Eve sinned when she came into agreement with Satan. She was persuaded and manipulated to do the one thing she was commanded not to. She agreed with the tempter and disagreed with God. She came under Satan's power and control.

"... Now the serpent was more crafty than any of the wild animals the LORD God had made. He said to the woman, "Did God really say, 'You must not eat from any tree in the garden'?" The woman said to the serpent, "We may eat fruit from the trees in the garden, but God did say, 'You must not eat fruit from the tree that is in the middle of the garden, and you must not touch it, or you will die.'" "You will not surely die," the serpent said to the woman. "For God knows that when you eat of it your eyes will be opened, and you will be like God, knowing good and evil." When the woman saw that the fruit of the tree was good for food and pleasing to the eye, and also desirable for gaining wisdom, she took some and ate it. She also gave some to her husband, who was with her, and he ate it. Then the eyes of both of them were opened, and they realized they were naked; so they sewed fig leaves together and made coverings for themselves." (Gen 3:1-7)

JOB AND THE BATTLE FOR AUTHORITY

Perhaps the most vivid example in the Bible of the authority vs. control battle is found in the story of Job. You'll recall that the story has to do with Satan being allowed to inflict great tragedy and suffering on Job.

115

The Walk Applied

We first note that Satan has direct access to God:

"One day the angels came to present themselves before the LORD, and Satan also came with them. The LORD said to Satan, "Where have you come from?" Satan answered the LORD, "From roaming through the earth and going back and forth in it." (Job 1:6-7)

"On another day the angels came to present themselves before the LORD, and Satan also came with them to present himself before him. And the LORD said to Satan, "Where have you come from?" Satan answered the LORD, "From roaming through the earth and going back and forth in it." (Job 2:1-2)

Next, we read that God initiates this, not Satan.

"All his brothers and sisters and everyone who had known him before came and ate with him in his house. They comforted and consoled him over all the trouble the LORD had brought upon him…" (Job 42:11)

"Then the LORD said to Satan, "Have you considered my servant Job? There is no one on earth like him; he is blameless and upright, a man who fears God and shuns evil." "Does Job fear God for nothing?" Satan replied. "Have you not put a hedge around him and his household and everything he has? You have blessed the work of his hands, so that his flocks and herds are spread throughout the land. But stretch out your hand and strike everything he has, and he will surely curse you to your face." (Job 1:8-11)

"Then the LORD said to Satan, "Have you considered my servant Job? There is no one on earth like him; he is blameless and upright, a man who fears God and shuns evil. And he still maintains his integrity, though you incited me against him to ruin him without any reason." "Skin for skin!" Satan replied. "A man will give all he has for his own life. But stretch out your hand and strike his flesh and

The Walk Applied

bones, and he will surely curse you to your face." The LORD said
*to Satan, "Very well, then, he is in your hands; but you must spare
his life."* (Job 2:3-6)

Job has no knowledge of this great spiritual "debate" that will affect
him in an intensely personal way. Job is allowed to be attacked
twice, so there is no mistaking God's intentions.

CURSING AND BLESSING

The 2 "wagers" between God and Satan have to do with whether or
not Job will curse God. The notion of cursing (and blessing) as it is
presented here is a lesson of the highest importance and is not to be
missed.

Satan asserts that Job worships God only because God is protecting
Job (Satan is ever the accuser!). Satan contends that if God were to
remove Job's "hedge of protection", Job would then curse God to
His face.

The understanding of what "curse" means is vital. A curse is the
issuance of a command to put that person under the power and
control of evil. It is the opposite of the blessing: which is to issue a
command to put someone under the authority of God. Satan wants
Job to come under his power and control. The Hebrew word used
here is "barak", and it is a most interesting word. First, we see where
the word curse ("barak") is used in the story:

"... he will surely curse you to your face." (Job 1:11)
"... he will surely curse you to your face." (Job 2:5)
"... Are you still holding on to your integrity? Curse God and die!
(Job 2:9)

117

The Walk Applied

Now, let's see what the word "barak" means as gleaned from Vine's Expository Dictionary:

1288. barak, to kneel; by implication. to bless God (as an act of adoration), and (vice-versa) man (as a benefit); also to curse (God or the king, as treason):"barak": blessing and cursing are primary biblical emphases, as reflected in the 516 uses of words such as bless (132), blessed (285), blesses (10), blessing (70), and blessings (19); and the 199 occurrences of such words as curse (97), cursed (74), curses (19), and cursing (9). The English word "bless" is often used to translate barak. The word means "to kneel" (2 chron. 6:13; ps. 95:6) and thus "to bless" (gen. 27:33; ex. 18:10; deut. 28:4)

1288. Barak, baw-rak'; a prim. Root; to kneel; by impl. **To bless god (as an act of adoration), and (vice-versa) man (as a benefit); also (by euphemism) to curse (god or the king, as treason)**:-- x abundantly, x altogether, x at all, blaspheme, bless, congratulate, curse, x greatly, x indeed, kneel (down), praise, salute, x still, thank.

So, we see that the real question is: who is Job going to kneel before: God or Satan? Who is Job going to worship? Will Job submit to the authority of God, or will he be seduced to come under power and control of Satan?

In the first incident, we see that Satan will use other people to affect you. Apparently, Satan can even manipulate nature when given permission to do so.

"One day when Job's sons and daughters were feasting and drinking wine at the oldest brother's house, a messenger came to Job and said, "The oxen were plowing and the donkeys were grazing nearby, and the Sabeans attacked and carried them off. They put the servants to the sword, and I am the only one who has escaped to tell you!" While he was still speaking, another messenger came and said, "The fire of God fell from the sky and burned up the

The Walk Applied

sheep and the servants, and I am the only one who has escaped to tell you!" While he was still speaking, another messenger came and said, "The Chaldeans formed three raiding parties and swept down on your camels and carried them off. They put the servants to the sword, and I am the only one who has escaped to tell you!" While he was still speaking, yet another messenger came and said, "Your sons and daughters were feasting and drinking wine at the oldest brother's house, when suddenly a mighty wind swept in from the desert and struck the four corners of the house. It collapsed on them and they are dead, and I am the only one who has escaped to tell you!" At this, Job got up and tore his robe and shaved his head. Then he fell to the ground in worship" (Job 1:13-20)

In the second incident we find that Satan can even inflict physical maladies, if given permission:

"So Satan went out from the presence of the LORD and afflicted Job with painful sores from the soles of his feet to the top of his head." (Job 2:7)

Satan left Job's wife alive to use her to tempt Job; Saran will even resort to using those closest to us:

"His wife said to him, "Are you still holding on to your integrity? Curse God and die!" He replied, "You are talking like a foolish woman. Shall we accept good from God, and not trouble?" In all this, Job did not sin in what he said." (Job 2:9-10)

WHAT CAN WE LEARN FROM JOB?

The spiritual realm is far more significant that the natural

As we ponder the tale of Job's suffering, it's helpful to also reflect on God's sermon in Job 38 – 41. God's series of questions all revolve around 2 distinct concepts: First, God wants us to know that

The Walk Applied

He controls the physical, natural world from the spiritual realm. Second, He purposely allows the natural to be uncontrollable and unpredictable. Without suffering and tragedy, what would make us yearn for the supernatural? Suffering and tragedy make us long for the perfection and love and security of God. Suffering and tragedy make us see the results of living in a sinful, fallen world, where evil is limited only by our imagination.

(Rom 1:28-32) Furthermore, since they did not think it worthwhile to retain the knowledge of God, he gave them over to a depraved mind, to do what ought not to be done. They have become filled with every kind of wickedness, evil, greed and depravity. They are full of envy, murder, strife, deceit and malice. They are gossips, slanderers, God-haters, insolent, arrogant and boastful; they invent ways of doing evil; they disobey their parents; they are senseless, faithless, heartless, ruthless. Although they know God's righteous decree that those who do such things deserve death, they not only continue to do these very things but also approve of those who practice them.

How else would we know we need God? For many, it's the only way to overcome our pride. Where is the hope, if this is such a wonderful place? The question is not "why does God allow this?" The statement is: This is what he protects us from. Suffering and tragedy are allowed so as to draw us closer to God. Indeed, many testimonies revolve around those who were at the lowest point of their lives. Ultimately, every circumstance, is designed to draw us closer to God:

"Have you not put a hedge around him and his household and everything he has? You have blessed the work of his hands, so that his flocks and herds are spread throughout the land. But stretch out your hand and strike everything he has, and he will surely curse you to your face." (Job 1:10-11)

The Walk Applied

"I gave you empty stomachs in every city and lack of bread in every town, yet you have not returned to me," declares the LORD. "I also withheld rain from you when the harvest was still three months away. I sent rain on one town but withheld it from another. One field had rain; another had none and dried up. People staggered from town to town for water but did not get enough to drink, yet you have not returned to me," declares the LORD. "Many times I struck your gardens and vineyards, I struck them with blight and mildew. Locusts devoured your fig and olive trees, yet you have not returned to me," declares the LORD. "I sent plagues among you as I did to Egypt. I killed your young men with the sword, along with your captured horses. I filled your nostrils with the stench of your camps, yet you have not returned to me," declares the LORD. "I overthrew some of you as I overthrew Sodom and Gomorrah. You were like a burning stick snatched from the fire, yet you have not returned to me," declares the LORD. (Amos 4:6-11)

Submission to God's authority is more important than the "sanctity of human life".

Sanctity of human life – yes, it's important, but far more important is obedience and our loving submission to God's authority. In Job's case, God allowed Job's family to be completely wiped out. We must begin to see our natural lives as the initial phase of a forever existence whereby we pass ultimately from what we know as our natural realm into the spiritual realm. Indeed, they both require complete loving submission to God, no matter what the circumstance. The beginning and end of our physical lives and the circumstances under which we live them is not nearly as important as how we serve Him. The notion that the sanctity of human life as the ultimate thing is the most important is rooted in idolatry. The ultimate is God, and service to him that is rooted in love! When we realize that our identity – the essence of who we are and what we're placed here for – is that we are children of God, saved only by His grace to:

The Walk Applied

"...for it is by grace you have been saved, through faith--and this not from yourselves, it is the gift of god - not by works, so that no one can boast. For we are God's workmanship, created in Christ Jesus to do good works, which God prepared in advance for us to do." (Eph 2:8-9)

This is exactly what Jesus came to do: he demonstrated that submission to heavenly authority is far more important than the sanctity of human life, or the conditions under which we live the natural, physical existence. Jesus of course, was the fitting example – a big part of why he suffered and died in the horrific way that he did. Jesus showed that His submission to His father's authority was what truly mattered. Jesus also died in the way he did to show us that there really was something worth going thru all that agony for.

We will be allowed to be put into circumstances as an example

Isaiah was subjected to 3 years of walking around naked and barefoot – not a pleasant way to live! Isaiah's suffering was used as a "sign and portent". To be sure, many times we are used in our suffering to show the rest of the world that no matter what, we still walk in faith, and we never lose hope.

"In the year that the supreme commander, sent by Sargon king of Assyria, came to Ashdod and attacked and captured it-- at that time the LORD spoke through Isaiah son of Amoz. He said to him, "Take off the sackcloth from your body and the sandals from your feet." And he did so, going around stripped and barefoot. Then the LORD said, "Just as my servant Isaiah has gone stripped and barefoot for three years, as a sign and portent against Egypt and Cush, so the king of Assyria will lead away stripped and barefoot the Egyptian captives and Cushite exiles, young and old, with buttocks bared--to Egypt's shame". (Isa 20:1-4)

The Walk Applied

"Then he said to them all: "If anyone would come after me, he must deny himself and take up his cross daily and follow me. For whoever wants to save his life will lose it, but whoever loses his life for me will save it. What good is it for a man to gain the whole world, and yet lose or forfeit his very self? If anyone is ashamed of me and my words, the Son of Man will be ashamed of him when he comes in his glory and in the glory of the Father and of the holy angels. I tell you the truth, some who are standing here will not taste death before they see the kingdom of God." (Luke 9:23-27)

Why did God set up our natural existence this way? He wanted to demonstrate that our own submission out of love to God as the ultimate authority was more important than anything we know in the natural - no matter what the circumstances. It is by faith that we have been saved and we must live by that faith regardless. Our true belief and hope are in God and His purpose because there is something far better. Our identity as a spiritual child of the living God is what matters, not what we know as a human being.

Christians will be used as an example. If we never suffered and the secular world did, then many, if not all, would come flocking to be a Christian simply out of selfish interest, not because of a hope in something much better as well as faith. If we didn't experience the same things they do, then people would simply become Christians to avoid suffering, not out of a fundamental need for repentance and salvation. Bearing up under suffering demonstrates our belief in the hope that's available to us. Knowing that we're being used to build up the kingdom and that our focus is on submission to the authority of God, even at the expense of our lives, is the priority. Christians must undergo the same things that the secular world does. Otherwise, how could we effectively witness? We must experience the same sufferings and maladies so that we can identify with what they go through. How else could we minister to them? How else could we serve them?

The Walk Applied

LIVING UNDER GODLY AUTHORITY

Prior to our salvation, we lived a natural, sinful life because we had no choice. We could not come into agreement with God, thus, we were incapable of thinking in a spiritual way. Why? We were under Satan's power and control! Paul addresses this idea forthrightly:

"Those who live according to the sinful nature have their minds set on what that nature desires; but those who live in accordance with the Spirit have their minds set on what the Spirit desires. The mind of sinful man is death, but the mind controlled by the Spirit is life and peace; the sinful mind is hostile to God. It does not submit to God's law, nor can it do so. Those controlled by the sinful nature cannot please God. You, however, are controlled not by the sinful nature but by the Spirit, if the Spirit of God lives in you. And if anyone does not have the Spirit of Christ, he does not belong to Christ. (Rom 8:5-9)

As saved Christians, we choose to live according to our true identity: Spiritual beings living a spiritual existence in the natural realm. We have discussed that salvation means much more than a free ticket to heaven. Loving submission to Godly Authority via faith in Jesus Christ becomes the fundamental drive of our lives. In the New Testament, Paul tells us that we need to know but one thing: Christ crucified.

THE BATTLE FOR AUTHORITY

The battle for authority is rooted in what we think and what we believe. How we think and see ourselves determines how we live – and that determines whose authority or power we come under! To live a life according to the sinful nature means to be subject to that nature, which leads to fear, anxiety, confusion, depression, hopelessness, and a dependence on performance and acceptance. To live according to the spiritual nature means to be subject to what

124

The Walk Applied

that nature desires: hope, peace, confidence, a sense of enormous value, love.

The spiritual being living a spiritual life in the natural understands that you submit to God's authority completely or you come under Satan's power and control. You cannot somehow coexist under both; you cannot serve 2 masters.

"...but if your eyes are bad, your whole body will be full of darkness. If then the light within you is darkness, how great is that darkness! "No one can serve two masters; either he will hate the one and love the other, or he will be devoted to the one and despise the other. You cannot serve both God and money..."* (Mat 6:23-24).

The spiritual being living a spiritual life in the natural understands that you desperately need God every second of every day! We fight an enemy that we cannot see and are totally helpless against were it not for God and his grace! Our enemy is extremely intelligent and highly organized. Demonic forces attack in a way that is purposed, planned and executed with one purpose in mind: to bring us under Satan's power and control so that we will believe anything but the truth of Jesus Christ as revealed in the bible. Ultimately, he wants to destroy us and our testimony. Satan and his minions tries to deceive us into believing that we have to earn and work for what has been freely given by God – thus our focus can easily become making ourselves "good enough" when our focus needs to be on communing with God in an ongoing, day to day relationship.

" ... grace and peace be yours in abundance through the knowledge of God and of Jesus our Lord. His divine power has given us everything we need for life and godliness through our knowledge of him who called us by his own glory and goodness." (2 Pet 1:2-3)

"...therefore, since we are surrounded by such a great cloud of witnesses, let us throw off everything that hinders and the sin that

The Walk Applied

so easily entangles, and let us run with perseverance the race marked out for us. Let us fix our eyes on Jesus, the author and perfecter of our faith, who for the joy set before Him endured the cross, scorning its shame, and sat down at the right hand of the throne of God." (Heb 12:1-2)

"...the word of the Lord came to me, saying, "before I formed you in the womb I knew you, before you were born I set you apart; I appointed you as a prophet to the nations." (Jer 1:4-5)

WE WILL BE HELD ACCOUNTABLE

To come under God's authority means we are accountable for our actions to fulfill our mission. Without accountability, there is no hope. If there is no accountability, then there is no authority. People are free to do as they choose in the natural, and chaos and anarchy will ensue as Genesis tells us.

"...the Lord saw how great man's wickedness on the earth had become, and that every inclination of the thoughts of his heart was only evil all the time. The Lord was grieved that he had made man on the earth, and His heart was filled with pain." (Gen 6:5-6)

"... the Lord came down to see the city and the tower that the men were building. The Lord said, "if as one people speaking the same language they have begun to do this, then nothing they plan to do will be impossible for them." (Gen 11:5-6)

The natural world tries so very hard to convince us that there's no God. We were made in the image of God, so try as we might, we cannot deny deep inside that there is indeed a sovereign God. Thus, the natural world convinces itself there is no ultimate authority, and in doing so, comes under the power and control of Satan.

The Walk Applied

To believe in falsehood does not change the truth. Romans 1 tells us that we can choose what we want and there are very real and significant consequences for choosing that which is false. To choose what is false brings us under the power and control of the evil one, and the evil we are capable of is limited only by our imagination. Truth matters; it is not relative. There is a right and a wrong. Truth is not dependent on our circumstances or whim. There is only one unalterable and unchanging truth – Jesus Christ as he is revealed in God's word, and this truth must be recognized as such.

To accept Satan's power and control is to accept chaos, confusion, hopelessness and no purpose. Without hope, there is no purpose. To come under Satan's power and control means to live in the natural without hope and purpose. Purpose is derived from the fulfillment of the eternal, spiritual mission to which we have been called - not to prove ourselves worthy depending on how well we perform, but performed eagerly because we know we are eminently qualified to perform the mission. To submit to God's authority is to acquire value, hope and purpose.

"Now fear the lord and serve him with all faithfulness. Throw away the gods your forefathers worshiped beyond the river and in Egypt, and serve the Lord. But if serving the Lord seems undesirable to you, then choose for yourselves this day whom you will serve, whether the gods your forefathers served beyond the river, or the gods of the Amorites, in whose land you are living. But as for me and my household, we will serve the Lord." (Josh 24:14-15)

The Walk Applied

THE SPIRITUAL MEANING OF
AUTHORITY & SUBMISSION

Most people, when asked to define the word "authority", will typically respond by saying something along the lines of "someone who is in charge" or "someone who knows more than most about a given subject". These definitions serve in daily usage. However, they have a different meaning in the spiritual realm of things and how it applies to us vis-à-vis God's sovereignty.

The word "authority" has a very interesting etymology. The word "author" comes from the Latin "auctorem", which translates to increase or augment". It means "one who causes to grow" or "one who creates the conditions for growth" or "the state of causing growth or increase". The suffix "ity" means the "ongoing state of". Thus, the word authority can more accurately be construed to mean "the constant and ongoing state of creating the conditions for growth".

The word "submission" has very interesting spiritual implications as well. "Submission" in the Greek word "huptasso" means to "to identify with" or "be in support of" or "line up under to support". "huptasso" evokes a vision similar to that of a concrete foundation of a house holding up the rest of the structure.

Taken together, the notions of authority and submission paint a picture of two parties working in tandem to create a mutually satisfying atmosphere whereby growth - indeed, life itself, can prosper and grow. The submitter makes the loving choice to submit to the authority. The authority is dependent on the submitter in that without the choice to submit, there can be no authority and no growth. The submitter is dependent on the authority for guidance, direction, and care. Without loving and tender care by the authority, the submitter will soon retreat from the authority. Truly, both submit to the other out of choice. This combination is exactly what

The Walk Applied

we see with God. God surely does not need us, but He chose to create us out of His infinite love because He wants to fellowship with us for eternity. Yet, God never forces himself on us. He does not force us to choose Him. Indeed, we are free to choose Him or simply walk away.

POWER & CONTROL

The polar opposite of authority and submission is power and control. This is the mechanism that Satan uses. He seeks to enslave us:

"It is for freedom that Christ has set us free. Stand firm, then, and do not let yourselves be burdened again by a yoke of slavery." (Gal 5:1)

Be it fear, manipulation, intimidation, seduction, coercion or a host of other methods, our great enemy, Satan and his army of demons seek to enslave us. The power-control logistic leads only to stagnation and death. Satan does not offer choice; he attempts to control by any means possible.

PSALM 23

The permanent and ongoing command is to bear fruit for the kingdom that will last. To produce fruit, you must have submission to Godly authority (although that is not all!). The relationship between authority and submission and bearing fruit is that there must be peace in order for lasting fruit to be borne. If the conditions for fruit bearing are not met, then only the conditions for chaos and death can be met. We can examine Psalm 23 in a non-traditional way to see that a Godly authority-submission structure needs to be in place. If we look at Psalm 23 in an If-Then syllogism, it becomes very revealing:

129

The Walk Applied

IF	The Lord is my shepherd
THEN	I will not be in want
	I will lie down in green pastures
	I will be lead to quiet waters
	My soul will be restored
	He will guide me in the paths of righteousness
	For His name's sake.
IF	The Lord is my shepherd,
THEN	I will walk thru the valley of the shadow of death
AND	I will fear no evil
	His rod and staff (his authority) will comfort me.
	He will prepare a table before me
	in the presence of my enemies
	He will anoint my head with oil
	and my cup will overflow
	Goodness and love will follow me
	all the days of my life
	I will dwell in the house of the Lord forever.

The psalmist tells us that if we come under Godly Authority we will have many good things. Of course, this does not mean that life will be a "cake walk" by any stretch. Jesus warned us that we will have problems, troubles and difficulties in this life. But we are also to take heart because Jesus has overcome, and so will we. The point of Psalm 23 is that when we accept Jesus as our shepherd, the stage will be set for us to produce fruit.

THE 4 LINES OF AUTHORITY IN THE NATURAL

There are 4 lines of authority in the natural established by God:

- Family
- Government
- Church
- Employment

The Walk Applied

FAMILY

The purpose of Family is to provide an atmosphere of love, acceptance and intimacy which are basic and fundamental emotional needs. Family is to provide the emotional security to lay the foundation. Family provides an atmosphere for the bringing up of children up in the 'training and admonition of the Lord". The New Testament lays out the Line of Authority for the family. The Husband is to be the Spiritual Authority of the Household. Why? The husband is the spiritual authority because he is the seed sower and the name giver. The wife is under the spiritual authority of the Husband because she is the seed receiver and the name receiver. The children are conceived via the father planting the seed in the mother and are next in line in the bloodline - an important biblical concept that we will cover in due course.

Obviously, not all parents are good and loving parents. Yet, we are explicitly told in the Bible to "honor our parents", along with some severe penalties for not doing so. There's no exceptions given for parents who do not hold their end of the bargain – we are to honor them regardless. How do we "honor" those who have caused us harm? We have already talked about the necessity for forgiveness. When it comes to our spiritual authority figures, we have to remember that we honor the position, even if the person occupying the position is far from exemplary. Some may express significant dissatisfaction with the president, but that does not change the fact that he is the president, and he deserves honor and respect by virtue of his position. It is the same with our parents - we are to honor and respect them by virtue of their spiritual authority position. As we discussed with forgiveness, this does not mean that we must put ourselves in position to be harmed. We are also to walk circumspectly; we have the right to defend ourselves.

The Walk Applied

As men and women, husband and wife, father and mother, we are to be particularly sensitive in our authority "offices" (more on that terminology later) of how we wield that authority. We are not to take up positions of power and control. We're not to "motivate to wrath" or "exasperate" those under our authority. But we are all sinners, and we all fall short; we all fail. That's why we need so desperately to be walking with Jesus day in and day out for guidance and wisdom.

GOVERNMENT

The purpose of Government is to provide peace, order, and security thru the law and the proper enforcement of the law. Government typically provides services that are needed by all. To facilitate the providing of shared community services, taxes or fees are usually levied. The Bible is clear: we are to submit to various Government officials as part of a Godly and orderly authority/submission structure. We reserve the right for peaceful protest when needed. Negotiation is sometimes called for. It is not uncommon for Christians to utilize judicial redress from time to time. Also, the bible does discuss violent protest under certain circumstances. In Esther, the Jews rebelled in order to save themselves form mass extermination. Jesus said that we are to "render to Caesar what is Caesar's.

As we discussed with Family, Government officials are not always fair, ethical or moral. Governmental powers are often abused by sinful individuals. Regardless of our expectations of fair and just treatment, we must never forget that Government offices are occupied by sinners. Sinners governing sinners is surely problematical. Still, we must respond to the spiritual authority of the position with honor and respect, and not necessarily the individual.

The Walk Applied

CHURCH

The purpose of the Church is so that we assemble together for common worship, prayer, and instruction. Perhaps a lesser understood purpose of why we gather together is so that we put ourselves in position to serve others - Isaiah 58 leads to this conclusion. In order to facilitate order and create a beneficial environment, churches need some form of structure. Given that, we are directed to submit to a Godly authority submission structure. In addition, we are to bring our tithes and offerings to the storehouse.

The sin problems that plague government can certainly be found in the church. Like Government official church officials are sinners, too. Just like government, sinful church officials abuse their privilege. Again, we must respond to the spiritual authority of the position with honor and respect, and not necessarily the individual.

EMPLOYMENT

The purpose of job and career is threefold: First, work helps to give us meaning and purpose as well as mental stimulation. Second, employment provides a way for God to funnel provision to us that He wants us to have. Third, working with others gives us an opportunity to be salt and light in a fallen world. Work should always be looked at as our mission field. Especially in our day and age, it's very rare to work in environment where there are all Christians. As we model salt and light, others will be drawn to us, and they will want what we have. If we are peaceful, no matter what our circumstances, fellow workers will take note. They will observe that we don't use four letter words. Coworkers will note that we never curse our superiors or the outfit we work for.

The Walk Applied

The sin problems that plague government and church are certainly present in the workplace. Organizations can be especially hostile to Christians. Supervisors, executives, co-workers, clients and customers are all sinners, too (just like you!). They most certainly can make your work environment chaotic and even fearful. While no one is asking you to purposely put yourself in harm's way, virtually all of us have had to deal with a bully boss or a very unpleasant co-worker or an abusive customer or client. Again, we must respond to the spiritual authority of the position with honor and respect, and not necessarily the individual. Even when you supervisors are blatantly unfair, can you submit?

SUBMITTING EVEN WHEN IT'S UNFAIR

Submission is usually a difficult notion for the vast majority of us. Let's face it: given our sinfulness and our idolatry, making the decision to submit is anything but easy. Of course, there will be times when we will be called on to assert ourselves. Indeed, we may have to be quite firm with those who have been called to submit to us. There is nothing wrong with lovingly and diplomatically expressing our authority when we have to. Yet, loving submission is the right thing to do in many instances. God certainly insists that we submit to Him in our relationship with Jesus. God's Word addresses it in any numbers of examples that are found in scripture.

But we want to examine a theme one final time that's found in the past few paragraphs: Can you submit to the authority that God allows in your life? Can you submit even when it's unfair? Verses like the following emphasize the import of true submission:

"A soft answer turns away wrath, but a harsh word stirs up anger. The tongue of the wise uses knowledge rightly, but the mouth of fools pours forth foolishness." (Pro 15:1-2 NKJV)

The Walk Applied

"There is an evil I have seen under the sun, the sort of error that arises from a ruler: Fools are put in many high positions, while the rich occupy the low ones. I have seen slaves on horseback, while princes go on foot like slaves." (Eccl 10:5-7)

The above two passages illustrate how we need to respond to unfair authority. Answer gently, just like Jesus did. The passage from Ecclesiastes shows us how we can and will be subject to unfair authority. We will be treated like slaves in some instances. The old adage "Life isn't fair" will become a very clear reality in that you will have to endure submission to those who have no interest in your welfare, and don't care one iota what you think. This will happen very likely many times in your life.

"Let everyone be subject to the governing authorities, for there is no authority except that which God has established. The authorities that exist have been established by God. Consequently, whoever rebels against the authority is rebelling against what God has instituted, and those who do so will bring judgment on themselves. For rulers hold no terror for those who do right, but for those who do wrong. Do you want to be free from fear of the one in authority? Then do what is right and you will be commended. For the one in authority is God's servant for your good. But if you do wrong, be afraid, for rulers do not bear the sword for no reason. They are God's servants, agents of wrath to bring punishment on the wrongdoer. Therefore, it is necessary to submit to the authorities, not only because of possible punishment but also as a matter of conscience. This is also why you pay taxes, for the authorities are God's servants, who give their full time to governing. Give to everyone what you owe them: If you owe taxes, pay taxes; if revenue, then revenue; if respect, then respect; if honor, then honor." (Rom 13:1-7)

The Walk Applied

SPIRITUAL OFFICES AND ROLES

As spiritual creatures living a spiritual existence in the natural realm, we are called upon to fill certain roles in the natural. The idea of roles is not explicitly defined as spiritual roles in the bible, but we need to start seeing our lives in a *spiritual context.* That's the idea behind our spiritual identity. These "roles" define the parameters of how we participate in a spiritual way in the natural realm. When we place roles into an authority/submission context and redefine and reframe how we see our participation in the natural, these roles can take on meanings that we have never thought of before. Indeed, it can revolutionize how we see our life experience.

My former pastor Marvin Busey deserves credit for introducing me to the concept of a "spiritual office". There are three kinds of offices that go along with the authority and submission construct: authority offices, submission offices and influencer offices.

Authority offices trains us to understand God's Authority/Submission structure. Submissive offices prepare us for Authority offices. Influencer offices are those that contribute to our life story in one way or another. Indeed, every office is an Influencer Office.

How we operate in these roles/offices and how we integrate our experiences in dealing with people who occupy these roles/offices in our life determines our life experience to a major degree. God is the final arbiter in our life experience, but it is critical that we understand the enormous effect vis-à-vis the Authority/Submission structure that people have on us. When we begin to understand how the Authority/Submission structure works, we can begin to see our lives in a totally different context.

The Walk Applied

We need to see our various statuses in life as spiritual roles that are integrated into the Authority/Submission construct. It is also important to understand that at any stage of our lives, we will almost always be in all 3 sets of roles.

Authority offices are those whereby people are put in authority positions over others. As we have discussed, it is the remit of those who are in authority positions to create the conditions for growth. Submissive offices require that we honor those who are placed in authority over us. Both should bless each other and never curse one another. Both should be aware that peace and growth can only occur when the authority blesses the submitter, and the submitter honors the authority. Because we live in a fallen world and we are all sinners, there will be numerous instances where the authority/submission dynamic will break down. No growth can occur when that happens. However, via the extraordinary power of forgiveness and repentance, the appropriate and proper authority/submission structure can be reclaimed. Ultimately, both parties must submit to one another for growth to occur and peace to reign.

Influencers contribute to our overall life experience and mold and shape our life story. These are individuals who we do not necessarily participate in an authority/submission relationship but exert influence in our lives to one degree or another. They provide companionship, wisdom, guidance, and ultimately, community. Just like authority/submissive structures, these relationships can be very satisfying and provide us with very positive life experiences. Unfortunately, very negative and traumatic scenarios are often seen as well. Influencers are also those who may have had a tragic or destructive influence on our life. An influencer can be the one who molested or seriously injured you. The bully who made your life miserable is an influencer as well. It can be the drunk driver who killed one of your parents or both as a child. Below is a listing of the various Spiritual offices and roles:

137

The Walk Applied

AUTHORITY OFFICES

Adult	Parent	Employer
Gov't. Official	Teacher	Judge
Grandparent	Supervisor	Husband/Wife
Clergy		

SUBMISSIVE OFFICES

Child	Student	Spouse
Employee	Citizen	Church member

INFLUENCER OFFICES

Extended family	Friends
Acquaintances	Strangers

SPIRITUAL OFFICES AND
LINES OF AUTHORITY & SUBMISSION

The preceding discussion of spiritual "offices" can seem very foreign. Yet, in several places in the New Testament (Ephesians 5 immediately comes to mind) the notion of authority and submission are very prevalent. The concept of submission is an integral concept that runs through scripture.

To review and re-phrase, submissive offices prepare us for authority offices via learned submission. Authority offices train us to understand God's authority/submission structure. Influencer offices contribute to your overall life experience and help to mold and shape your life story. They provide companionship and give wisdom and guidance. They also provide community. Influencer offices also many times expose us to evil and wrongdoing. In a larger sense, all the offices influence others in one way or another. The Bible is explicit when it comes to certain offices as authority offices and submission offices, so we will discuss them separately.

The Walk Applied

LINES OF AUTHORITY:
THE BLESSING-HONORING-FRUIT BEARING CYCLE

The Authority Blesses the Submitter
The Blessing enables the Submitter to submit.
The Conferred Blessing brings the
    Authority and the Submitter In line with God's authority
The Submitter Honors the Authority
The Authority Prepares the Submitter to Become an Authority
The Authority Prepares the Submitter to Become Fruit Bearers

THE PARENT-CHILD LINE OF AUTHORITY

Father – Mother – Children:
The Family provides the emotional foundation:
    The love and security we fundamentally need
    Provides the basic emotional needs.
The Husband is the Authority:
    He is the Seed Sower and the Name Giver.
The Wife is the Submitter to the Authority of the Husband
    She is the Seed Receiver and the Name Receiver.
The Husband Blesses the Wife
The Wife Honors the Husband
The Parents are the Name Givers to the Children
    The Parents are the Authorities over the Children
The Parents bless the Children
The Children are Submitters to the Parents
The Children Honors the Parents
The Parents Prepare the Children to become Authorities.
The Parents Prepare the Children to be Fruit Bearing vessels.

The Walk Applied

THE MASTER/SERVANT LINE OF AUTHORITY
(SUPERVISOR/EMPLOYEE) or (TEACHER/STUDENT)

The Master Blesses the Servant
The Master Names the Servants position
The Servant Honors the Master
The Servant Accepts the Name of the Position
The Master Prepares the Servant to become the Master
The Master Prepares the Servant to be a Fruit Bearing vessel

THE CHURCH LINE OF AUTHORITY

The New Testament supports 3 distinct positions in the church authority structure: The Pastor, The Elder, and The Deacon. The Pastor is typically considered the CEO of the church. The Pastor is responsible and ultimately accountable for the day-to-day operations of the church. Elders are similar to a Board of Directors and oversee the Pastor. Elders assist the pastor and guide and give input and advice. Ultimately, the Elders represent the people of the church. Deacons are those who are appointed for specific functions that are needed for the operations of the church. In a very large sense we are all deacons as we perform functions in the service of the Pastor and the Church. Typically, Deacons are appointed and do represent an authority in the church, as do the Elders.

The Pastor, Elders, Deacons are the Authorities
The Pastor blesses the Congregants.
The Congregants are the Submitter to the Authority of Pastor
The Congregants Honor the Pastor.
The Pastor prepares the Congregants to become the Authorities.
The Pastor prepares the Congregants to be Fruit Bearing vessels.

The Walk Applied

THE GOVERNMENT LINE OF AUTHORITY

Local, State, and National entities represent a different form of authority and submission. Systems of laws and the structures that constitute Government spring from the notion that we recognize that we are in need of mechanisms to maintain order and provide for the common good. Laws, enforcement of laws, and appropriate consequences for those who choose to break the law are required so that anarchy does not reign. Government is also tasked with defending our borders against hostile invaders and providing services that contribute to the overall benefit and welfare of the citizenry.

In the New Testament, we are directed to submit to the governing authorities. In our day, submission to the government has come to be highly controversial in many instances. Here in America, many policies and laws have been implemented which directly conflict with Biblical principles. How and when individual Christians choose to submit is a personal decision – but it should be rooted in solid scriptural principles.

Typically, we would not think of Government entities in the vein of the Blessing and Honoring, as we have discussed others. Government can be significant blessing and has been used by God, indeed:

The Officials are the Authority
 The Officials Bless the citizens
The Citizens are the Submitters
 The Citizens Honor the Officials
The Officials prepares the Citizens to become the Officials
The Officials prepare the Citizens to be Fruit Bearing vessels.

The Walk Applied

CHAPTER 6
THE PERSONAL AND
EFFECTUAL CALL

The Walk Applied

The Walk Applied

CHAPTER 6
THE PERSONAL AND
EFFECTUAL CALL

We all have a call given to us by God. Indeed, God has a purpose plan and will for each and every one of us. Scripture tells us that "Where there is no vision, the people perish" (Pro 29:18).

The question we might be posing in prayer is this: What is God's overall plan for me? How do I enter into that call? When we are saved, the Spirit inhabits us. As we pursue Him, His call on your life is what fills you and gives you purpose. All good things flow from the throne of God, and your call and purpose are most assuredly a part of that. Recall we talked about the personal, effectual call earlier when we discussed the Spiritual Identity. We'll repeat it here for convenience:

SANCTIFICATION, STAGE 2:
YOUR CALLING REVEALED

"I consider my life worth nothing to me; my only aim is to finish the race and complete the task the Lord Jesus has given me—the task of testifying to the good news of God's grace." (Acts 20:24)

"This is what the Lord says: "Stand at the crossroads and look; ask for the ancient [eternal] paths, ask where the good way is, and walk in it, and you will find rest for your souls." (Jer 6:16)

"And let us run with perseverance the race marked out for us" (Heb 12:1-2)

"I will instruct you and teach you in the way you should go" (Ps 32:8)

"Where there is no vision, the people perish…" (Pro 29:18, KJV)

The Walk Applied

Isaiah tells us we will lie down in torment (torment!) when we try and go our own way:

"Who among you fears the Lord and obeys his servant? If you are walking in darkness, without a ray of light, trust in the Lord and rely on your God. But watch out, you who live in your own light and warm yourselves by your own fires. This is the reward you will receive from me: You will soon lie down in great torment."
(Isa 50:10-11)

God has an overall purpose, plan and will that is specific to you. We maintain that every single person has an individual call on their life. For some, it may be a one-time call that you will have been prepared for. A good example of this is Phillip in Acts 8, where he was used mightily of God. Some are called for a lifetime of service, like Paul, Moses, or Samuel. Typically, we find in the Bible that those who were called out for service wound up serving in that calling for the remainder of their lives.

Your personal call is what will give you meaning and purpose and fill you like nothing else. God will move heaven and earth to ensure you have everything you need to fulfill your calling. The contention from here is that what God will ask each and every one of us: Did you seek and follow the call?

Indeed, each person's call is as important as the next. No one's call is any more important than anyone else's. Some have been called to be a prayer warrior and labor in obscurity. Some are called to be powerful men and women of God called to preach the word of God fearlessly. Others may be called to be great evangelists or erudite theologians. What is important is that you seek your calling and follow your call.

The Walk Applied

THE PERSONAL, EFFECTUAL CALL REVEALED:
THE VEIL IS REMOVED

"...even to this day when Moses is read, a veil covers their hearts, but whenever anyone turns to the Lord, the veil is taken away." (2 Cor 3:15-16)

Moses turned, looked and saw the burning bush. He pursued it and encountered the Living God. He heard God and understood Him. The course of His life was truly changed. Moses resisted, but it was clear that his life would never be the same. Moses was launched on an adventure he certainly never expected. There are a number of instances in the scripture where we see that the veil was removed, and the personal, effectual call was revealed:

- Moses encountered God at the burning bush.
- The two men who walking on the road to Emmaus
- Paul's encounter on the road to Damascus
- Phillip in Acts 8

As we ponder the passage from Corinthians cited earlier, we note some similarities:

- God engineered circumstances in their lives
- They encountered God
- They heard God speak to them
- They understood what God had to say
- They were forever changed by God
- The course of their lives was changed God

The Walk Applied

BEAR FRUIT FOR THE KINGDOM

The purpose of the personal, effectual call is to provide meaning and purpose in our lives. Your calling is the primary way that God wants to use you to bear lasting fruit for His Kingdom. Your calling is "your specialty", if you will. God wants to use you to be a "people changer" via your specialty. Changed people – people who have been discipled and are more like Christ – is the fruit that will last.

The permanent and ongoing command is to bear fruit for the kingdom that will last. To produce fruit, you must have submission to Godly authority (although that is not all!). The relationship between authority and submission and bearing fruit is that there must be peace in order for lasting fruit to be borne. If the conditions for fruit bearing are not met, then only the conditions for chaos and death can exist.

BEARING FRUIT FOR THE KINGDOM: MAKE DISCIPLES AND BE A "PEOPLE CHANGER"

Bearing fruit is a running theme in the New Testament, as it is mentioned literally dozens of time. In the Great Commission, Jesus commanded His disciples (as well as us in the present day) to go forth and make disciples. The disciples clearly understood what Jesus meant implicitly: Go and do exactly what Jesus did with them. In short, Jesus wants us to go and find people who want to be changed – and then allow God to use you to change them. When Jesus sent out the 72, this is exactly what He had in mind. You can read all about it in Luke 10. Use your gifts and operate in your call so that Jesus can use you to change people according to His purpose, plan, and will. Changed people are the fruit of your personal ministry. If you are faithful to follow your call, some will be saved. Others will be healed or restored. Many will see Jesus in you and be inspired. Still others will walk away, unchanged. Whether they are changed or not is really none of your concern (although it will matter to you). Your job is to walk the path (Jer 6:16) and operate in your gifts and your call. Bless them. Depend upon God to provide for the journey. Meet others at their point of need. Intentionally invest in others. Demonstrate Christ in your life. Love others genuinely.

BEARING FRUIT FOR THE KINGDOM: EVANGELISM

Evangelism means to share the Good News of Jesus Christ by sharing the gospel story with others. Many people make way too much out of how one goes about evangelizing. Well-meaning Christians either want to avoid it entirely (typically because they are afraid of offending others among many reasons) or they overdo it. Many find it very easy to share the story of the Gospel – it just seems to come naturally to them. For the most part, evangelism or "witnessing" simply means telling others what you know about how Jesus has made the difference in your life. It's typically as simple as that.

THE INTENTIONAL INVESTMENT

What is the "intentional investment"? What does it mean to "intentionally invest" in others? How do we go about in such a way that we become "people changers"?

BEARING FRUIT FOR THE KINGDOM: THE INTENTIONAL INVESTMENT

When we examine Christ's ministry closely, a theme begins to emerge. What Christ did was to ask His Father to send him individuals that He would invest in. Over the next 3½ years, what Christ did was pour Himself into 12 men, and taught them how to do this "Jesus thing". Now, no one is asking you to do the same thing that Christ did (truly, no one can!) No one is expecting you to

The Walk Applied

take 3 to 4 years out of life to leave everything behind to go perform miracles and disciple others. What Jesus is asking you to do is to mimic what He did. Ask the Father to send you those who you can invest in for a season that may last a week or may last several years –perhaps even a lifetime.

JESUS & THE INTENTIONAL INVESTMENT

Christians love to talk about all the wonderful things that Jesus did and how he changed the world. Jesus took flawed sinners and turned them into fearless champions. Those unlikely men carried on an anointed movement that Jesus started. It continues to this day.

Jesus had a call, and He followed that call on his life. Jesus was called to go with the intention of discipling very flawed men who would go forward to change the world. Jesus made an *intentional investment.* Jesus *intentionally invested* by pouring himself into 12 men for 3 years. He showed them how this "Jesus thing" was to be done. The great commission tells us to go and be people changers. Luke tells us that Jesus commanded us to go and proclaim the kingdom and heal them. Judas is the tragic example that show us it won't always go as planned.

THE INTENTIONAL INVESTMENT:
KNOW YOUR CALL

We reiterate that we all have a call given to us by God. God has a specific purpose plan and will for each of us. Your call is your purpose, so you must ask God to show you your calling:

This is what the Lord says: "Stand at the crossroads and look; ask for the ancient paths, ask where the good way is, and walk in it, and you will find rest for your souls. (Jer 6:16-17)

"Where there is no vision, the people perish" (Pro 29:18).

The Walk Applied

"...let us run with perseverance the race marked out for us"
(Heb 12:1)

"I will instruct you and teach you in the way you should go"
(Ps 32:8)

You need to know your call. Your call is how you will influence and change people. Ask God what your call is. The passages above from Jeremiah tells us to ask, so ask! God will reveal your call to you.

THE INTENTIONAL INVESTMENT:
ACCEPT GOD'S CALL ON YOUR LIFE

Let's re-visit the powerful passage below from Luke 2. You'll recall that this incident is where Jesus, at the age, of 12 stayed behind in Jerusalem. Jesus is sitting among the teachers at the Temple.

"When his parents saw him, they were astonished. His mother said to him, "Son, why have you treated us like this? Your father and I have been anxiously searching for you." Why were you searching for me?" he asked. "Didn't you know I had to be in my Father's house?" But they did not understand what he was saying to them. Then he went down to Nazareth with them and was obedient to them. But his mother treasured all these things in her heart. And Jesus grew in wisdom and stature, and in favor with God and man.
(Luke 2:48-52)

Jesus is acknowledging his true submission to his Heavenly father. He is preparing to be groomed for his call. Jesus is teaching us that there comes a time when we need to unequivocally accept our Heavenly Father as our true father and take on the mantle of preparing for the call.

The Walk Applied

The apostles accepted the call and submitted willingly to Jesus who trained them for 3 years. Pentecost came, and they were then anointed to go. They went out and changed the world.

Paul, on the road to Damascus, was confronted by Jesus. God made it quite difficult for Paul to refuse the call He had on Paul's life. Paul subsequently went into the desert for many years to be trained. After his time of preparation and training, Paul went out and changed the world.

Moses' early years prepared him for what was ultimately to come. God waited 40 years before He interrupted Moses' life in a most unexpected way. Moses submitted to God's call on his life and he subsequently changed the world.

Joseph, in the Old Testament, endured great suffering that prepared him for God's work. He accepted God's call on his life and he changed the world.

Some will be called like Phillip in Acts 8. Phillip accepted the call and used his training. He didn't know it at the time, but his "chance" meeting resulted in the start of the evangelization of Africa. He followed the call and the result was the world was changed.

The length of your personal call can vary. Phillip is an example of a one-time call. Gideon had a one-time call that he had been prepared for. Jesus was called for a season. Samuel was called for a lifetime. The apostles were called for a lifetime.

THE INTENTIONAL INVESTMENT:
HONOR THE SABBATH

Many like to think of Isaiah 58 as the "fasting chapter." Yet, a close reading of the stirring and profound narrative found in Isaiah 58 has much more to say than mere fasting. The passage tells us that by

The Walk Applied

honoring the Sabbath, we are putting ourselves in position to serve. The passage emphasizes service without judgement. When we comply with the admonitions found in Isaiah's writings, we are creating opportunities to intentionally invest in others. Indeed, Isaiah forcefully details how we can allow God to minister to us so as to heal our own personal hurts while we pursue our personal call by being intentional. The passage firmly conveys the message that as we encounter those who we can minister to and invest in without judgement, there is much to be gained from sincere and compassionate service.

"Is not this the kind of fasting I have chosen: to loose the chains of injustice and untie the cords of the yoke, to set the oppressed free and break every yoke? Is it not to share your food with the hungry and to provide the poor wanderer with shelter— when you see the naked, to clothe them, and not to turn away from your own flesh and blood? Then your light will break forth like the dawn, and your healing will quickly appear; then your righteousness will go before you, and the glory of the Lord will be your rear guard. Then you will call, and the Lord will answer; you will cry for help, and he will say: Here am I. "If you do away with the yoke of oppression, with the pointing finger and malicious talk, and if you spend yourselves in behalf of the hungry and satisfy the needs of the oppressed, then your light will rise in the darkness, and your night will become like the noonday. The Lord will guide you always; He will satisfy your needs in a sun-scorched land and will strengthen your frame. You will be like a well-watered garden, like a spring whose waters never fail. Your people will rebuild the ancient ruins and will raise up the age-old foundations; you will be called Repairer of Broken Walls, Restorer of Streets with Dwellings. "If you keep your feet from breaking the Sabbath and from doing as you please on my holy day, if you call the Sabbath a delight and the Lord's holy day honorable, and if you honor it by not going your own way and not doing as you please or speaking idle words, then you will find your joy in the Lord, and I will cause

153

The Walk Applied

you to ride in triumph on the heights of the land and to feast on the inheritance of your father Jacob." For the mouth of the Lord has spoken. (Isa 58: 6-14)

BEARING FRUIT FOR THE KINGDOM: MUCH MORE THAN EVANGELISM

Bearing fruit for the Kingdom means far more than evangelizing people to Christ, as important as that is. You will notice there is precious little in this book about evangelism. That is by design. There are numerous books and methodologies and tutorials for bringing people to Christ, and it's highly important that we make witnessing a priority. Indeed, evangelism is a crucial step in changing people. However, it is important to remember that evangelizing them is only a step in the process. Admittedly, converting people may, in fact, be our only role in some people's lives. That is all well good and fine. Yet, we have far too many examples of people coming to Christ and then being left to fend for themselves without any effort to disciple them. If we truly want to imitate Jesus and what He did, then we need to emulate what He did: ask the Father to bring us people that we can invest in and mentor them thru change – all according to God's perfect purpose and will for both you and the individual you invest in.

BEARING FRUIT FOR THE KINGDOM: DO WHAT YOU CAN WHEN YOU CAN WITH WHAT YOU HAVE BY BEING IN POSITION TO SERVE

In the New Testament, a little boy was in position to serve and did what he could when he could with what he had. The young boy offered to Jesus what he had at the time: five loaves of bread and a couple of fishes. Jesus took that humble offering and fed thousands.

154

The Walk Applied

The story of the Good Samaritan tells us of the Samaritan who stopped to help a hurting man. The Good Samaritan was in position to do what he could when he could with what he had and saved a man's life. Mary accepted the overwhelming responsibility to be the mother of Jesus. She was in position to do what she could when she could with what he had.

In Acts 8, Phillip responded to a supernatural call which ultimately resulted in the start of the evangelism of Africa. Philip had no idea what he was getting involved with. He trusted God and went and did what was asked. Phillip was in position to do what he could when he could with what he had.

A common theme we note is that they were in position to serve, and responded when God called, no matter what the consequences. They were in position to serve. They did what they were could when they could with what they had at the time.

A common thread we note in all these instances is that these people were interrupted in their lives. They certainly weren't expecting what happened. They were in position to serve; they did what they could when they could with what they had.

It's a huge error to think that we somehow have to be overtly profound to be effective for the Kingdom. Simple, random acts that we can do every day can be huge keys in others' lives. Visiting the sick, making a meal for a new mother, taking someone to the doctor – these and a thousand other similar acts are the mark of a humble servant. Do what you can when you can with what you have.

Jesus told us that we would do greater things then Him. Jesus crafted amazing miracles, yet we are told we would do greater things. What Jesus meant was that people would see our testimony of selfless acts done out of a genuine, loving heart – and that those actions would be far more meaningful than miracles. Never underestimate how significant your "little" contribution might be!

THE CONDITIONS FOR BEARING FRUIT
FOR THE KINGDOM

ABIDE IN CHRIST

"I am the true vine, and my Father is the gardener. He cuts off every branch in me that bears no fruit, while every branch that does bear fruit he prunes so that it will be even more fruitful. You are already clean because of the word I have spoken to you. Remain in me, as I also remain in you. No branch can bear fruit by itself; it must remain in the vine. Neither can you bear fruit unless you remain in me. "I am the vine; you are the branches. If you remain in me and I in you, you will bear much fruit; apart from me you can do nothing. If you do not remain in me, you are like a branch that is thrown away and withers; such branches are picked up, thrown into the fire and burned. If you remain in me and my words remain in you, ask whatever you wish, and it will be done for you." (John 15:1-7)

What John is talking about here is that we must maintain a relationship with Christ. Jesus is clearly communicating that not having an intimate relationship with Christ is not an option. This relationship with Jesus is the key to bearing fruit. Jesus is emphasizing in no uncertain terms that the object is to bear fruit: which means changed people. Jesus is also flatly stating that whatever we need according to his purpose, plan, and will for us will be supplied.

The Walk Applied

REPENTANCE

"Produce fruit in keeping with repentance." (Mat 3:8)

Just prior to Jesus's baptism John the Baptist issues a stern warning to all of us. He is essentially making the claim that only when you have aligned yourself with Christ can you produce lasting fruit that is meaningful. In Matthew 3:10 John the Baptist draws the final line in the sand: If you don't produce fruit by following the Father's purpose plan and will, then *"...every tree that does not produce good fruit will be cut down and thrown into the fire."* What John is proclaiming here is that if you are truly saved, you will pursue Jesus, and you will produce fruit. If you were never truly saved, you will not produce fruit, because your pursuit of Jesus was non-existent.

STUDY OF THE WORD

"But his delight is in the law of the LORD, and on his law he meditates day and night. He is like a tree planted by streams of water, which yields its fruit in season and whose leaf does not wither. Whatever he does prospers." (Psa 1:2-3)

Study of God's word is required in our pursuit of Jesus to become "people-changers" and fruit-bearers. The Word – preached or read – is what changes us over time. It is a vital part of the sanctification process and cannot be overlooked.

ROOTED IN THE WORD

"But since he has no root, he lasts only a short time. When trouble or persecution comes because of the word, he quickly falls away. The one who received the seed that fell among the thorns is the man who hears the word, but the worries of this life and the deceitfulness of wealth choke it, making it unfruitful. But the one who received the seed that fell on good soil is the man who hears the word and

157

understands it. He produces a crop, yielding a hundred, sixty or thirty times what was sown." (Mat 13:21-23)

DIE TO THE NATURAL LIFE:
UNDERSTAND YOUR TRUE IDENTITY

"Jesus replied, "The hour has come for the Son of Man to be glorified. I tell you the truth, unless a kernel of wheat falls to the ground and dies, it remains only a single seed. But if it dies, it produces many seeds. The man who loves his life will lose it, while the man who hates his life in this world will keep it for eternal life. Whoever serves me must follow me; and where I am, my servant also will be. My Father will honor the one who serves me. "Now my heart is troubled, and what shall I say? 'Father, save me from this hour'? No, it was for this very reason I came to this hour.

GODLY DISCIPLINE

"Endure hardship as discipline; God is treating you as sons… No discipline seems pleasant at the time, but painful. Later on, however, it produces a harvest of righteousness and peace for those who have been trained by it." (Heb12:7)

THE "7-FOLD" MINISTRY

"So Christ himself gave the apostles, the prophets, the evangelists, the pastors and teachers, to equip his people for works of service, so that the body of Christ may be built up until we all reach unity in the faith and in the knowledge of the Son of God and become mature, attaining to the whole measure of the fullness of Christ." (Eph 4:11-13 NIV)

This above passage has no small degree of notoriety within many christian circles. It is usually referred to as the "5-fold ministry". Many ministries, large and small, have been built around this

158

The Walk Applied

profound and purposeful concept. In the passage above, Paul lays out 5 distinct calls for service within the body of Christ that we will discuss momentarily.

We need to make an important distinction here. One of the issues with the application of the five-fold ministry is that many have assumed that all members of Christ's flock must fit within one of the 5 general calls. The problem is that the passage never says that. The passage reports that Christ has equipped people with those calls, but nowhere does it assert that every person in God's family has one of these 5 callings. For that reason, I add two categories: worshippers and servers. We will examine what I like to call the 7-fold ministry.

APOSTLE: The word apostle means "one sent forth". This would include missionaries and church planters. Apostles go and set up ministries. An apostle can also be that person who also ministers outside of the congregation by setting up "quasi–ministries" that can be either formal or informal. An example might be Jeanette, an older woman who ministers to younger people where she works. Her ministry is in no way "official", but the evidence that she is ministering to others is unmistakable. She even refers to it as her "bathroom ministry". Some of the younger girls even follow her into the bathroom to seek her counsel! Young people are just drawn to her. She might be considered an evangelist, but her ministry goes deeper than that by virtue of how people seek her out for her advice and guidance.

PROPHET: A prophet is one who "proclaims a divine message ". In the Old Testament, prophets were typically not very popular, as they usually sternly warned the populace. In the modern day, we might think of them as theologians. Virtually every church has them. They are usually the men and women who always seem to have a good answer for your questions when it comes to God and the Bible.

159

The Walk Applied

EVANGELIST: is one who "spreads the good news". These people seem to be able talk about Jesus in ways that others can't. These "soul winners" are perhaps more properly referred to as "seed-sowers". They are good at seizing opportunities to work Jesus into the conversation at just the right time. By sowing "verbal seed", they influence others and bring people closer to Christ.

PASTOR: is one who "shepherds the flock". These are people who are called to insure the general welfare of the flock. They usually are responsible for the day to day operations of the church and handle the vast majority of the peaching and teaching chores. They might also be considered to be healers or counselors or mentors. Certainly, this calling can also be extended easily to parents or spouses. Not as easily seen is the idea that Christian employers and supervisors can also be seen as shepherds in their various employment capacities.

TEACHER: is one who explains God's word and how to apply it in our lives. They tend to lead Bible studies, Sunday school classes and the like. Those who have been called to teach pursue a high calling indeed. They typically spend a great deal of time seeking God for revelation and wisdom and discernment. They are a vital part of the development of God's people via their instruction.

WORSHIPERS are those who find great satisfaction in the simple act of worshipping God. Be it music, prayer, intense meditation, these people are typically called by God to seek Him. The musician, the prayer warrior and those who meditate on God and His word are much more than just a vital part of His Kingdom. Indeed, these children of God pursue a high and mighty calling. In the Old Testament, David employed 4,000 Levites whose purpose was to simply worship God. If David ("the man after God's own heart") could recognize and understand the overwhelming significance of worship, then we need to recognize its importance as a separate "ministry fold".

The Walk Applied

SERVER: These dedicated servants find their niche as "helpers". They are the greeters, those who set-up the church; do clean up; maintain the church, help with parking, and assist with zillion other details that help a church function. Many of these awesome people of God simply enjoy serving in a myriad of ways.

It's important to remember that these ministry archetypes often overlap, as many enjoy participating in several of the ministries at the same time.

YOUR "OIKOS"

An important concept that we might introduce here is the notion of the "oikos"- a Greek term that refers your various "people circles", such as family, work, and social. The way you negotiate these people groups in your life give you opportunity to exercise various callings in your life. As a parent, you are almost certainly a pastor. As an employee, you might think of yourself as an apostle or an evangelist. In your various social and family circles, you might think of yourself as a teacher or a prophet. It's important to remember that you don't need to "force it" or assume a role that you're just not suited for. Your witness to others is based upon you simply being you. (If you need to you, use words…) Let God use you as He deems.

THE FRUIT OF THE SPIRIT

*"So I say, **live by the Spirit**, and you will not gratify the desires of the sinful nature. For the sinful nature desires what is contrary to the Spirit, and the Spirit what is contrary to the sinful nature. They are in conflict with each other, so that you do not do what you want. But if you are led by the Spirit, you are not under law…. **But the fruit of the Spirit** is love, joy, peace, patience, kindness, goodness, faithfulness, gentleness and self-control. Against such things there is no law."* (Gal 5:16-26)

The Walk Applied

"Those who belong to Christ Jesus have crucified the sinful nature with its passions and desires. <u>Since we live by the Spirit, let us keep in step with the Spirit</u>. Let us not become conceited, provoking and envying each other." (Gal 5:24-26)

"His divine power has given us everything we need for life and godliness through our knowledge of him who called us by his own glory and goodness. Through these he has given us his very great and precious promises, so that through them you may participate in the divine nature and escape the corruption in the world caused by evil desires. For this very reason, make every effort to add to your faith goodness; and to goodness, knowledge; and to knowledge, self-control; and to self-control, perseverance; and to perseverance, godliness; and to godliness, brotherly kindness; and to brotherly kindness, love. For if you possess these qualities in increasing measure, they will keep you from being ineffective and unproductive in your knowledge of our Lord Jesus Christ." (2 Pet 1:3-8)

"For you were once darkness, but now you are light in the Lord. Live as children of light (for the fruit of the light consists in all goodness, righteousness and truth) and find out what pleases the Lord." (Eph 5:8-10)

"And this is my prayer: that your love may abound more and more in knowledge and depth of insight, so that you may be able to discern what is best and may be pure and blameless until the day of Christ, filled with the <u>fruit of righteousness</u> that comes through Jesus Christ--to the glory and praise of God." (Phil 1:9-11)

" But the wisdom that comes from heaven is first of all pure; then peace-loving, considerate, submissive, full of mercy and good fruit, impartial and sincere". (James 3:17)

The Walk Applied

THE FRUIT OF THE SPIRIT (GALATIANS 5)

We reiterate from chapter 4: A fundamental aspect of a truly intimate relationship with Jesus means we will change over time. Sanctification tells us that as we pursue Jesus, we will begin to look more like Jesus in thought and deed. In his letter to the Galatians, Paul details 9 areas we will develop in over time. Paul's caution to us is that we not try to hurry the Sprit's work in us; instead, he tells us to "keep in step with the Spirit", and not try to work around or get ahead of the Spirit, The Holy Spirit's leads us into all truth: He knows best how and when to develop us as the Father sees fit.

Loving, Joyful, Peaceful: Christian habits of mind.
Patient, Kind, Good: Christian social virtues.
Faithful, Gentle, Self-controlled: Christian traits of the Heart.

SPIRITUAL GIFTS

To know your spiritual gifts is to be seeking how you are equipped in your role to build up the kingdom. If you don't know your gifts, how are you going to effectively serve the kingdom? It is through the use and expression of the gifts that God satisfies your God given desire to achieve! Following are various scriptures that instruct us about the spiritual gifts.

"Just as each of us has one body with many members, and these members do not all have the same function, so in Christ we who are many form one body, and each member belongs to all the others. We have different gifts, according to the grace given us. If a man's gift is prophesying, let him use it in proportion to his faith. If it is serving, let him serve; if it is teaching, let him teach; if it is encouraging, let him encourage; if it is contributing to the needs of others, let him give generously; if it is leadership, let him govern diligently; if it is showing mercy, let him do it cheerfully.

The Walk Applied

(Rom 12:4-8)
"Now about spiritual gifts, brothers, I do not want you to be ignorant. You know that when you were pagans, somehow or other you were influenced and led astray to mute idols. Therefore I tell you that no one who is speaking by the Spirit of God says, "Jesus be cursed," and no one can say, "Jesus is Lord," except by the Holy Spirit. There are different kinds of gifts, but the same Spirit. There are different kinds of service, but the same Lord. There are different kinds of working, but the same God works all of them in all men. Now to each one the manifestation of the Spirit is given for the common good. To one there is given through the Spirit the message of wisdom, to another the message of knowledge by means of the same Spirit, to another faith by the same Spirit, to another gifts of healing by that one Spirit, to another miraculous powers, to another prophecy, to another distinguishing between spirits, to another speaking in different kinds of tongues, and to still another the interpretation of tongues. All these are the work of one and the same Spirit, and he gives them to each one, just as he determines. The body is a unit, though it is made up of many parts; and though all its parts are many, they form one body. So it is with Christ. For we were all baptized by one Spirit into one body--whether Jews or Greeks, slave or free--and we were all given the one Spirit to drink. Now the body is not made up of one part but of many. If the foot should say, "Because I am not a hand, I do not belong to the body," it would not for that reason cease to be part of the body. And if the ear should say, "Because I am not an eye, I do not belong to the body," it would not for that reason cease to be part of the body. If the whole body were an eye, where would the sense of hearing be? If the whole body were an ear, where would the sense of smell be? But in fact God has arranged the parts in the body, every one of them, just as he wanted them to be. If they were all one part, where would the body be? As it is, there are many parts, but one body. The eye cannot say to the hand, "I don't need you!" And the head cannot say to the feet, "I don't need you!" On the contrary, those parts of the body that seem to be weaker are indispensable, and the

The Walk Applied

parts that we think are less honorable we treat with special honor. And the parts that are unpresentable are treated with special modesty, while our presentable parts need no special treatment. But God has combined the members of the body and has given greater honor to the parts that lacked it, so that there should be no division in the body, but that its parts should have equal concern for each other. If one part suffers, every part suffers with it; if one part is honored, every part rejoices with it. Now you are the body of Christ, and each one of you is a part of it. And in the church God has appointed first of all apostles, second prophets, third teachers, then workers of miracles, also those having gifts of healing, those able to help others, those with gifts of administration, and those speaking in different kinds of tongues. Are all apostles? Are all prophets? Are all teachers? Do all work miracles? Do all have gifts of healing? Do all speak in tongues? Do all interpret? But eagerly desire the greater gifts. And now I will show you the most excellent way." (1 Cor 12)

"It was he who gave some to be apostles, some to be prophets, some to be evangelists, and some to be pastors and teachers, to prepare God's people for works of service, so that the body of Christ may be built up until we all reach unity in the faith and in the knowledge of the Son of God and become mature, attaining to the whole measure of the fullness of Christ. Then we will no longer be infants, tossed back and forth by the waves, and blown here and there by every wind of teaching and by the cunning and craftiness of men in their deceitful scheming. (Eph 4:11-16)

"So it is with you. Since you are eager to have spiritual gifts, try to excel in gifts that build up the church". (1 Cor 14:12)

"Each one should use whatever gift he has received to serve others, faithfully administering God's grace in its various forms." (1 Pet 4:10)

165

The Walk Applied

SPIRITUAL ROLES	SPIRITUAL CALLINGS	SPIRITUAL GIFTS: PETER WAGNER[1]
CHILD	PRIEST	PROPHECY
STUDENT	APOSTLE	SERVICE
ADULT	PROPHET	TEACHING
SPOUSE	HEALER	EXHORTATION
PARENT	HELPER	GIVING
GRANDPARENT	ADMINISTRATOR	LEADERSHIP
WORKER	TEACHER	MERCY
EMPLOYER	SHEPHERD (PASTOR)	WISDOM
FRIEND	EVANGELIST	KNOWLEDGE
RELATIVE		FAITH
ACQUAINTANCE		HEALING
STRANGER		MIRACLES
		DISCERNMENT
		TONGUES
		INTERPRETING TONGUES
		APOSTLE
		ADMINISTRATION
		EVANGELIST
		PASTOR
		CELIBACY
		POVERTY
		MARTYRDOM
		PEACEMAKER
		HOSPITALITY
		MISSIONARY
		INTERCESSION
		EXORCISM
		CRAFTMANSHIP
		MUSIC

There are numerous spiritual gift inventories that you can access online or purchase. Numerous books have been written on the subject. I chose Wagner's because I felt it was the most complete; you can take Wagner's inventory of spiritual gifts online for free.

The Walk Applied

I'll comment briefly here as to what each gift is and what it can potentially mean in your life. I want to emphasize that the interpretation of what the gifts are and how they are manifested in our lives can vary widely. You certainly may agree with my brief thoughts or not. In any case, the Bible is certainly clear in that we are to seek our gifts and callings. I have purposely left out the giftings that are the same as the sevenfold ministry, as they are discussed above.

SERVICE: This gift is evident in those who want to "DO": parking, clean up, construction, serve meals, assist the pastor and staff, church set-up, etc. These marvelous saints typically want to tend to all the "little things" and the tedious details that need to be taken care of in today's modern church. They can also typically be seen when they assist a new mother, help a church attendee who is ill, or drive someone to church or an appointment. They usually want to labor anonymously. They typically take great satisfaction in seeing the finished results. Some may refer to this gift as the gift of helps, buts it's all borne out of a heart's desire to serve.

EXHORTATION: Means to "strongly encourage or urge (someone) to do something." People who exhibit this gift will come along side and encourage you, especially if you are wavering in your faith. Their gifting is such that what they say will come across as genuine and authentic as they minister to you.

GIVING: This gift means far more than just giving money. They are typically very hospitable and love to give material gifts as well. They give simply because they want to honor God through their giving.

LEADERSHIP: Gifted leaders know how to motivate and inspire.

The Walk Applied

MERCY: People with this gift can minister very effectively with those who are hurting. Their compassion and empathy will be very genuine and sincere.

WISDOM: In Proverbs, wisdom means to "master the art of living". In other words, it means to see your life from an overall perspective that is Godly. It means to appreciate in a deep and convicted way how the spiritual realm and the natural realm work together and have an understanding of how it applies to our lives - even on a day to day basis.

KNOWLEDGE: People with the gift of knowledge have a good overall working knowledge of scripture and its applications to living our daily lives. It differs from wisdom in that those with wisdom may not have a deep knowledge of scriptures, but just seem to always know the right thing to do or have the wise approach. Teachers typically have the gift of knowledge. If you have the gift of knowledge, be careful. Paul, in the New Testament, wants us to be wary of knowledge. Paul warns us that *"Knowledge puffs up, but love builds up"* (1 Cor 8:1)

FAITH: Those with the gift of faith see Jesus as the basis for virtually everything in life. They see themselves as true spiritual creatures living in the natural.

HEALING: Healing can mean many things, not just miraculous physical changes in people's bodies. Healings can and do happen. I myself watched my daughter's leg lengthen. I have heard numerous testimonies of people who have experienced what can only be described as a miraculous physical healing. I am also aware of verifiable instances of people who were raised from the dead after an extended period of prayer. While I do not believe that every request made of God will result in a miraculous healing, I do believe that there are Godly people who are capable of healing others. I do not subscribe to the idea that these individuals have the actual gift of healing at will. However, I do believe that certain people have been raised up by God to perform healing, and that God does work through then at His choosing to heal certain individuals.

What can be terribly problematic vis-à-vis healing is that when someone does not get healed there can be the "why not me?" question. The discussion can get very complex and emotional when the "you-don't-have-enough-faith" accusation is raised. Then, there's the "you-must-have-unconfessed-or-secret-sin-or-God-would-have-healed-you" claim. A myriad of other reasons ("You didn't pray hard enough" or "you didn't pray right") can also be raised when someone does not experience the desired healing.

The position from here is that not everyone gets "healed" as we think we should. Or perhaps people do not experience healing on their "timetable". Many walk a path whereby they experience physical maladies of one sort or another. Joni Erickson Tada (paralyzed from the neck down in her teens in a swimming accident) is but one example of many very Godly people who believe that God allowed major physical difficulties in their lives so as to portray His honor and glory regardless of circumstances. Ms. Tada has built a stunning worldwide ministry that is extraordinarily blessed by God. She firmly believes without question that she has been allowed to walk this life in her condition so as to be a witness to God's grace and mercy.

MIRACLES: Christians believe that God can intervene at any moment in time according to His purpose plan and will. As I stated earlier, I watched my daughter's leg lengthen, and she will testify to it. Numerous sincere and compelling stories and anecdotes from around the world paint a picture of a sovereign God who is intervening all the time in various ways. I do believe there are individuals who can and will be used by God to do miraculous things. We note that it is God working through them to perform the miracle.

The Walk Applied

DISCERNMENT: To discern means to judge wisely. Those who have the gift of discernment will be able to discern if something is of God or not. There are those who will be able to examine a situation and determine if that situation is rooted in God's will, or if the situation is designed to seduce someone into evil. Spiritualgiftstest.com has this to say:

"The spiritual gift of discernment is also known as the gift of "discernment of spirits" or "distinguishing between spirits." The Greek word for the gift of discernment is Diakrisis. The word describes being able to distinguish, discern, judge or appraise a person, statement, situation, or environment. In the New Testament it describes the ability to distinguish between spirits as in 1 Corinthians 12:10, and to discern good and evil as in Hebrews 5:14. The Holy Spirit gives the gift of discernment to enable certain Christians to clearly recognize and distinguish between the influence of God, Satan, the world, and the flesh in a given situation. The church needs those with this gift to warn believers in times of danger or keep them from being led astray by false teaching. See also I Corinthians 12:10, Acts 5:3-6; 16:16-18; 1 John 4:1."

ADMINISTRATION: Those blessed with gift of administration are good at handling the various logistical, clerical, and managerial functions that exist in the modern-day church.

CELIBACY: Those who are celibate are those who can dedicate themselves to a life that has no sexual partner and rejects physical intimacy. Celibacy is really much more of a calling as opposed to a gift. Paul talks about being celibate, and how he believed that it is truly a preferred lifestyle. Most would acknowledge this gift/lifestyle is quite difficult. For those who can relate to this gift, Paul implies that it is a high calling indeed. I have also heard the testimonies of a few Christians who truly believe that they are lesbian or homosexual. They freely admit that they do interpret their sexual attraction/preference as God's call to enter the celibate life.

The Walk Applied

One was quoted that sex is not necessary for life, but intimacy is. In that instance she professes that she has rejected a sexual lifestyle while acknowledging her need for intimacy. She talks about a most intimate walk with Jesus as well having intimate, yet non-sexual relationships.

POVERTY: There are those who have this gift who choose an ascetic lifestyle. Much like celibacy, to choose poverty is really to choose a lifestyle calling. They eschew most earthly comforts and live minimally. There are those who choose to give most of what they have to the causes God has called them to give to.

HOSPITALITY: Many identify this gifting with the important notion of accepting visitors into their home for either a short or lengthy period of time. Hosting visiting missionaries or church planters or evangelists are worthwhile pursuits. Delivering meals to the sick or visiting shut-ins are wonderful extensions of this gift. Yet, it's more than that. Henri Nouwen points out that the German and Dutch words for hospitality actually means to "create the safe place". When you look at it that way, hospitality takes on a completely different tenor and tone. Indeed, it can be a most significant first step in providing emotional healing in numerous instances. By creating the "safe place" for healing, you help to give the emotionally hurting person the impetus and the foundation for healing.

MISSIONARY: Missionaries leave their comfort zone to go to exotic and potentially dangerous places to spread God's word. It doesn't have to mean that they go halfway around the world to the jungles of the Amazon or the Middle East. For some, it may mean living among the poor in the inner city. It can also imply that the missionary goes to rural Alaska or Appalachia. They live and work among the residents, helping out locals in numerous ways and spreading the word. In most cases - not all - they must raise financial support their efforts.

The Walk Applied

INTERCESSION: These Christian prayer warriors have the very special gift of being able to pray for one another and seeing spectacular results. It is as if they have been "commissioned" by Jesus to be "prayer soldiers". While we should all be about the business of intercession, these individuals in particular are very passionate about prayer, and they revel in praying for others.

PEACEMAKERS: The term "peacemakers" appears twice in the New Testament, once in Matthew 5:9 and also in James 3:18. "Peacemakers" is not found in the usual scriptures for spiritual gifts. We include it here because the tone of the two passages imply that more than just a few people have this capability, or gift. The passages hint at someone who can bring peace by the exercise of this gift. That Jesus himself mentions the term also gives it a significantly greater weight.

CRAFTMANSHIP: Those who have this wonderful and awesome service gift are the ones who serve diligently as the carpenters, plumbers and electricians in many local churches. They are also the ones who make things festive at the appropriate times of the year. They serve in various ways to help keep the local churches going.

MUSIC: Vocalists and instrumentalists make up a vital part of worship as they lead us in praise and worship most every Sunday, and on other special occasions as well.

TONGUES / INTERPRETING TONGUES: These gifts can be very controversial in Christian circles. Like miracles, there is nothing in scripture to indicate that these gifts were ever taken away. Indeed, many of God's people believe implicitly in a "prayer language" and actively practice a prayer language. Great care must be exercised as you pursue and utilize these gifts according to the Spirits leading. It is my opinion that scripture teaches that these gifts are valid, but not everyone will get them. Paul warns us that while these giftings are important, they are among the "least" of God's giftings - love is far more important. In other words, if you have one or the other or both of these gifts, use them with great discernment, but do not be deluded into thinking that they are the end all be all.

EXORCISM: This gift should be approached with great care and discernment. Possession by the demonic is a very scary notion and is not to taken lightly. I have talked to several sensible and level-headed individuals who have witnessed actual possessions and exorcisms. Demonic possession in its sensationalized form tends to happen rarely - but there are many documented cases whereby grotesque manifestations of evil are exhibited. However, many people (including Christians) can allow themselves to be "demonized" and give demons a foothold in their lives. As Neil Anderson talks about in his books, large percentages of people have admitted to hearing voices. Typically, we use the term "deliverance" to denote the routing of these demonic spirits from our minds. We can be taught how to deliver others from the influences of evil spirits, and given the prevalence of these beings, it's something that we all should learn how to do.

MARTYRDOM: While the joke is that "you can only use this gift once", in actual practice this gift is all about defending and advocating Jesus fearlessly. A former pastor of mine tells of a very petite woman he knew in Baltimore, Md., who would go to the inner city and walk among the pimps and the drug dealers fearlessly and would talk about Jesus to anyone who cared to listen. She got respect from these people because of her bravery.

The Walk Applied

THE MARTYRDOM CALLING

The gift of martyrdom is actually a unique, special, and very high calling. Included in this calling would be those who:

-Suffer from incurable diseases that are typically quite painful.
-They may have experienced tragedies in their life that suddenly changed the course of their lives such that they will endure physical suffering the rest of their lives.
-Unexpectedly wind up caring for others who cannot help themselves and labor in obscurity for years.
-Spend many years in jail or other confinement as a political pawn because of their faith.
-Endure great suffering, torture, and/or death for their faith. Many times, their deaths are quite horrific.

A good example of a martyr would be Joni Ericson Tada. She was paralyzed from the neck down for life after she hit her head on a rock when she dove into the Chesapeake Bay. After going thru a couple of years of grieving (and all that entailed) she learned to draw and paint with pens or brushes in her mouth. Her martyrdom has led to a ministry that is world famous. According to Wikipedia, "… she has written over forty books, recorded several musical albums, starred in an autobiographical movie of her life, and is an advocate for people with disabilities."

In our day and age, there are thousands around the world who endure great suffering for their faith. We need to pray for these courageous men and women who endure horrific conditions that we cannot even begin to imagine.

CHAPTER 7
THE KINGDOM

The Walk Applied

The Walk Applied

CHAPTER 7
THE KINGDOM

The Bible makes many stunning claims, not the least of which is that there exists a spiritual Kingdom – God's Kingdom. We are told that ultimately Jesus is in authority over this Kingdom. This idea spawns many questions, to be sure, but perhaps we might first ponder the following: Who was Jesus? Why did He come? What's the point? Who is this Jesus such that He has authority over this Kingdom?

WHO WAS JESUS?

Jesus is, without question, THE central figure in human history. He was God in the flesh, the Word come to life in the form of a man. He was conceived by the Holy Spirit and born of a virgin. He died a brutal, agonizing death on the cross and rose to life again after 3 days. He lived a perfect life and shed His blood in the ultimate sacrifice for us. He paid the heavy price for mankind's sin that only He could pay, thus paving the way for us to have eternal life with Jesus in heaven. We will reign with Him as His Bride forever. Jesus is also understood to be the second person of the Trinity.

20 REASONS WHY JESUS CAME

Here's a list of reasons as to why Jesus came to live among us:

1) Jesus fulfilled prophecy. The Old Testament make numerous claims as to a Messiah who would come.
2) Jesus came to prove the existence of the One True Eternal Supreme God. Jesus often talked of His Father and who He was. Jesus proved via His miracles and His teachings that his claims about His Father were absolutely true, and that His Father stood alone as the Ultimate Entity in the universe – past, present and future.

177

The Walk Applied

3) Jesus proved the existence of the Trinity. He told us that He must go to the Father so that the Holy Spirit could come and inhabit us.
4) Jesus proved God's infinite love for us by sacrificing himself so that we might have eternal life.
5) Jesus proved that God understands what we go through.
6) Jesus showed us how to deal with temptation. He was tempted just like us and experienced a wide variety of emotions.
7) Jesus paid the price we could never pay for our sin. God was insistent that the price of our sin would have to be death, and that blood would have to be shed. Only the perfect lamb would do.
8) Jesus paved the way to make salvation available to us.
9) Jesus established the basis of the new covenant through his death and resurrection.
10) Jesus instructed us in the operation of the spiritual and how we could interact with it.
11) Jesus showed us how to use spiritual methods in the natural.
12) Jesus taught us how to bear fruit that will last.
13) Jesus achieved the victory that only He could bring about.
14) Jesus let us know that he is indeed coming back for his bride.
15) Jesus conferred authority on us as believers.
16) Jesus proved that the spiritual controls the natural. He manipulated weather. He changed the very nature of substances. He raised people from the dead. He cured people of various infirmities. He did all these things by merely saying words. Jesus demonstrated conclusively that the spiritual controls the natural.
17) Jesus paved the way for the Holy Spirit to come to us. Jesus had to go so that we could have the spirit in order to experience the spiritual in a personal and intimate way.
18) Jesus taught us of the Father's Kingdom and how it operates.
19) Jesus taught us how we are to operate within the Kingdom.
20) Jesus proved that there is a supernatural realm that's far above anything we can even begin to conceive of.

The Walk Applied

KINGDOM STRUCTURE AND METHODS

Christians are absolutely committed to the truth that there is one sovereign supreme God who is eternal. We believe firmly that He has always existed and will always exist. He was not created or somehow "made". He is absolutely sovereign over all things. He is all-powerful; He can do whatever He chooses to do; none can stay His hand. He creates simply by speaking whatever He wants into existence. His limitation is that He cannot and will not do something that is not of His nature. He cannot lie; therefore, whatever He says stands as pure unadulterated truth. Whatever He chooses to do is perfect without qualification. There is nothing that He does not know. He controls everything at His discretion.

We see God as absolutely perfect with no possibility for even the slightest imperfection. The overall panorama of scripture reveals a God who has an ongoing and overriding purpose, plan, and will. God is never arbitrary or capricious. As we proposed at the beginning of this book, God's purpose for us is to prepare and groom a bride for Jesus. We do not know why Jesus needs or wants a bride or the circumstances surrounding the wedding feast of the Lamb (Rev 19), but the Bible tells us that we who are saved will be the bride and will be forever unified in fellowship with Jesus.

God is an infinite God, and it will take an eternity to even begin to appreciate Him. God is immutable; He is eternally unchangeable. God is sovereign over all things. God is perfect love; He is omnipotent, omnipresent, and omniscient.

THE TRINITY

The large majority of Christians firmly believe in the Trinity. Although the Bible never actually uses the word "trinity", the overall context of God's Word tells of a sovereign entity that exists as 3 persons in one that we know as the Trinity. We know the Trinity as consisting of The Father, The Son (Jesus), and the Holy Spirit. These 3 "actors" compromise a sovereign "Godhead" in a way that we cannot begin to comprehend. They are to be considered co-equals. That said, Jesus and the Holy Spirit are presented in the Word in such a way as to imply submission by the Holy Spirit and Jesus to the Father's will. Jesus is depicted in Scripture not only as our Savior as well as our advocate in Heaven. We are told that the Holy Spirit is the Spiritual entity that takes up residence in our Spirit Man when we are saved. He communicates with us and, as the Word tells us, "leads us into all truth".

THE KINGDOM

This natural existence that God created as the foundation for grooming Jesus bride is no accident. His Kingdom is purposed, planned, and executed according to His will. Jesus proclaimed that He came at the behest of His Father to proclaim the coming of His Kingdom. Indeed, the book of Matthew focuses on the establishment of that Kingdom. The Bible has much to say about the characteristics of His Kingdom. God's Kingdom has order and structure. His kingdom is operating precisely the way He wants. To be sure, there are times we may disagree with the way He wants to do things, but part of our submission to God is to accept His perfect ways without question as an expression of our faith. Indeed, it is up to us to study His Word and seek the Holy Spirit to discern His methods and His ways.

THE DEFINTION OF EARTHLY SUCCESS:
THE DAY TO DAY WALK WITH JESUS

Jeremiah 6:16 proclaims the definition of success and the goal of our relationship with Jesus Christ:

The Walk Applied

"This is what the LORD *says: "Stand at the crossroads and look; ask for the ancient paths, ask where the good way is, and walk in it, and you will find rest for your souls."* (Jer 6:16)

"And let us run with perseverance <u>the race marked out for us"</u> (Heb 12:1-2)

"I will instruct you and teach you in the way you should go" (Ps 32:8)

We've seen these passages several times before. These passages tell us that we will have peace as we seek our calling. We must not forget that the object of our existence is to refresh ourselves in our ongoing, intimate relationship with Jesus daily. We are here to bear fruit that will last for the Kingdom. Our primary focus should be on what God has commissioned us to do.

6 KINGDOM KEYS

In Matthew 16, we are told that Jesus would give Peter the "Keys to the Kingdom". What Jesus meant is open to conjecture as Jesus did not specify exactly what those keys were. For our purposes here, we will look at keys as being aspects of what we believe about God and how that belief is expressed. As we delve into the properties of the Kingdom as written in the Word, we will define 6 keys that form the basis of how we operate in God's kingdom here in the natural. Perhaps you can come up with others.

SALVATION: The entry point into the Kingdom. The promise covenant of salvation adopts us in the family, assures our place as the Bride, secures forgiveness of sin, along with a host of other gifts.

LOVE: One of the true hallmarks of those who are saved, this aspect is masterfully summarized in chapter 13 of first Corinthians. Love is a <u>*daily decision*</u> to be what the chapter proscribes. We

181

The Walk Applied

decide to be patient when we love. We make a conscious choice to avoid envy. And so on. To read that awesome missive summarizing love as a series of decisions is to view love in a most powerful way:

"If I speak in the tongues of men or of angels, but do not have love, I am only a resounding gong or a clanging cymbal. If I have the gift of prophecy and can fathom all mysteries and all knowledge, and if I have a faith that can move mountains, but do not have love, I am nothing. If I give all I possess to the poor and give over my body to hardship that I may boast, but do not have love, I gain nothing. Love is patient, love is kind. It does not envy, it does not boast, it is not proud. It does not dishonor others, it is not self-seeking, it is not easily angered, it keeps no record of wrongs. Love does not delight in evil but rejoices with the truth. It always protects, always trusts, always hopes, always perseveres. Love never fails. But where there are prophecies, they will cease; where there are tongues, they will be stilled; where there is knowledge, it will pass away. For we know in part and we prophesy in part, but when completeness comes, what is in part disappears. When I was a child, I talked like a child, I thought like a child, I reasoned like a child. When I became a man, I put the ways of childhood behind me. For now we see only a reflection as in a mirror; then we shall see face to face. Now I know in part; then I shall know fully, even as I am fully known. And now these three remain: faith, hope and love. But the greatest of these is love."

FAITH: The foundational requirement. God requires that we believe in what we can't see, or touch. Yet any faithful Christian knows implicitly that God is always with us and seeks Him based solely on faith. In the love chapter (above), Paul tells us that nothing else counts if you don't have love, but without faith you cannot be saved.

The Walk Applied

HOPE: If you don't have faith, it is hard to conceive that you have hope. What do you hope in if you don't have faith? Hope is the logical extension of Faith. Our hope is in Jesus Christ, our Lord and savior.

INTIMACY WITH GOD: If you are truly saved, then you will desire a relationship with the Father. This is starkly different than trying to see how good you can be to please Him. In the same vein, trying to see how well you can avoid sinning is essentially the same notion. Isaiah tells us that our efforts - our works - to show God how good we are nothing but filthy rags to Him. In all truthfulness, if you do not desire to have a relationship with the creator God of the Universe, then I would question your salvation.

WORSHIP is the sincere, heartfelt expression of adoration of the One True Living Creator God. God requires our submission to His authority out of love. He asks us to love Him; He does not force it. In return, we get the fellowship that fills our deepest needs. Don't make the mistake of thinking that worship is just some abstract concept in God's Kingdom. True worship is far more. True worship should be seen as an emotional experience. Worship is truly at the root of our fellowship with Jesus. Worship can be expressed thru prayer, praise, and expressing thankfulness.

KINGDOM PILLARS

God's Kingdom is structured; nothing is random or left to chance. These kingdom pillars describe the foundations of how we commune and work within His Kingdom. Each one of these topics is very complex; this listing of kingdom pillars is merely a very brief overview of concepts that are most significant in how a Christian operates within the Kingdom. This list is subjective, of course; you can probably come up with some of your own.

The Walk Applied

GRACE, MERCY & FAVOR: God's grace regarding us is overwhelming. Grace means "unmerited favor". Despite our sinful condition, He extends great mercy to us. We deserve nothing from God, yet He gives us all He has, and promises us eternal fellowship with Him forever. God is pure Love. He loves us absolutely - enough to send His Son to suffer and die for us. His heaven is absolutely pure, and the admission of even one infinitesimal speck of sin in Heaven would destroy the purity of Heaven, and it would no longer be purely holy. To allow us into Heaven, we must be declared and judged perfect. God, at the moment of Salvation, declares us fully accepted and fully forgiven. We are fully loved by the Creator of the Universe. God's favor is evident as He meets our needs according to His purpose plan and will.

AUTHORITY & SUBMISSION: God's Authority-Submitter dynamic brings growth. God's Kingdom proscribes, without exception, positive growth through His Authority-Submitter dynamic. We choose to be a Submitter to the perfect Authority, who creates the ongoing conditions for growth.

PEACE: A fulfilling relationship with Jesus Christ will, over time, bring increasing degrees of peace. We will think and act and believe differently. It's through peace that we can experience God's joy no matter what our circumstance. When we have the peace of Jesus, we have patience to wait for what he has for us. God's peace gives us the foundation for self-control as well.

SONSHIP: We are adopted as sons and made citizens of the Kingdom. The import of this cannot be underestimated. As Paul tells us, we are grafted into His Kingdom. Once we are truly saved, our salvation is guaranteed. This means that our future is absolutely assured.

The Walk Applied

PURPOSE: Each one of us has a call on our lives. As we learn and pursue our call, God fills us with purpose. Purpose is what brings true meaning to our lives.

WISDOM: Covers a number of topics that are significant in our Christian walk: instruction, knowledge, discernment and discipleship. Wisdom connotes any number of notions, but perhaps the best is to define wisdom as "to master the art of living". Another way of looking at wisdom would be to say "Wisdom is knowing what to do with knowledge".

GIVING & SERVICE: Be it money, time, expertise, helping or just good old fashioned "grunt work", these all embrace the same thing: a person with a servant's heart that chooses to contribute to the Kingdom simply because they want to serve God in whatever way they can.

STEWARDSHIP: One of the major belief shifts that we must make as a Christian is that we own NOTHING. We are mere custodians of whatever God gives us. God has a plan and a calling for our lives. As we pursue that plan and our call, we can be assured that we will never lack what we need to accomplish what He wants us to do.

SUFFERING: To one degree or another, suffering is part of the program. Jesus told us that we would have "difficulty in this life but take heart for I have overcome the world". Indeed, we will be tested. The world is a sinful place much of the time, and we will not be insulated from it. Some of us will suffer more than others. The question is not "why we suffer?" The proper question is: How do we portray God's honor and glory through our suffering? Jesus suffered greatly for us, and we have numerous stories in the Bible of how people suffered and died for God's Kingdom.

185

The Walk Applied

PSALM 119: THE LAW

To truly understand God's Kingdom here in the Natural, it's vital that we have an appreciation of God's law and how it works. For that, we turn to Psalm 119. Ps. 119 is an acrostic Psalm. It is comprised of 22 "sets" of eight verses each. Each set of eight verses begin with the same first letter of the Hebrew alphabet. Verses 1 thru 8 all begin with aleph, the first letter of the Hebrew alphabet. The second set of 8 verses begin with the second letter (bet) of the Hebrew alphabet and so on. All 22 letters of the Hebrew alphabet are depicted in this Psalm. Because it is an acrostic in the Hebrew language, the Psalm will not work the way God designed it to work in any other language. Scholars have suggested that it was a way for Hebrew children to learn their Hebrew "ABC's". The psalm certainly gives every indication that it was used in the way. However, Ps.119 is much, more than a mere child's recitation.

Psalm 119 is nothing less than a majestic treatise on God's Law and how it operates in the natural realm. Several legal terms are included in Ps. 119 which we will cover here. The same words are repeated numerous times, and the style and the tone of the psalm seems to convey something far deeper than just different words for law. As we examine the text and what each of the words mean, an overall picture begins to emerge: different words are used to point out various aspects of the structure of God's law. It's God's way to instruct us as to how God's law is invoked and implemented.

THE LAW: FORMAL INSTRUCTION AND TEACHING OF THE LAW GIVES DIRECTION

In Psalm 119 the word "Law" is used 25 times. It comes from the Hebrew "torah" which means instruction or direction. In other words, the Law is the basic instruction in how we are to live.

The Walk Applied

PRECEPTS: THE FORMAL BASIS OF GOD'S LAW THAT IS ESTABLISHED BY GOD'S AUTHORITY

The Hebrew "piqqudim" appears 21 times in Psalm 119. Precepts is foundational in that it refers not only to God's authority to lay down the principles of Law, but also incorporates the idea of God's unbreakable covenants. The inferences of both "covenant" and "authority" that are inherent in the Hebrew "piqqudim" contributes to the overall thrust and significance of the term. God wants us to understand that it by His authority that He gives us the law. God has absolute sovereignty and ultimate authority – He is the absolute apex of any and all existence. His precepts give us the foundation of the legal system.

TESTIMONY: THE ORAL COMMUNICATION OF GOD'S LAW THAT IS TO BE ESTABLISHED IN WRITING

The word used by the translators here for testimony ("edut") indicates that the law will be spoken by God Himself, and that it must be written down. It is the next logical step after establishing God's bases of the Law. God alone will speak (testimony/testify) the foundations (the precepts), and the particulars(statutes) must be written down for all to see. The notion of covenant embodied in the Hebrew "edut" conveys and reinforces the absolute seriousness of what God is communicating.

WORD: HIS WORD IS DIVINE REVELATION THAT GOVERNS ALL THINGS.

The Hebrew "imrah" and "dabar" refer to anything that God has spoken, commanded, or promised. What God speaks is true and perfect and uncontestable. We may not always understand what He speaks and establishes and commands, but we are free to inquire of Our Lord and ask for wisdom and discernment (Eph. 1:17)

187

The Walk Applied

STATUTES: THE TESTIMONY OF THE SPECIFICS OF THE LAW OF GOD'S WORD IS WRITTEN OUT FOR ALL TO SEE

The Hebrew word translated statutes is "eduwth". Eduwth communicates the notion that the specifics of the Law will be written down. Because they will be the written testimony of God, these ordinances - the statutes - are to be considered as unchanging and constant as the Supreme Author of this magnificent body of Law. There is no deviation, no wavering. Statutes refer to the specific laws that are to be listed and enumerated for us. The statutes of the law refer to such statements as "Do not murder" or "Do not steal".

DECREES: ESTABLISHES THAT THEY ARE ENGRAVED OR INSCRIBED: i.e., THEY ARE "SET IN STONE"

The Hebrew for the word Decrees is "huqqim" which is derived from the root for "engrave," or "inscribe." "huqqim" communicates that it is His direction that the statutes will be physically written down for all to see. There will be no questioning, because His Statutes will be "engraved in stone".

COMMANDS: CERTIFIES THE LAWS

Command(s) is the translation of the Hebrew "mitswah" or "mitswoth". "Mitswah" communicates the idea that God is "certifying" His law as good and right and true. God is the sole source of all that is good. He is the foundation of anything that can bring justice, order, and peace. He has orally given His Law and it has been written down for all to see. Now, He certifies (gives His stamp of approval) the Law. All is in His order, and it is good and right and true.

188

The Walk Applied

JUDGEMENTS: CASE LAW

The Hebrew "sapat" refers to the adjudication of legal disputes and form the basis for case laws that are a part of most legal systems. The term communicates the notion that there will be disputes and that He will give us wisdom to settle those contested cases.

KINGDOM LAW:
A BLESSED, PRINCIPLED LIFE

We have been examining the basic structure and foundations of God's Kingdom as we operate within it here in the natural realm. God is a God of order - He is never chaotic. He does not do anything out of whim. God's Kingdom operates in certain proscribed ways that He dictates according to His purpose plan and will. The following "laws" help us to understand how the Kingdom works, and how we operate within it.

LAW OF LOVE: James 2:8: *"If you really fulfill the royal law according to the Scripture, 'You shall love your neighbor as yourself,' you do well;"*

LAW OF FAITH: Romans 3:27: *"Where is boasting then? It is excluded. By what law? Of works? No, but by the law of faith."*

THE LAW OF SOVREIGNTY: God controls all things; He is in total and absolute command at all times. To some, this may appear to be counter-intuitive and imply that this would exclude free will on our part. Yet, we are free to make our choices - God does not force anything He does not want to. Even within that, God is in total and complete command at all times.

The Walk Applied

THE LAW OF AUTHORITY: Willing submission to God's authority will bring peace, love, hope, blessing and clarity. Submission to Satanic power will bring chaos, confusion, depression, and hopelessness. What this law describes is that God wants us to worship Him as the sovereign king of our lives. To do so brings us into the center of His authority. Satan tempts us by virtually every means imaginable to bring us out of Godly authority in order to ruin our testimony and bring us to a state of disorder. When we find ourselves drifting away from God's authority, we can always repent, thus "resetting" our submission to Godly authority.

THE LAW OF PRAYER: This law gives us the key to getting a "yes" answer to virtually every prayer. It is not meant to be a "magic formula" by any stretch, and we should never interpret this law that way. What this very profound law should instruct us is that we need to be submissive to God's purpose plan and will in everything - no exceptions. God knows our heart and our intent. We may be reticent to pray for God's will to be done in our lives at times, but true submission in all things of God is always the best way. Praying in the name of Jesus is akin to "notarizing" your submission to Jesus - you acknowledge your true submission to Him by specifying His name.

"This is the confidence we have in approaching God: that if we ask anything according to his will, he hears us. And if we know that he hears us - whatever we ask - we know that we have what we asked of him." (1 John 5:14-15)

Stated another way, we can formulate the law in a syllogism:

If: You say it and You believe it and
You trust that God will do it and
It's God's will and You pray it in the name of Jesus
Then:
It will happen in God's way in God's time.

The Walk Applied

THE LAW OF GOD'S WORD: Faithful pursuit of God's Word with an open heart will change you.

" All Scripture is God-breathed and is useful for teaching, rebuking, correcting and training in righteousness ". (2 Tim 3:16).

When you invest yourself in God's word with an open heart, you will change, and you will be more Christ like. There is simply no substitute for reading the Bible on a consistent basis. Some might say that it is prayer that changes a person, but I would contend that unless you about the business of consistently reading God's word, your approach to prayer will remain stifled. You can only grow as you read the manual with a heart for God. Preaching and teaching are other ways of receiving God's word, to be sure, and it is important that we pursue those avenues. Devotionals, books, articles, etc. are all offshoots of good preaching and teaching, and provide enormously beneficial inputs to our walk with Christ, with the proviso that they are truly Biblically based. Others sharing what God is communicating to them is essential to our walk and provide us with inspiration to reach into the Word. They help us deepen our understanding of the Word. There is no substitute for investing in God's word out of a heart that hungers to know Him. There are those who do not have access to God's word, and there are those who, due to physical limitations, cannot read the Word. Yet, God will always find a way to make His Word available to those who seek it.

THE LAW OF BLESSING: To bless is to bring under Godly authority. To curse is to bring under Satanic control. In Biblical times, the notion of blessing and cursing was considered very serious business. The book of Job is rooted in what it means to bless and curse. In the Old Testament, the Hebrew word "barak" is used to convey both blessing and cursing (polar opposites). The word could mean one or the other depending on the context. Barak means "to kneel" or "to kneel in front of". The word is translated

191

The Walk Applied

"blessing" over 500 times in the Old Testament and translated just under 200 times to mean "a curse". The word "barak" is the word that is used Job 1 & 2, where Satan insists that Job will "curse god and die". Job's wife, you may recall, urges Job to simply curse God and get it over and done. "Barak" connotes: who are you going to kneel before? Who are you going to worship? Who are you going to submit to: God or Satan? To understand the extraordinary significance of the spoken blessing in biblical times, we can refer to Roy Honeycutt's article in Holman's encyclopedia:

"The unique concept of the spoken word... is important for understanding the significance of both cursing and blessing. According to Old Testament thought patterns, the formally spoken word had both an independent existence and the power of its own fulfillment. The word once spoken assumed a history of its own, almost a personality of itself ... The Word of God exists as a reality and has within itself the power of its own fulfillment. Formal words of blessing or cursing also had the same power of self-fulfillment.... Blessing and cursing released suprahuman powers which could bring to pass the content of the curse or the blessing ...The Lord was the source of all blessing..."

As Honeycutt points out, when Isaac mistakenly blessed Jacob rather than Esau, he could not recall the blessing. That blessing now existed in history (Gen. 27:18-41) because it had acquired an identity of its own. In other words, when you blessed someone, you were ostensibly bringing them under God's authority, bringing them peace and prosperity. If you cursed them, you were issuing a command that would bring them under Satan's power and control, arguably bringing them chaos and ruin. To the ancients, these concepts were as real as if you shot them or gave them a million dollars. To them, there was no difference whatsoever. As Honeycutt tells us, you cannot underestimate what these concepts meant – and still mean for us today.

192

The Walk Applied

THE LAW OF THE SEED: Seed reproduces after its own kind. God makes it perfectly clear that all species of life can only reproduce after their own kind. Monkeys produce other monkeys; they do not produce human beings. Dogs give birth to other dogs. Seeds from apple trees produce more apple trees. In recent human history, we have seen how genetic manipulation can produce new and distinct species of plants and animals. However, these can only happen when there is human intervention. Indeed, there has NEVER been an observable change of one species changing into a new, different species.

THE LAW OF GIVING: You will reap what you sow. To sow under Godly authority is to reap blessing; to sow under Satanic authority is to reap cursing. This has impact far beyond merely giving money. Whenever and whatever you give, the blessing becomes a significant spiritual component of your gift – be it acts of service, money, time, or something of value. That's why we must be cheerful givers. To give cheerfully and bless your gift without expecting to be recompensed reflects a Godly attitude that goes far beyond your gift.

THE LAW OF SIN: To sin means to "miss the mark" or more plainly, disagree with God. To sin is to come out of Godly authority. Most believe that sin means to "do the wrong thing." Some will extend the idea by saying our sin is offensive to God. That is all true, but it is also a very limited notion of the full extent of sin and what it all means. When we define sin as doing the wrong thing and offending God, we are putting the concept of sin into a performance context. This tends to propagate the idea of sin as a "works-oriented", performance theology. In other words, we might say "I sinned – I did the wrong thing. I need to ask forgiveness, and hopefully I won't do that anymore. I offended God, and I should not do that". As sincere as this might be, this performance and works mindset minimizes the overall destructive nature of sin and can tend to make a mockery of grace.

The Walk Applied

Sin means to disagree with God, which is an entirely different idea then "I did the wrong thing". Obviously that notion comprises that we "did the wrong thing" and we "offended God". However, when we identify sin as coming out of Godly authority (read: rebellion against God), the true horror of sin and the gravity of transgression becomes much more apparent. As we discussed in the authority submission dynamic, to rebel and come out of Godly authority has significant consequences. James 1 discusses the sin process:

"When tempted, no one should say, "God is tempting me." For God cannot be tempted by evil, nor does he tempt anyone; but each person is tempted when they are dragged away by their own evil desire and enticed. Then, after desire has conceived, it gives birth to sin; and sin, when it is full-grown, gives birth to death."

Sin is not just the act, but the process as well. Note the strong language James uses. Indeed, sin needs to be defined in terms of where we are in the Authority/Submission relationship structure with God to begin to appreciate how devastating it is.

THE LAW OF PROVISION: God will supply your needs to fulfill your call. The Law of Prayer instructs us as to how God meets our legitimate needs. The Law of Provision is similar:

If	You ask for it and trust that God will provide and
	It is God's will that you have it and
	It is required for your mission
Then	God will get you what you need when you need it
	He will likely bring it in abundance
But	You must ask in faith.

It is God's desire that you fulfill your mission and calling. He will do what is necessary to ensure that you have whatever you need.

The Walk Applied

DON'T confuse this with "prosperity theology". Some falsely believe the heresy that God wants all of us to be wealthy. Indeed, God has called some Christians to be wealthy, but that is quite rare. That said, we are all called to a given mission. What the Law of Provision tells us is that whatever we are called to, God will make sure we have what we need to fulfill it. This does not say that our lives will be easy or glamorous. Jesus told us that we will have difficulties in this world. Many of us will be tested severely. However, as we pursue our calling and mission, God will ensure that we will have what we need to accomplish it.

THE LAW OF SUFFERING: We will experience trials and suffering in this life. We will all go through times when we will lack or suffer. During those times we are expected to trust in God. As difficult as it might be we need to recognize that our suffering does have a purpose. Some experiences may be truly horrific, but God assures us that we will never be asked to endure more than we can bear. The way we walk through these times is to lean into our faith in God. There will be times when it may seem like God is not providing or is saying "no" to our prayer. He may be saying "no" in that what we think is necessary is not really needed. Perhaps God has a different way of resolving the problem. Maybe He wants us to wait for reasons known only to Him. Daniel experienced this (see Daniel 10). Or perhaps He is testing us and strengthening our faith. The point is that God is always faithful, no matter what the situation looks like. Rest assured, God hears you, and His response is always the right one.

THE LAW OF SALVATION: You come under Godly authority when you truly believe on Jesus. The Salvation Covenant is a promise covenant that guarantees your status as the Bride of Christ. To be saved means you have truly recognized Jesus as your Lord and Savior and submit willingly to His Authority. You also acknowledge that you are a sinner and that you have been in rebellion against God.

195

The Walk Applied

THE LAW OF JUDGEMENT: Judgement is reserved for God alone, except where authority to judge has been delegated by God. To judge is to improperly exercise spiritual authority. Only God is to judge. We have discussed four lines of spiritual authority, where God has allowed for the delegation of spiritual authority: Family, Church, Government, and Employment. When we judge outside of the lines of spiritual authority, we are guilty of assuming power and control. Romans 2 tells us that when we judge others, self-seeking is the result, and that wrath, anger, trouble, and distress will be the result. When we elect to not forgive those who have offended us, we are choosing to sit in judgement on them. To not forgive is to judge and self-seek, which will bring on "wrath, anger, trouble, and distress". Thus, it is imperative that we forgive, as we are commanded to do.

THE LAW OF REPENTANCE AND FORGIVENESS: Repentance applies to false belief systems (idolatry); thus, we repent of wrong beliefs. We repent before God for believing the wrong things. True repentance means to change direction. The implication is that we start down the road of changing our belief system. It does not mean that the symptomatic, sinful behavior will stop right away. True repentance means we commit to go thru the process of change. We may need to repent many times in order to truly change the belief.

Forgiveness applies to people. To not forgive says that you are judging. Sincere forgiveness is a legal statement that asserts that you have taken yourself out of a position of power and control over another individual. By doing so, you "reset" the authority structure to its appropriate place. You take yourself out of judgement on that individual. Forgiveness is a "one and done" sincere statement removing any expressed or implied emotional "debt".

The Walk Applied

THE LAW OF TEMPTATION: Fight temptation with spiritual tools. It's an interesting exercise to compare how Jesus and Eve dealt with temptation.

EVE VS. JESUS: DEALING WITH TEMPTATION
TEMPTATION: NOT EVEN JESUS WAS EXEMPT

God's Word is clear in that we will be allowed to be tempted. Even Jesus was not exempt.

JESUS vs. SATAN (Matt 4:1-11)

"Then Jesus was led by the Spirit into the desert to be tempted by the devil. After fasting forty days and forty nights, he was hungry. The tempter came to him and said, "If you are the Son of God, tell these stones to become bread." Jesus answered, "It is written: 'Man does not live on bread alone, but on every word that comes from the mouth of God.'" Then the devil took him to the holy city and had him stand on the highest point of the temple. "If you are the Son of God," he said, "throw yourself down. For it is written: '"He will command his angels concerning you, and they will lift you up in their hands, so that you will not strike your foot against a stone."' Jesus answered him, "It is also written: 'Do not put the Lord your God to the test.'" Again, the devil took him to a very high mountain and showed him all the kingdoms of the world and their splendor. "All this I will give you," he said, "if you will bow down and worship me." Jesus said to him, "Away from me, Satan! For it is written: 'Worship the Lord your God, and serve him only.'" Then the devil left him, and angels came and attended him.

WE WILL BE TEMPTED IN 3 GENERAL WAYS

The account given in Matthew 4 is "Temptation 101". The purpose of the passage is to illustrate the 3 general ways that we will be tempted.

197

The Walk Applied

TEMPTATION #1: LOOK INTO THE NATURAL

The first temptation has to do with food. It shows us that Jesus is dealing with temptation in his human state, while "the tempter" is apparently in a spiritual form. Jesus was obviously hungry and weak after His 40 day fast. Note how the tempter prompts Jesus to mentally engage with his misleading question: "If you are the Son of God …" Jesus is propositioned to "prove" he is the Son of God by turning the stones into bread - something Jesus could easily do. Jesus lived the credo that the Father would supply Jesus' every need. This temptation illustrates is that we will often want to fulfill our natural desires/needs on our own, rather than depending on God.

TEMPTATION #2: MANIPULATE GOD

Here, Jesus allows himself to be taken to the top of the temple. This time, it's "the devil" - presumably the same as "the tempter" - who transports Jesus to this very high place that overlooks the "Holy City". The devil quotes Psalm 91 to entice Jesus to "prove" He is the Son of God by jumping ("IF" you are the Son of God…). Given that it is not Jesus appointed time or way to die, Jesus could not and did not comply. Had Jesus accommodated the proposition, it would have falsified prophecy in the Old Testament. The attempt here was to manipulate God by forcing His hand - in essence, to control God.

TEMPTATION #3: COME UNDER SATAN'S POWER

Finally, Jesus allows "the devil" to take him to a "very high place". Jesus tells us it is Satan himself, and Satan is apparently quite exasperated at this point! Satan offers Jesus our world, if only Jesus will bow down before Satan. Our world already belongs to Jesus. He is a member of the Trinity, after all. This temptation further illustrates the fundamental strategy of how we will be tempted to move away from the spiritual into the natural where Satan is in authority!

The Walk Applied

EVE vs. SATAN

"Now the serpent was more crafty than any of the wild animals the LORD God had made. He said to the woman, "Did God really say, 'You must not eat from any tree in the garden'?" The woman said to the serpent, "We may eat fruit from the trees in the garden, but God did say, 'You must not eat fruit from the tree that is in the middle of the garden, and you must not touch it, or you will die.'" "You will not surely die," the serpent said to the woman. "For God knows that when you eat of it your eyes will be opened, and you will be like God, knowing good and evil." When the woman saw that the fruit of the tree was good for food and pleasing to the eye, and also desirable for gaining wisdom, she took some and ate it. She also gave some to her husband, who was with her, and he ate it. Then the eyes of both of them were opened, and they realized they were naked; so they sewed fig leaves together and made coverings for themselves. (Gen 3:1-7)

HOW EVE HANDLED TEMPTAION

The first thing you might notice about the passage above is that Eve let herself get involved in a conversation with "the serpent". Eve focused on the object of the temptation, and we have paid the price ever since. Her thought processes as presented indicate that she rationalized reasons why she should comply with the serpent's request. She clearly knew it was forbidden to eat of the fruit; she had said so. The consequences of her rationalization were staggering and mindboggling. We also note that Adam was either not paying attention or, more likely, chose not to intervene. Some commentators contend that Adam was indeed very likely close by. The phrase "Then the eyes of both of them were opened..." is compelling in that is tells us that the Fall was not complete until Eve's husband - her spiritual leader - also fell.

199

The Walk Applied

THE STRATEGY: GET US TO FOCUS
ON THE OBJECT OF THE TEMPTATION

Note how both temptation scenarios begin: Both Jesus and Eve were prompted to draw their attention to the object of the temptation. Note how the questions that were posed played on legitimate natural desires. The temptations were designed to focus into the natural, where Satan is "the prince of this world". Consider the following passages that show God has elected to allow Satan rule of the earth for a time:

" ... the prince of this world will be driven out." (John 12:31)
" ... the prince of this world is coming." (John 14:30)
"... the prince of this world now stands condemned." (John 16:11)

THE RESPONSE: FIGHT TEMPTATION WITH
SUPERNATURAL WEAPONS, NOT NATURAL

Jesus is the notable example of how to approach the supernatural. Note how Jesus handled the situation in His weakened state:

-Jesus didn't acknowledge what was asked of Him.
-Jesus didn't look at the object of the temptation.
-Jesus used the word of God.
-Jesus didn't "debate" the issue.
-Jesus didn't acknowledge Satan's name, except to rebuke him.
-Jesus used his God-given authority to rebuke Satan.

In Ephesians, Paul wants to emphasize that the fight is in the spiritual and not the natural:

"For our struggle is not against flesh and blood, but against the rulers, against the authorities, against the powers of this dark world and against the spiritual forces of evil in the heavenly realms."
(Eph 6:12-16)

The Walk Applied

In Corinthians, Paul again highlights that the fight is in the spiritual realm:

"For though we live in the world, we do not wage war as the world does. The weapons we fight with are not the weapons of the world. On the contrary, they have divine power to demolish strongholds. We demolish arguments and every pretension that sets itself up against the knowledge of God, and we take captive every thought to make it obedient to Christ." (2 Cor 10:3-5)

The objective is to get us to lose our focus by looking into the natural, where Satan is in power. In doing so, we come out of peace into anxiety and chaos. We will be tempted to look at the object of the temptation, and it will likely be at our weakest point. To come into agreement with Satan is to be out of agreement with God and come under Satan's power and control! Satan's aim is to modify what you believe at any cost. We emphasize that He wants to get you to agree with him - that brings you under his power and control!

"IT IS WRITTEN"

We note that Jesus said "it is written" on all 3 temptations. The contention is that when you use the word in response to tempting thoughts, you must first identify it as God's word. This is what ushers in God's anointing on your speech. It's virtually the same thing as pulling the sword out of the scabbard (Eph 6:17) where the Word is described as "the sword of the Spirit".

The temptation here is to think that using the Word will bring about automatic relief to anxiety that might be accompanying the temptation. The account in Matthew never indicates that Jesus used the word to avoid any anxiety he may have been experiencing. Certainly, we should not expect that result. The lesson to be garnered from this passage is that the use of God's word is

The Walk Applied

something that we need to master over time. Remember, there are no pat solutions. God does not want us dependent on a technique! God wants us dependent on Him and Him alone!

GOD'S BOOKS:

God keeps a very distinctive library. The Bible tells us of different books that God keeps. As citizens of His Kingdom, it's valuable to reflect on what the Word tells us about these books, and what we might be able to deduce about the books.

1: THE BOOK OF LIFE

Allaboutgod.com has this to say about the Book of Life:

"The Book of Life (also called The Lamb's Book of Life) is a record containing the names of those who have overcome sin through accepting Jesus as Christ (having a spiritual rebirth). In other words, the Book of Life is the names of the redeemed—those who will live with God forever in heaven."

The import of the Book of Life is established in Revelation:

"If anyone's name was not found written in the book of life, he was thrown into the lake of fire." (Rev 20:15)

This is an eternal sentence. The lake of fire is the destination created for Satan and those who reject God. This is foretold in the vision that is written in Revelation 13:8:

"All inhabitants of the earth will worship the beast—all whose names have not been written in the book of life belonging to the Lamb that was slain from the creation of the world."

The Walk Applied

The verse above partners with the vision in <u>Revelation 17:8</u> given to John:

"The beast, which you saw, once was, now is not, and will come up out of the Abyss and go to his destruction. The inhabitants of the earth whose names have not been written in the book of life from creation of the world will be astonished when they see the beast, because he once was, now is not, and yet will come."

2: THE BOOK OF REMEMBRANCE

Amazingdiscoveries.org says this:

"This Book of Remembrance holds every act of faithful service done for the Lord. Every encouraging word, every unselfish deed, every sacrifice made, the Lord has carefully placed there as a witness to the universe that you are indeed His child." (Mal 3:16)

It would seem to make sense that if you are in the Book of Life, you will have deeds and utterances recorded in the great Book of Remembrance.

Ecclesiastes 12:14 reports that *"For God shall bring every work into judgment, with every secret thing, whether it be good, or whether it be evil".*

3: THE BOOK OF TRUTH

"...but first I will tell you what is written in the Book of Truth. (Dan 10:21)

Daniel contains the only reference to this particular book. What most commentators seem to believe is that God wants to communicate to us that He has written things down in advance. We are not given the scope or content of what God has recorded, but it seems plausible that we can assume God has written down much more of what is to happen in the future.

Daniel 10 is so very interesting in that it gives us insight into the Spiritual realm that we really do not find anywhere else in Scripture. It talks of princes of various geographic entities and alludes to a spiritual war that is apparently raging as we speak. It describes how sometimes our prayers are answered, but that there are greater priorities hindering the answers coming to us in a more timely fashion.

4: THE BOOK OF WORKS

Rev 20:12-13 tells us of this book. In this book are recorded all the works of non-believers. Their works will be used as judgement against them to show how they fell short.

5: THE BOOK OF WORDS

Matt 12:33-37 tells us that we will be judged by our words. It seems logical to infer that this book is similar to the Book of Works. Perhaps our own words are included in the Book of Works. It also speaks of "every idle word" being brought into account. While the context of the passage would seem to indicate that Jesus was referring to the Pharisees and by implication the unsaved, we cannot be completely certain of that. In any case, a word to the wise: be careful what you say!

The thrust of the book appears to serve 2 purposes. The first purpose is in the Book of Truth. God wants us to know that He is absolutely sovereign over time, even to the point of having written the future in advance of when it happens. Only God could do such a thing.

The second purpose seems to be judicial. Whether or not we are saved is recorded. Apparently, our words, works, and our acts of

The Walk Applied

service have been recorded for all to see. If we are not saved, our words and works will be used as the benchmark. The unsaved may even get the opportunity to defend themselves. If we are saved, our names will appear in the Book of Life, and our sins will very likely be unreadable - obliterated by the deep rich red blood of Jesus.

THE 5 CROWNS

The Bible specifies 5 different "crowns" that will apparently be "awarded". The idea that we might be "awarded trophies" is hard to ignore here, although we should certainly not jump to conclusions. Gotquestions.org concludes that "we should see the crowns as perhaps more symbolic than physical". That position would seem to make sense, indeed. These crowns will be awarded in the spiritual realm and we are not told exactly what they are. We can only conjecture as to what they really are and how they are awarded. The narrative surrounding each one is very broad which makes it difficult to narrow it down. My particular take is that we will all enjoy most of these. There appears to be special treatment when it comes to Pastors in particular as well as those who experience extraordinary suffering and persecution.

THE INCORRUPTIBLE CROWN

"Do you not know that in a race all the runners run, but only one gets the prize? Run in such a way as to get the prize. Everyone who competes in the games goes into strict training. They do it to get a crown that will not last, but we do it to get a crown that will last forever." (1 Cor 9:24-25)

This passage implies endurance and discipline, two hallmarks of the Christian life. Mathew 24:13: *"...but the one who stands firm to the end will be saved"*. This crown would seem to commemorate a spiritual hallmark of one who lived out their salvation, no matter what they went through.

205

The Walk Applied

THE CROWN OF REJOICING

"For what is our hope, our joy, or the crown in which we will glory in the presence of our Lord Jesus when he comes? Is it not you?" (1 Thess 2:19)

Gotquestions.org tells us that "The crown of rejoicing will be our reward where: *"God will wipe away every tear . . . there shall be no more death, nor sorrow, nor crying. There shall be no more pain, for the former things have passed away"* (Revelation 21:4)."

This crown would seem to cover all who are saved, as the text in both passages seem inclusive of all who are saved. Our reward, in this case, would be the resolution of all of our suffering, hurts, and disappointments.

THE CROWN OF LIFE

"Do not be afraid of what you are about to suffer. I tell you, the devil will put some of you in prison to test you, and you will suffer persecution for ten days. Be faithful, even to the point of death, and I will give you life as your victor's crown." (Rev 2:10)

This particular crown seems to include the faithful who suffer or deal with severe persecution - up to and including death. The phrase "I will give you life as your victor's crown" is difficult to understand. It does appear that the passage implies an exclusive club of those who have (or will) experienced great suffering and trials.

The Walk Applied

THE CROWN OF RIGHTEOUSNESS

"For I am already being poured out like a drink offering, and the time for my departure is near. I have fought the good fight, I have finished the race, I have kept the faith. Now there is in store for me the crown of righteousness, which the Lord, the righteous Judge, will award to me on that day—and not only to me, but also to all who have longed for his appearing". (2 Tim 4:6-8)

Paul makes it abundantly clear that we are all eligible for this crown. The crown seems to correspond with salvation ("all who have longed for His appearing"). What is intriguing about this passage is that Paul seems to be hinting at an "award" for his faithfulness.

THE CROWN OF GLORY

"To the elders among you, I appeal as a fellow elder and a witness of Christ's sufferings who also will share in the glory to be revealed: Be shepherds of God's flock that is under your care, watching over them—not because you must, but because you are willing, as God wants you to be; not pursuing dishonest gain, but eager to serve; not lording it over those entrusted to you, but being examples to the flock. And when the Chief Shepherd appears, you will receive the crown of glory that will never fade away. In the same way, you who are younger, submit yourselves to your elders. All of you, clothe yourselves with humility toward one another, because, "God opposes the proud but shows favor to the humble." Humble yourselves, therefore, under God's mighty hand, that he may lift you up in due time. Cast all your anxiety on him because he cares for you. (1 Peter 5:4)

As we read this passage, the Crown of Glory appears to be reserved for the elders - and perhaps more specifically: Pastors. We deduce this by how the word shepherd is used in this passage.

The Walk Applied

Why God has instituted these crowns is not disclosed to us. Nor do we know how they will be awarded. Paul hints at an award ceremony of some sort, but that seems to be somewhat of a stretch. Somehow, I just cannot bring myself to picture an "awards ceremony" in heaven. When the momentous day comes, we'll all find out!

THE AGES

There are numerous references in both Testaments to Biblical "ages". Several are listed below for reference. Interpretations vary widely as to what is meant by "ages". Translating the Hebrew and the Greek seem to indicate that these terms refer or imply a long period of time. A close read of these passages seems to strongly imply ages that occurred before our natural existence and will take place after what we know as our physical existence. Since we trust in a forever God who wants us to live with Him forever, it's not out of line to claim that there were past "ages" prior to the creation that we live in. In the same vein, we can predict that there will be future "ages" to come. Paul Billheimer says as much in His book "Destined for the Throne":

"It is God's way of giving the church on-the-job-training... this world is a laboratory in which those destined for the throne are learning...as an apprenticeship for an eternity of reigning with Christ...what foes will be left to overcome in the eternal ages, we do not know..." "Therefore, from all eternity, all that precedes the marriage supper of the lamb is preliminary and preparatory. Only thereafter will God's program for the eternal ages begin to unfold... up and until then, the entire universe under the Son's regulation and control is being manipulated by God for one purpose - to prepare and train the bride"

208

The Walk Applied

Billheimer's stunning assertion is no less than that we are being trained for something in the future - once we get to heaven. Obviously, this is quite subjective; no one really knows for sure. But the thought that there is more than what we know of here is quite compelling, to be sure. The logical implication is that Heaven may be a lot more than we have even dared to imagine. Study the following passages and decide for yourself. Of particular note is Matthew 13:38-39, which tends to support Billheimer's contention:

"The field is the world, and the good seed stands for the people of the kingdom. The weeds are the people of the evil one, and the enemy who sows them is the devil. <u>The harvest is the end of the age</u>, and the harvesters are angels."

PAST AGES

"Now to him who is able to establish you by my gospel and the proclamation of Jesus Christ, according to the revelation of the mystery hidden for long ages past, (Rom 16:25)

"and to make plain to everyone the administration of this mystery, which for ages past was kept hidden in God, who created all things." (Eph 3:9)

"the mystery that has been kept hidden for ages and generations, but is now disclosed to the saints." (Col 1:26)

"to the only God our Savior be glory, majesty, power and authority, through Jesus Christ our Lord, before all ages, now and forevermore! Amen." (Jude 1:25)

209

The Walk Applied

"This is how it will be at the end of the age. The angels will come and separate the wicked from the righteous." (Mat 13:49)

"As Jesus was sitting on the Mount of Olives, the disciples came to him privately. "Tell us," they said, "when will this happen, and what will be the sign of your coming and of the end of the age?" (Mat 24:3)

"We do, however, speak a message of wisdom among the mature, but not the wisdom of this age or of the rulers of this age, who are coming to nothing." (1 Cor 2:6)

"None of the rulers of this age understood it, for if they had, they would not have crucified the Lord of glory." (1 Cor 2:8)

"It teaches us to say "No" to ungodliness and worldly passions, and to live self-controlled, upright and godly lives in this present age," (Titus 2:12)

The Walk Applied

"a day of darkness and gloom, a day of clouds and blackness. Like dawn spreading across the mountains a large and mighty army comes, such as never was of old nor ever will be in ages to come." (Joel 2:2)

"Anyone who speaks a word against the Son of Man will be forgiven, but anyone who speaks against the Holy Spirit will not be forgiven, either in this age or in the age to come." (Mat 12:32)

"... will fail to receive a hundred times as much in this present age... and in the age to come, eternal life." (Mark 10:30)

"...will fail to receive many times as much in this age and, in the age to come, eternal life. " (Luke 18:30)

"far above all rule and authority, power and dominion, and every title that can be given, not only in the present age but also in the one to come." (Eph 1:21)

"in order that in the coming ages he might show the incomparable riches of his grace, expressed in his kindness to us in Christ Jesus." (Eph 2:7)

The Walk Applied

CHAPTER 8
COMMUNING
WITH CHRIST:
LIVING INTENTIONALLY

The Walk Applied

The Walk Applied

CHAPTER 8
COMMUNING WITH CHRIST:
LIVING INTENTIONALLY

One of the great themes of the Bible is that Jesus desires a relationship with us. That the Sovereign Creator God of the Universe would want and covet a relationship with us is indeed a stunning revelation. Since God deeply desires a relationship with us, He lets us know how He wants us to commune with Him. In this chapter we will develop how He wants us to relate to Him.

Brian McLaren, in his book "Finding Our Way Again", expresses the sentiment that that it's nowhere near enough to see the walk with Jesus as a mere system of belief. He points out that a relationship with Jesus means to live life in a completely different way. It's far more than putting on a pretty face and acting righteous and doing less bad things and going to church and praying and what all else. A rewarding relationship with Jesus means to experience a totally new way to live on a daily basis – and that's what the Walk Applied is all about. It means that we approach life as a spiritual creature and no longer as a natural creature, as we have previously discussed.

McLaren calls some of the ways we approach Christ "practices". Many have referred to them as "disciplines". In the Walk Applied, we much prefer the term "commune". We get to "commune" with Jesus because WE WANT TO! The isn't about being obligated or experiencing drudgery. A rich relationship is all about the extraordinary privilege of being able to approach the Supreme Being of all eternity in the ways He wants us to. Abba Father (literally, "Daddy") wants us to encounter Him with excitement and joy. The sovereign Lord of all creation wants us to encounter Him expecting to come away from our encounters with Him refreshed and more like Jesus.

The Walk Applied

A rewarding relationship with Jesus is firmly rooted in the idea that we must be intentional in our pursuit of Him. The Bible gives us numerous ways to approach Him. If you believe that the ways He has proscribed for us to relate to Him are onerous, then your relationship with Jesus will reflect that - dull, boring, and meaningless. In Revelations, God says be "hot or cold", anything but lukewarm. Otherwise, He says He will simply "spit us out"!

RELATING TO JESUS

It's important to note that the vast majority of what follows should be thought of as ways to simply get to know Our Lord and Savior, as well as to express our love, admiration, worship as well as our deep respect. That's why we call it communing. In the New Testament, we frequently see the term Abba Father. (Again, loosely translated, it means "Daddy"). You read that right. It gives us an idea of how we are to approach Him, and how deeply He wants to relate to us. God is a highly relational being. He is our heavenly Father, and He wants us to know Him and walk with Him daily. Larry Crabbe, in his book. "Soul Talk", maintains that the deepest desire of our hearts is to "know God and be known by Him." Never forget that every single one of us needs Jesus desperately and absolutely.

Jesus can and should be approached on a number of levels. We can approach Him formally by kneeling. Some prefer to lay down. Others simply sit and enjoy His presence. However you feel led to approach Him, it should always be done with profound respect and with an attitude of worship.

The Walk Applied

PRAYER: THE SIMPLE ACT OF TALKING WITH GOD.

Prayer is an ongoing, continuous conversation with God. Indeed, we should think of prayer as a lifestyle that you choose to live all day, every day. Prayer is the way we make known to God our desires, and prayer signifies our dependence on Him. Prayer is a way that God communes with us, as well. Prayer means that we understand that <u>are to commune with Jesus.</u> To be sure, we can pray anywhere, anytime. However, prayer really should to be *scheduled*; otherwise it typically only happens sporadically. Scheduling prayer means you have made it a priority in your life. It means you are being intentional!

MAKING TIME FOR PRAYER: THE 1% SOLUTION

Some Christians find that once they have committed to prayer in one way or another, there never seems to be enough time in the day. The complaint "I just can't find the time!" is not uncommon. Yet, this is easily overcome - especially if you're serious about it. One way to look at it is that we have 96 15-minute periods each and every day - just under 100. So, if you can't find 1% of your day - 15 minutes - to commune with the Creator of the Universe, the contention from here is that you're not really serious about your relationship with Jesus, or you simply don't see the value of it.

There's any number of ways to carve out time for what's important. One of my early mentors advised me to get up earlier, which I did. Lunch time on the job can work. When I was working, I used to dedicate my drive time to prayer or listening to worship music; I still do that to this day. Turning off the TV at night is another viable solution. Trust me, it was a struggle in our household…

Even though I am retired, I still find it's all too easy to blow off my time with God – although in 2016, I celebrated 25 years of being saved. I finally decided to start having "a cup of coffee" with Jesus.

217

The Walk Applied

After my wife leaves for work, I finally C-O-M-I-T-T-E-D to having that next cup of coffee with Jesus. Here are some scriptures that will help you formulate your prayer life.

"But when you pray, go into your room, close the door and pray to your Father, who is unseen. Then your Father, who sees what is done in secret, will reward you. And when you pray, do not keep on babbling like pagans, for they think they will be heard because of their many words. Do not be like them, for your Father knows what you need before you ask him. "This, then, is how you should pray: "'Our Father in heaven, hallowed be your name, your kingdom come, your will be done on earth as it is in heaven. Give us today our daily bread. Forgive us our debts, as we also have forgiven our debtors. And lead us not into temptation but deliver us from the evil one.' (Mat 6:6-15)

"Look to the LORD and his strength; seek his face always." (1 Chr 16:11)

"Watch and pray so that you will not fall into temptation. The spirit is willing, but the body is weak." (Mat 26:41)

"Then Jesus told his disciples a parable to show them that they should always pray and not give up." (Luke 18:1)

"One day Jesus was praying in a certain place. When he finished, one of his disciples said to him, "Lord, teach us to pray, just as John taught his disciples." He said to them, "When you pray, say: "'Father, hallowed be your name, your kingdom come. Give us each day our daily bread. Forgive us our sins, for we also forgive everyone who sins against us. And lead us not into temptation." Then he said to them, "Suppose one of you has a friend, and he goes to him at midnight and says, 'Friend, lend me three loaves of bread, because a friend of mine on a journey has come to me, and I have nothing to set before him.' "Then the one inside answers, 'Don't

218

The Walk Applied

bother me. The door is already locked, and my children are with me in bed. I can't get up and give you anything.' I tell you, though he will not get up and give him the bread because he is his friend, yet because of the man's boldness he will get up and give him as much as he needs. "So I say to you: Ask and it will be given to you; seek and you will find; knock and the door will be opened to you. For everyone who asks receives; he who seeks finds; and to him who knocks, the door will be opened. "Which of you fathers, if your son asks for a fish, will give him a snake instead? Or if he asks for an egg, will give him a scorpion? If you then, though you are evil, know how to give good gifts to your children, how much more will your Father in heaven give the Holy Spirit to those who ask Him!"
(Luke 11:1-13)

SCHEDULING TIME

We continue with the important notion of scheduling and being intentional. We cannot emphasize enough that the import of being intentional should mean that we schedule time for Him. This practice should never take on a tone of obligation. Rather, scheduling reflects what is important to us. The vast majority of us are careful to schedule any number of activities in our lives because they are important. When we stop and think about it, there lots of things that we schedule without even thinking about it. I make sure I pay our bills on the 5th of the month. We set the alarm clock to make sure we get up in time to go to work. We schedule birthdays and anniversaries and weddings. Church attendance is scheduled on Sunday. We recognize that these things are important, so we set aside specific dates and times because they are meaningful.

So, scheduling time with Jesus should not be considered odd. It's just a way to make sure that we carve out time for Him. Many might think that prayer time should be somehow spontaneous, but those who schedule time will tell you that it becomes a time they sincerely look forward to. Most like to set aside the first thing in the morning.

The Walk Applied

For some it may be lunch time (excellent time to fast, by the way!). Others may pray before retiring. The Bible does teach we should rise early. Setting aside time for a personal audience with the King of Kings on a consistent ongoing basis is one of the most important things you can do.

THE LAW OF PRAYER

Let's repeat the Law of Prayer here for review:

"This is the confidence we have in approaching God: that if we ask anything according to his will, he hears us. And if we know that he hears us—whatever we ask—we know that we have what we asked of him." (1 John 5:14-15)

Let's review the law in outline format:

> If: You say it and
>   You believe it and
>   You trust that God will do it and
>   It's God's will and
>   You pray it in the name of Jesus
> Then:
>   It will happen in God's way in God's time

This law gives us the key to getting a "yes" answer to virtually every prayer. It is not meant to be a "magic formula" by any stretch, and we should never interpret this law in that way. What this very profound law should instruct us is that we need to be submissive to God's purpose plan and will in everything - no exceptions. God knows our heart and our intent. We may be reticent to pray for God's will to be done in our lives at times, but true submission in all things of God is always the best way. Praying in the name of Jesus is akin to "notarizing" your submission to Jesus - you acknowledge your true submission to Him by specifying His name

The Walk Applied

THANK HIM NOW FOR PRAYERS
ANSWERED IN THE FUTURE

An important aspect of praying God's will is He will always honor sincere prayer that His will be done in your life. This is a singularly profound notion that bears far more than just a passing thought. Following is a line of thought that we need carefully consider. If you follow the law of prayer, then you know you will receive a yes answer. Remember that God is omnipresent: past, present and future. Since God is present in the future, then He has *already answered your prayer – you just haven't reached the time yet!* You read that sentence correctly: Your prayer has already been answered in the future! Therefore, you can thank Him now for the answer to your prayer.

SOME SUGGESTED PRAYERS

"Father, in the name of Jesus, I thank you that …"

"…are making me into the Godly person you want me to be."
"…I/we are out of debt."
"…you are making our marriage into the Godly marriage
        you want it to be."
"…you are bringing me the person you want me to marry."
"…you are examining me and showing me any wicked way in me."
"…that you are revealing the truth to me about my situation…"

These are all scriptural prayers whereby you are praying God's will for your life. You are praying that you are giving it over to God and letting Him take the helm. You are honoring God with assertive prayers like this by trusting in Him to do what needs to be done - without reservation.

The Walk Applied

NOT "NAME IT CLAIM IT"
OR "PROSPERITY THEOLOGY"

This prayer logistic that we have been discussing entails that we proceed in faith. This mode of prayer is NOT to be interpreted as "name it and claim it". This is NOT the heresy of "prosperity theology" whereby some believe that God wants us all to be wealthy or at least very well off - a blatantly heretical theology.

What we are advocating here is that God will answer affirmatively any prayer that ask for His purpose plan and will to be done. Becoming the Godly man or woman He wants is certainly his will. We believe that He does not want us handicapped by debt, but that does not mean a huge bag of money will appear on our doorstep tomorrow morning. I am aware of a situation whereby an individual went before God and thanked God for providing a substantial amount of money to help his church out. He hit the state lottery for a substantial amount of money. He played the lottery for several months, and then won. It was seen by many to be a move by God. Gambling is not prohibited by His word, and the money spent each week was minimal, and the individual involved could well afford the $5 per week he spent. Now God may operate like that again - and He may not. I suspect provision like that is quite rare.

I am aware of several similar testimonies. I know of several who have thanked God for resolving their debt issues and they are now out of debt. Now, some have walked in faith, and they have given according to what they believe God wants them to give. Two of them felt it was important to tithe regularly; others did not tithe. Some got out of debt in short order; others took several years. The way it happened was different for all involved.

The Walk Applied

PRAY BELIEVING:
PRAY THE ANSWER, NOT THE REQUEST

We just discussed thanking Him now for prayers He will answer in the future. Yet another take on this idea is as follows: Pray believing: pray the answer, not the request. If you say it/ask it + believe it + trust fully that God will do it + it's in God's will, then it happens in God's way in God's time. If it's His will as promised in His word, you can pray it, and believe and expect it to happen, and it will happen - in His way and in His time! If it's not specifically in the Word, then pray believing and expecting for revelation and wisdom regarding the situation, and it will be given you. To be sure, we need to be praying God's will in any case.

This profound notion bears repeating: God is ahead of us in the future. He has already answered your prayer in the future – *you simply have not yet reached the time!* So, when you pray God's will, you can simply thank Him for granting your request! Daniel 10:12-14 gives an example:

"Then he continued, "Do not be afraid, Daniel. Since the first day that you set your mind to gain understanding and to humble yourself before your God, your words were heard, and I have come in response to them. But the prince of the Persian kingdom resisted me twenty-one days. Then Michael, one of the chief princes, came to help me, because I was detained there with the king of Persia. Now I have come to explain to you what will happen to your people in the future, for the vision concerns a time yet to come."

This remarkable passage gives us a truly stunning insight into the Spiritual realm and how it works. In Daniel's case, the emphasis is on how an intense level of activity in the spiritual realm has delayed the answer to Daniel's request. We note how an angel has been dispatched to answer Daniel's request. The lesson here is well-

223

The Walk Applied

taken: God's will *WILL* happen. If you pray God's will, it will happen in your life. Pray God's will into your life, and it will happen in His way in His time. Here are more passages about our assurances when it comes to prayer:

"Again, I tell you that if two of you on earth agree about anything you ask for, it will be done for you by my Father in heaven." (Mat 18:19)

"Jesus replied, "I tell you the truth, if you have faith and do not doubt, not only can you do what was done to the fig tree, but also you can say to this mountain, 'Go, throw yourself into the sea,' and it will be done. If you believe, you will receive whatever you ask for in prayer." (Mat 21:21-22)

"If any of you lacks wisdom, he should ask God, who gives generously to all without finding fault, and it will be given to him. But when he asks, he must believe and not doubt." (James 1:5-6)

"Ask and it will be given to you; seek and you will find; knock and the door will be opened to you. For everyone who asks receives; he who seeks finds; and to him who knocks, the door will be opened. "Which of you, if his son asks for bread, will give him a stone? Or if he asks for a fish, will give him a snake? If you, then, though you are evil, know how to give good gifts to your children, how much more will your Father in heaven give good gifts to those who ask him!" (Mat 7:7-11)

PRAYING SCRIPTURE

There is enormous value in praying God's word on a continuous basis. As we discussed earlier, Honeycutt's article in the Holman Bible encyclopedia highlighted how the ancients understood speaking the word to be a living, breathing, spiritual entity that took

The Walk Applied

on a life of its own once it left your lips. Praying scripture is a way of returning God's Word to Him.

"[God's] word that goes out from my mouth: It will not return to Me empty, but will accomplish what I desire and achieve the purpose for which I sent it." (Isa 55:1)

"For the word of God is living and active. Sharper than any double-edged sword, it penetrates even to dividing soul and spirit, joints and marrow; it judges the thoughts and attitudes of the heart." (Heb 4:12)

"Is not my word like fire," declares the LORD, *"and like a hammer that breaks a rock in pieces?"* (Jer 23:29)

"I am not ashamed of the gospel, because it is the power of God for the salvation of everyone who believes: first for the Jew, then for the Gentile." (Rom 1:16)

"The Spirit gives life; the flesh counts for nothing. The words I have spoken to you are spirit and they are life." (John 6:63)

We repeat it here for emphasis: To understand the extraordinary significance of the spoken blessing in biblical times, we repeat Roy Honeycutt's article in Holman's encyclopedia:

"The unique concept of the spoken word... is important for understanding the significance of both cursing and blessing. According to Old Testament thought patterns, the formally spoken word had both an independent existence and the power of its own fulfillment. The word once spoken assumed a history of its own, almost a personality of itself ... The Word of God exists as a reality and has within itself the power of its own fulfillment. Formal words of blessing or cursing also had the same power of self-fulfillment.... Blessing and cursing released suprahuman powers which could

The Walk Applied

bring to pass the content of the curse or the blessing ...The Lord was the source of all blessing..."

As Honeycutt points out, when Isaac mistakenly blessed Jacob rather than Esau, he could not recall the blessing, for it existed in history (Gen. 27:18-41); it had acquired an identity of its own.

PRAYER:
PERSONALIZING SCRIPTURE
IN THE PRESENT TENSE

There are those who like to pray scripture by personalizing it and praying it in the present tense. This is an excellent prayer method. It takes a bit of practice to get the idea, but it is well worth mastering the technique. Here's how you might pray Psalm 91:

I am dwelling in the shelter of the Most High
I am resting in the shadow of the Almighty.
The LORD is my refuge and my fortress,
  He is my God, in whom I trust.
He is saving me from the fowler's snare
  and from the deadly pestilence.
He is covering me with His feathers,
  and under his wings I find my refuge;
His faithfulness is my shield and rampart.
I don't fear the terror of night,
  nor the arrow that flies by day,
  nor the pestilence that stalks in the darkness,
  nor the plague that destroys at midday.
A thousand might be falling at my side,
  ten thousand at my right hand,
But it will not come near me.
I will only observe with my eyes
  and I will see the punishment of the wicked.

The Walk Applied

I say this: "The LORD is my refuge,"
and the Most High is my dwelling,
Therefore, no harm will overtake me,
and no disaster will come near my tent.
The Lord is commanding His angels concerning me
to guard me in all my ways;
They are lifting me up in their hands,
so that I won't strike my foot against a stone.
I am treading on the lion and the cobra;
and I am trampling the great lion and the serpent.
I know The Lord is rescuing me because I love Him
The Lord is protecting me, because I acknowledge His name.
I am calling on the Lord, and He is answering me;
The Lord is with me in trouble,
He is delivering me and honoring me.
The Lord is satisfying me with long life and
The Lord is showing me my salvation.

THE PRAYER JOURNAL

Many people like to keep a prayer journal. Think of it as a personal prayer diary. Your journal can be whatever you want it to be as you express your thoughts, concerns, emotions, etc. You can record prayer requests, sermon notes; what you believe God is communicating to you - whatever you want!

PRAY TOGETHER WITH YOUR SPOUSE

"Husbands, in the same way be considerate as you live with your wives, and treat them with respect as the weaker partner and as heirs with you of the gracious gift of life, so that nothing will hinder your prayers." (1 Pet 3:7)

"Again, I tell you that if two of you on earth agree about anything you ask for, it will be done for you by my Father in heaven. For

227

The Walk Applied

where two or three come together in my name, there am I with them." (Mat 18:19-20)

If you trust and believe, you can pray and expect that He will make your marriage a Godly one. Surely, that is God's will for your marriage that it prosper and grow in Him. Richard Burr, in his book, *"Developing Your Secret Closet of Prayer"*, makes this compelling statement: *"In my many years of ministry…I have never heard of a marriage that ended in divorce if the husband and wife prayed together regularly.*

Many years ago, I attended a seminar where an event occurred that made a most vivid impression on me. At one point, the leader asked married women to comment on what they thought about their husbands praying with them. The raw emotion that came from these women was truly illuminating - I never expected to see such a reaction, I assure you. It taught me a lesson I will never forget!

Recently, I heard in a radio interview from a ministry leader who works with married couples. I wish I could remember who it was, so I could give proper credit. He noted that in his seminars and ministry, sadly only about 5% of the couples he ministers to pray together.

Kathy and I set the alarm for 10 minutes before we need to get up. During that time, we cuddle and pray together and bless one another and our daughters. We pray believing that He is making us the Godly couple He wants us to be. We pray believing that He is making us the Godly people He wants us to be. We pray for those on our mind, and we bless our day and set it aside to Him. We also pray for people that are on our minds as well as those God brings to mind.

The Walk Applied

COMMUNING WITH GOD CONTINUALLY: PRAISE

The following two passages are very daunting, indeed. How do we pray continually? Is it really possible to pray "on all occasions"?

"...pray continually" (1 Th 5:17)
"...pray in the Spirit on all occasions" (Eph 6:18)

It seems far more likely that what the passages are referring to are a lifestyle of prayer as opposed to a 24/7/365 100 percent uttering of prayer. The Bible advises us how to acquire a lifestyle of prayer.

(*Note: the credit for the remainder of this section on praise goes to Paul Billheimer, the author of "Destined for the Throne).*

"The answer apparently lies in developing a habit of praising God on a consistent, ongoing basis. Yes, the answer is praise! Consistent, ongoing praise is the key to praying all the time! Praise and exaltation are found almost 450 times in the bible." ... *"To be most effective, then, praise must be massive, continuous, a fixed habit, a full-time occupation, a diligently pursued vocation, a way of life... This suggests a premeditated and predetermined habit of praise... This kind of praise depends on something more than temporary euphoria...based upon principle, not impulse...based upon something more than fluctuating circumstances or ephemeral emotional states. .... It's praise that becomes a full-time occupation, reflecting the pattern of unceasing praise in the celestial sphere."*

If they can praise God in heaven 24/7, why can't we?

"Each of the four living creatures had six wings and was covered with eyes all around, even under his wings. Day and night they never stop saying: "Holy, holy, holy is the Lord God Almighty, who was, and is, and is to come." (Rev 4:8)

The Walk Applied

Psalms instructs us that we should be praising God all day long!

"My tongue will speak of your righteousness ... praises all day long." (Ps 35:28)
"My mouth is filled with your praise, declaring your splendor all day long." (Ps 71:8)
"I will always have hope; I will praise you more and more. My mouth will tell of your righteousness, of your salvation all day long..." (Ps 71:14-15)
"My tongue will tell of your righteous acts all day long" (Psa 71:24)
"Blessed are those who have learned to acclaim you, who walk in the light of your presence, O LORD. They rejoice in your name all day long" (Psa 89:15-16)
"I will sing praise to my God as long as I live." (Psa 104:33)
"Every day I will praise you and extol your name for ever and ever." (Psa 145:2)
"I will sing praise to my God as long as I live." (Psa 146:2)
"It is good to praise the LORD ... to proclaim your love in the morning and your faithfulness at night" (Psa 92:1-2)

David, in psalm 57, while he was hiding in a cave, wrote this:

"My heart is fixed, O God, ... I will sing and give praise."

Hebrews 13:15 makes a similar point:

"let us continually offer to God a sacrifice of praise...

The Old Testament highlights the significance of continual praise:

-1 Chronicles 23: David appointed 4,000 Levites, whose sole purpose was to praise God.
-2nd Chronicles 20: A huge army was wiped out when Jehoshaphat and the people fasted and praised God!

The Walk Applied

Why does this "work?" It retrains our mind via the constant repetition - it replaces the constant messages coming in. It also makes it possible for us to praise under any circumstances. We are to praise God at all time - good and bad. If we only praise Him when life is good, how can we expect to praise Him when things don't go well? It also replicates what they do in heaven, repeated here for emphasis:

"Each of the four living creatures had six wings and was covered with eyes all around, even under his wings. Day and night they never stop saying: "Holy, holy, holy is the Lord God Almighty, who was, and is, and is to come." (Rev 4:8)

COMMUNING WITH GOD: THE WORD

God's Word is His anointed communication to His people; it's His instruction manual for *living a spiritual existence!* God's word is His infallible, inerrant, and anointed will for our lives. Thus, the study of God's Word will, in God's time and in God's way, plant itself and grow in you. You will be changed, healed, instructed, and trained on how to live a Godly, spiritual life.

"As the rain and the snow come down from heaven, and do not return to it without watering the earth and making it bud and flourish, so that it yields seed for the sower and bread for the eater, so is my word that goes out from my mouth: It will not return to me empty but will accomplish what I desire and achieve the purpose for which I sent it." (Isa 55:10-11)

"The Spirit gives life; the flesh counts for nothing. The words I have spoken to you are spirit and they are life." (John 6:63)

The Word renews your mind; it is a living, breathing, spiritual entity that carries with it God's anointing and authority. His Word changes

231

The Walk Applied

us by changing what we think and believe! God changes people who want to be changed. God uses changed people to change people. Just like prayer, worship, preaching, and teaching, the Word of God is a major component in Godly change.

God's Word needs to be read, studied, and mulled over at least 3- 4 times per week. There a numerous Bible study and reading plans that you can find on the 'net. Bible study groups that meet on a regular basis where the Word is explored should be a regular part of your communing with the Father.

COMMUNING WITH GOD: THE WORD HEALS

"Then they cried to the LORD in their trouble, and he saved them from their distress. He sent forth his word and healed them; he rescued them from the grave." (Psa 107:19-20)

"Do not let this Book of the Law depart from your mouth; meditate on it day and night, so that you may be careful to do everything written in it. Then you will be prosperous and successful." (Josh 1:8)

TWO TESTAMENTS

The word "Testament" means "covenant". In other words, the Bible is the story of the Old Covenant and the New Covenant. The Old Covenant describes in vivid detail what it was like to live under works, and the abject futility of our attempts to satisfy God's requirements through observance of the Law. The New Covenant details the covenant of grace. In the Sermon on the Mount, Jesus emphasized that "You used to think and believe "x", but now you need to think and believe "y". Jesus and the writers of the New Testament explained to us what it meant to live under grace.

Ultimately, the Word of God tells us of our absolute need of Jesus. The Old Testament tells us that works are totally insufficient; we

The Walk Applied

needed a Savior - the one perfect intercessor who could pay the price we never could. That intercessor, of course, was Jesus. The New Testament tells us the story of Jesus and His apostles and how we can live under the covenant of grace.

COMMUNING WITH GOD:
SPEAKING IN A GODLY WAY

What we say and how we say it are vitally important. The spiritual realm is conceptual and operates completely differently than the physical, natural realm that we know. How we deal and interact with the spiritual realm is dependent on our thoughts, beliefs, attitudes, and speech. We need to understand how the spiritual realm works as it operates in the natural, so we can operate properly as a spiritual creature living in the natural. We have seen how the Law of Prayer works: when we say it, believe it, and it's in God's will, then it will happen in God's way in God's time. However, God has temporarily ceded intermediate control over this world to Satan. Thus, by our mouth and what we think and believe, we can be deceived into coming under Satan's power and control. When we utter negative things and believe them that will almost always put us under Satan's control. It is vital that we learn to speak in a Godly way. The following numerous passages instruct us and reflect the overriding, significant emphasis that we are to speak in a Godly manner that reflects our faith.

"Anyone who speaks a word against the Son of Man will be forgiven, but anyone who speaks against the Holy Spirit will not be forgiven, either in this age or in the age to come. "Make a tree good and its fruit will be good or make a tree bad and its fruit will be bad, for a tree is recognized by its fruit. You brood of vipers, how can you who are evil say anything good? For out of the overflow of the heart the mouth speaks. The good man brings good things out of the good stored up in him, and the evil man brings evil things out of the evil stored up in him. But I tell you that men will have to give

233

The Walk Applied

account on the day of judgment for every careless word they have spoken. For by your words you will be acquitted, and by your words you will be condemned." (Mat 12:32-37)

"From the fruit of his mouth a man's stomach is filled; with the harvest from his lips he is satisfied. The tongue has the power of life and death, and those who love it will eat its fruit." (Prov 18:20-21)

"He who guards his lips guards his life, but he who speaks rashly will come to ruin." (Prov 13:3)

"Do you see a man who speaks in haste? There is more hope for a fool than for him." (Prov 29:20)

"He who walks righteously and speaks what is right, who rejects gain from extortion and keeps his hand from accepting bribes, who stops his ears against plots of murder and shuts his eyes against contemplating evil-- this is the man who will dwell on the heights, whose refuge will be the mountain fortress. His bread will be supplied, and water will not fail him." (Isa 33:15-16)

"Their tongue is a deadly arrow; it speaks with deceit. With his mouth each speaks cordially to his neighbor, but in his heart he sets a trap for him. Should I not punish them for this?" declares the LORD. "Should I not avenge myself on such a nation as this?"* (Jer 9:8-9)

"Brothers, do not slander one another. Anyone who speaks against his brother or judges him speaks against the law and judges it. When you judge the law, you are not keeping it, but sitting in judgment on it". (James 4:11)

"If anyone speaks, he should do it as one speaking the very words of God." (1 Pet 4:11)

The Walk Applied

"Reckless words pierce like a sword, but the tongue of the wise brings healing." (Prov 12:18)

"If anyone considers himself religious and yet does not keep a tight rein on his tongue, he deceives himself and his religion is worthless." (James 1:26)

"Likewise, the tongue is a small part of the body, but it makes great boasts. Consider what a great forest is set on fire by a small spark. The tongue also is a fire, a world of evil among the parts of the body. It corrupts the whole person, sets the whole course of his life on fire, and is itself set on fire by hell. All kinds of animals, birds, reptiles and creatures of the sea are being tamed and have been tamed by man, but no man can tame the tongue. It is a restless evil, full of deadly poison. With the tongue we praise our Lord and Father, and with it we curse men, who have been made in God's likeness. Out of the same mouth come praise and cursing. My brothers, this should not be." (James 3:5-10)

COMMUNING WITH GOD:
THINKING IN A GODLY WAY

What we think are perhaps more significant than what we speak. What we think governs what we say. What we honor and what we believe constitute what we will submit to. Indeed, the Word instructs us to think in Godly ways.

"But the things that come out of a person's mouth come from the heart." (Matt 15:18)

"For though we live in the world, we do not wage war as the world does. The weapons we fight with are not the weapons of the world. On the contrary, they have divine power to demolish strongholds. We demolish arguments and every pretension that sets itself up

235

The Walk Applied

against the knowledge of God, and we take captive every thought to make it obedient to Christ." (2 Cor 10:3-5)

"But when Jesus... rebuked Peter. "Get behind me, Satan!" he said. "You do not have in mind the things of God, but the things of men." (Mark 8:33)

"All the believers were one in heart and mind. No one claimed that any of his possessions was his own, but they shared everything they had." (Acts 4:32)

"The mind of sinful man is death, but the mind controlled by the Spirit is life and peace; the sinful mind is hostile to God. It does not submit to God's law, nor can it do so." (Rom 8:6-7)

"Do not conform any longer to the pattern of this world but be transformed by the renewing of your mind." (Rom 12:2)

"Therefore, let us stop passing judgment on one another. Instead, make up your mind not to put any stumbling block or obstacle in your brother's way." (Rom 14:13)

"I appeal to you, brothers, in the name of our Lord Jesus Christ, that all of you agree with one another so that there may be no divisions among you and that you may be perfectly united in mind and thought." (1 Cor 1:10)

""For who has known the mind of the Lord that he may instruct him?" But we have the mind of Christ." (1 Cor 2:16)

"Their destiny is destruction, their god is their stomach, and their glory is in their shame. Their mind is on earthly things." (Phil 3:19)

The Walk Applied

"Finally, brothers, whatever is true, whatever is noble, whatever is right, whatever is pure, whatever is lovely, whatever is admirable--if anything is excellent or praiseworthy--think about such things." (Phil 4:8)

"But when he asks, he must believe and not doubt, because he who doubts is like a wave of the sea, blown and tossed by the wind. That man should not think he will receive anything from the Lord; he is a double-minded man, unstable in all he does." (James 1:6-8)

"Rather, clothe yourselves with the Lord Jesus Christ, and do not think about how to gratify the desires of the sinful nature." (Rom 13:14)

"Therefore, prepare your minds for action; be self-controlled; set your hope fully on the grace to be given you when Jesus Christ is revealed." (1 Pet 1:13)

An intense read of Romans 1 and 2 details for us what happens when our thought life goes awry. Even though God's authority is clearly seen, men choose out of their sinful, idolatrous nature to come under the power and control of Satan:

"their thinking became futile and their foolish hearts were darkened. ... They exchanged the truth of God for a lie, and worshiped and served created things rather than the Creator--who is forever praised.... Furthermore, since they did not think it worthwhile to retain the knowledge of God, he gave them over to a depraved mind, to do what ought not to be done. They have become filled with every kind of wickedness, evil, greed and depravity. They are full of envy, murder, strife, deceit and malice. They are gossips, slanderers, God-haters, insolent, arrogant and boastful; they invent ways of doing evil; they disobey their parents; they are senseless, faithless, heartless, ruthless. Although they know God's righteous decree that those who do such things deserve death, they not only

The Walk Applied

continue to do these very things but also approve of those who practice them…

Ephesians reflects the same theme:

"So, I tell you this, and insist on it in the Lord, that you must no longer live as the Gentiles do, in the futility of their thinking. They are darkened in their understanding and separated from the life of God because of the ignorance that is in them due to the hardening of their hearts." (Eph 4:17-18)

As we conclude our discussion of Godly speech and thinking, it's handy to have a quick summary. The diagram below shows us what happens when we allow our speech and inputs to go unchecked. The same logistic applies when we seek Godly speech and thinking:

Changed speech & inputs:
➡**Changed thinking**
  ➡**Changed agreement**
    ➡**Changed beliefs**
      ➡**Changed submission**

If we change our speech and our "inputs", we will change our thinking and what we agree with. When that happens, our belief system changes. When that happens, we change our authority. Speak and think in a Godly way, and you will ultimately come under Godly Authority. We take in thousands of "inputs" every day! It is up to us to *regulate and moderate* what comes in – and it's virtually impossible to defend against the onslaught of incoming messages from the modern media. The conscious attempt to regulate and moderate what comes in will actually change what you believe!

The Walk Applied

More to the point, the overwhelming number of media "inputs" that besiege us each and every day make it virtually impossible to "take captive every thought". There's simply too many messages that most of us take in each and every day. I hope what you have caught from these past few pages is that it is incumbent upon each and every one of us to create our own inputs via prayer, praise and worship.

A wise old Indian was telling his grandson about two wolves that fight within us – a good & bad wolf. The grandson asked: "who will win?" The grandfather answered: "the one you feed".

COMMUNING WITH GOD: WORSHIP

Worship is the recognition of God's sovereignty and holiness and our response of celebrating submission to him. Worship is expressed in any number of ways. We tend to think of singing and music as worship, but prayer, praise, service, and giving out of a Godly heart are all expressions of worship:

"Worship the LORD your God, and his blessing will be on your food and water." (Exo 23:25)

"Do not worship any other god, for the LORD, whose name is Jealous, is a jealous God." (Exo 34:14)

"When the LORD made a covenant with the Israelites, he commanded them: "Do not worship any other gods or bow down to them, serve them or sacrifice to them." But the LORD, who brought you up out of Egypt with mighty power and outstretched arm, is the one you must worship. To him you shall bow down and to him offer sacrifices. You must always be careful to keep the decrees and ordinances, the laws and commands he wrote for you. Do not worship other gods. Do not forget the covenant I have made with you, and do not worship other gods. Rather, worship the LORD

239

The Walk Applied

your God; it is he who will deliver you from the hand of all your enemies. " (2 Ki 17:35-39)

"Ascribe to the LORD, O families of nations, ascribe to the LORD glory and strength, ascribe to the LORD the glory due his name. Bring an offering and come before him; worship the LORD in the splendor of his holiness. Tremble before him, all the earth!" (1 Chr 16:28-30)

COMMUNING WITH GOD:
THE FELLOWSHIP OF THE BELIEVERS

It is the bond of common purpose, devotion and unity that binds Christians together and to Christ. The fellowship of believers is what gives you opportunities to give and serve to build up the body. The fellowship of the believers is what allows them to serve you in your time of need, as well. Isaiah 58 elaborates on how the observing the Sabbath puts us in position to serve. The fellowship of believers also provides for corporate prayer. Acts 2:42 talks about how powerful that fellowship is:

"They devoted themselves to the apostles' teaching and to the fellowship, to the breaking of bread and to prayer. Everyone was filled with awe, and many wonders and miraculous signs were done by the apostles. All the believers were together and had everything in common. Selling their possessions and goods, they gave to anyone as he had need. Every day they continued to meet together in the temple courts. They broke bread in their homes and ate together with glad and sincere hearts, praising God and enjoying the favor of all the people. And the Lord added to their number daily those who were being saved." (Acts 2:42-47)

The Walk Applied

"And let us consider how we may spur one another on toward love and good deeds. Let us not give up meeting together, as some are in the habit of doing, but let us encourage one another- and all the more as you see the Day approaching." (Heb 10:24-25)

"But you are to seek the place the LORD your God will choose from among all your tribes to put his Name there for his dwelling. To that place you must go; there bring your burnt offerings and sacrifices, your tithes and special gifts, what you have vowed to give and your freewill offerings, and the firstborn of your herds and flocks." (Deu 12:5-6)

"Two are better than one, because they have a good return for their work: If one falls down, his friend can help him up. But pity the man who falls and has no one to help him up! Also, if two lie down together, they will keep warm. But how can one keep warm alone? Though one may be overpowered, two can defend themselves. A cord of three strands is not quickly broken." (Eccl 4:9-12)

COMMUNING WITH GOD: FASTING

Fasting is denying oneself to achieve a greater intimacy with God. It is abstaining from a basic natural need in order to get closer to God. Fasting often applies to food, but it can also apply to simply abstaining from other needs. Some may choose to abstain from intimate physical relations; some may choose to have a prayer vigil that lasts all night long (sleep fast). There are numerous excellent fasting resources that one can research, and there are various viewpoints that commentators have when it comes to fasting. Thus, don't expect that you will find any one source to be the end-all be-all of fasting. You are urged to study what God's Word has to say about fasting. For our purposes, we will use Wallis's excellent book *"God's Chosen Fast"*.

241

The Walk Applied

Matthew tells us that fasting is something that we all should be doing. Fasting should be done such that as few people as possible know. We do not have to be "called" to fast. Anyone can decide to fast whenever they want to.

"When you fast, do not look somber as the hypocrites do, for they disfigure their faces to show men they are fasting. I tell you the truth, they have received their reward in full. But when you fast, put oil on your head and wash your face, so that it will not be obvious to men that you are fasting, but only to your Father, who is unseen; and your Father, who sees what is done in secret, will reward you" (Mat 6:16-18).

Fasting is also a way to break free from habitual sin:

"Is not this the kind of fasting I have chosen: to loose the chains of injustice and untie the cords of the yoke, to set the oppressed free and break every yoke?" (Isa 58:6)

Fasting intensifies our prayers because it symbolizes it reflects a total dependence on God:

"There, by the Ahava Canal, I proclaimed a fast, so that we might humble ourselves before our God and ask him for a safe journey for us and our children, with all our possessions. I was ashamed to ask the king for soldiers and horsemen to protect us from enemies on the road, because we had told the king, "The gracious hand of our God is on everyone who looks to him, but his great anger is against all who forsake him." So, we fasted and petitioned our God about this, and he answered our prayer." (Ezra 8:21-23)

Fasting can be a part of true repentance declaration experience

The Walk Applied

"'Even now,' declares the LORD, 'return to me with all your heart, with fasting and weeping and mourning.'(Joel 2:12)

WALLIS 5 TYPES OF FASTS:

ABSOLUTE FAST: NO FOOD NO WATER

This fast should be conducted over no more than 3 days. Moses (twice) and Elijah both participated in an absolute fast for 40 days. Divine intervention enabled them to fast in such a way.

"Saul got up from the ground, but when he opened his eyes he could see nothing. So, they led him by the hand into Damascus. For three days he was blind and did not eat or drink anything. (Acts 9:8-9)

THE NORMAL FAST: WATER ONLY

The normal fast is what most people think of when they fast. The length of the fast can vary. Research this fast before you attempt it. There is no Biblical injunctive that says you must fast for 40 days. One day, 7 days, etc. are fine. Fast as God leads you.

"Jesus, full of the Holy Spirit, returned from the Jordan and was led by the Spirit in the desert, where for forty days he was tempted by the devil. He ate nothing during those days, and at the end of them he was hungry." (Luke 4:1-2)

THE PARTIAL FAST:
ABSTAIN FROM CERTAIN TYPES OF FOOD

This fast involves choosing different foods to abstain from. A variant is choosing a very limited variety of food, such as bread and water only for a certain period of time. A popular fasting choice for many Christians is "The Daniel fast". You can research it on the Internet, and you will find numerous resources.

243

The Walk Applied

"At that time, I, Daniel, mourned for three weeks. I ate no choice food; no meat or wine touched my lips; and I used no lotions at all until the three weeks were over". (Dan 10:2-3)

THE REGULAR FAST:
ABSTAIN ON A CONSISTENT BASIS:

This fast involves choosing a certain day or time period to fast. Some may elect to not eat and drink on a given day of the week consistently. Some may decide to not eat lunch during the week.

"The LORD said to Moses, "The tenth day of this seventh month is the Day of Atonement. Hold a sacred assembly and deny yourselves, and present an offering made to the LORD by fire. Do no work on that day, because it is the Day of Atonement, when atonement is made for you before the LORD your God. Anyone who does not deny himself on that day must be cut off from his people. I will destroy from among his people anyone who does any work on that day." (Lev 23:26-30)

THE PUBLIC FAST: FASTING TOGETHER TO
ACHIEVE A COMMON PURPOSE

This fast occurs when a group of people decide to fast in common. Esther gives us an example of such a fast:

"Go, gather together all the Jews who are in Susa, and fast for me. Do not eat or drink for three days, night or day. I and my maids will fast as you do. When this is done, I will go to the king, even though it is against the law. And if I perish, I perish." (Est 4:16)

The Walk Applied

COMMUNING WITH GOD: HONOR THE SABBATH

To honor the Sabbath is to honor one of God's great commandments. For our purposes, we will consider the Sabbath as a weekly gathering of God's people on Sundays in a church setting. The Sabbath is meant to be a day of rest taken weekly. We maintain that God expects us to observe the Sabbath on a regular and consistent basis for reasons that will become apparent.

You could conceivably never attend church and you can be saved. Church attendance is not a requirement of the salvation covenant. That said, if you do not feel any need to attend a Bible believing church, or simply refuse to go, we might suggest that you examine yourself and your relationship with Jesus Christ. The Bible clearly expects us to gather in the fellowship of believers on a regular basis.

Recall that earlier we discussed Isaiah 58 in depth. Honoring the Sabbath via regular church attendance was seen to be most profound. Putting yourself in position to serve as well as being able to help meet others at their point of need were two prime reasons for honoring the Sabbath. It was also emphasized that honoring the Sabbath was important regarding our personal healing. The passages given below indicate that God is most emphatic about keeping the Sabbath holy:

"Then God blessed the seventh day and made it holy, because on it he rested from all the work of creating that he had done." (Gen 2:3)

"Remember the Sabbath day by keeping it holy. Six days you shall labor and do all your work, but the seventh day is a Sabbath to the Lord your God. On it you shall not do any work, neither you, nor your son or daughter, nor your male or female servant, nor your animals, nor any foreigner residing in your towns. For in six days the Lord made the heavens and the earth, the sea, and all that is in

245

The Walk Applied

them, but he rested on the seventh day. Therefore, the Lord blessed the Sabbath day and made it holy." (Ex 20:8-11)

"Observe the Sabbath day by keeping it holy, as the Lord your God has commanded you. Six days you shall labor and do all your work, but the seventh day is a sabbath to the Lord your God. On it you shall not do any work, neither you, nor your son or daughter, nor your male or female servant, nor your ox, your donkey or any of your animals, nor any foreigner residing in your towns, so that your male and female servants may rest, as you do." (Duet 5:12-14)

"I am the Lord your God; follow my decrees and be careful to keep my laws. Keep my Sabbaths holy, that they may be a sign between us. Then you will know that I am the Lord your God." (Ez 20:19-20)

"If you keep your feet from breaking the Sabbath and from doing as you please on my holy day, if you call the Sabbath a delight and the Lord's holy day honorable, and if you honor it by not going your own way and not doing as you please or speaking idle words, then you will find your joy in the Lord, and I will cause you to ride in triumph on the heights of the land and to feast on the inheritance of your father Jacob." For the mouth of the Lord has spoken. *(Isa 58:13-14)*

COMMUNING WITH GOD: TEACHING/PREACHING

A significant part of the Christian experience is that of being taught the Word of God by experienced and wise teachers. Sermons, Sunday school, seminars, devotionals, books, articles, conferences, etc. are most important in the believers walk. The Bible clearly advocates that we need to be under consistent Godly teaching that is congruent with the Word of God. Acts talks about the Bereans who exhibited the kinds of devoted students that we all need to be.

260

The Walk Applied

"Now the Berean Jews were of more noble character than those in Thessalonica, for they received the message with great eagerness and examined the Scriptures every day to see if what Paul said was true." (Acts 17:11)

As we pursue the teaching and exposition of Gods' word, it's important that we study and ponder the teaching. This is where commentaries, concordances, books, tapes, and cd's all contribute to our knowledge and increase our faith.

COMMUNING WITH GOD:
GIVING & SERVICE

Giving means to offer your time, talents or money simply because you love God. Giving and service are first and foremost spiritual acts. Giving needs to be seen as the planting of spiritual seeds for growth, so that it will produce fruit spiritually. They are far more than physical actions. Acts of giving and service must be blessed and never cursed.

Giving and service do not require that you have to perform some Herculean task. It's most often as simple as using what you have when opportunity presents itself. Recall "do what you can when you can with what you have?" Scripture talks of the little boy who offered 2 loaves of bread and 5 fishes. One women gave her last 2 coins without any expectation of return. The Good Samaritan saved the life of a man who was robbed and beaten.

You can create your own opportunities. Volunteer at any one of dozens of worthwhile places in your community. The local nursing home. Your church. The widow down the street. The young couple who just had a baby - you can prepare a meal. Opportunities abound all around you - all you have to do is look.

The Walk Applied

"Command them to do good, to be rich in good deeds, and to be generous and willing to share. In this way they will lay up treasure for themselves as a firm foundation for the coming age, so that they may take hold of the life that is truly life." (1 Tim 6:18-19)

"You will be made rich in every way so that you can be generous on every occasion, and through us your generosity will result in thanksgiving to God. This service that you perform is not only supplying the needs of God's people but is also overflowing in many expressions of thanks to God. Because of the service by which you have proved yourselves, men will praise God for the obedience that accompanies your confession of the gospel of Christ, and for your generosity in sharing with them and with everyone else."
(2 Cor 9:11-13)

"Ever since the time of your forefathers you have turned away from my decrees and have not kept them. Return to me, and I will return to you," says the LORD Almighty. "But you ask, 'How are we to return?' "Will a man rob God? Yet you rob me. "But you ask, 'How do we rob you?' "In tithes and offerings. You are under a curse--the whole nation of you--because you are robbing me. Bring the whole tithe into the storehouse, that there may be food in my house. Test me in this," says the LORD Almighty, "and see if I will not throw open the floodgates of heaven and pour out so much blessing that you will not have room enough for it. (Mal 3:7-10)

DO WHAT YOU ARE EQUIPPED AND ENABLED TO DO

No one is asking you to step outside of what you are capable of doing. Do what you are good at. Perform the simplest of tasks. Cook a meal. Give a ride. Visit a shut in. Cleanup the yard of the elderly man or the elderly widow around the block. Mow their lawn. Again, opportunities present themselves all the time.

248

The Walk Applied

COMMUNING WITH GOD:
GIVING & MONEY

Scripture is very clear when it comes to giving money. We should offer money, and we should give cheerfully. However, there is often great debate regarding whether or not we must tithe – giving a certain percentage of your income (usually 10%) to your church. We believe that the New Testament teaching about giving is best summed up in the following passage:

"Let each one do just as he has purposed in his heart; not grudgingly or under compulsion; for God loves a cheerful giver" (2 Cor. 9:7)

The New Testament emphasizes a relationship with Jesus Christ. Rules and legalism are no longer the guidelines. If we have a close walk with Jesus, we can expect that Jesus will put it on our hearts what we should give. Seek the Lord, decide what you wish to give and who you want to give it to, and give cheerfully! That said, we believe that it is important that you should give to your home church first. Your pastor and the other employees of the church should not have to scrape by. Feel led to tithe? Then by all means do so.

COMMUNING WITH GOD: STEWARDSHIP

The Bible is very forthright in that it tells us that God will meet our needs according to His purpose plan and will:

"And my God will meet all your needs according to the riches of his glory in Christ Jesus." (Phil 4:19).

We are expected to exercise proper stewardship over what we are given and blessed with. We really own nothing - we only have what God has given us. In actuality, the notion of ownership is truly somewhat dubious when you think about it. I may "own" my car –

249

The Walk Applied

after all, I signed for it and paid for it - but what that really means is I am the one who governs the use of the vehicle. The idea of ownership is truly a spiritual one. It is a conceptual idea that gives me the *"feeling"* that I "own it". The reality is that God owns all things, and He provides what we need. We might be better off thinking of ourselves as custodians, actually.

COMMUNING WITH GOD: THANKFULLNESS

Giving thanks is something that is easily forgotten. We are adopted, anointed and appointed as a spiritual creature, and we need to be thankful for all the good things God has given us! Being thankful, like praising God, needs to be a 24x7x365 proposition!

"Give thanks to the LORD, call on his name; make known among the nations what he has done. Sing to him, sing praise to him; tell of all his wonderful acts. Glory in his holy name; let the hearts of those who seek the LORD rejoice. Look to the LORD and his strength; seek his face always. Remember the wonders he has done, his miracles, and the judgments he pronounced" (1 Chr 16:8-12)

"Sacrifice thank offerings to God, fulfill your vows to the Most High, and call upon me in the day of trouble; I will deliver you, and you will honor me." (Psa 50:14-15)

"always giving thanks to God the Father for everything, in the name of our Lord Jesus Christ." (Eph 5:20)

"Do not be anxious about anything, but in everything, by prayer and petition, with thanksgiving, present your requests to God." (Phil 4:6)

"And whatever you do, ... do it all in the name of the Lord Jesus, giving thanks to God the Father through him." (Col 3:17)

The Walk Applied

"And we pray this in order that you may live a life worthy of the Lord and may please him in every way: bearing fruit in every good work, growing in the knowledge of God, being strengthened with all power according to his glorious might so that you may have great endurance and patience, and joyfully giving thanks to the Father, who has qualified you to share in the inheritance of the saints in the kingdom of light. For he has rescued us from the dominion of darkness and brought us into the kingdom of the Son he loves" (Col 1:10-13)

"Let the peace of Christ rule in your hearts, since as members of one body you were called to peace." (Col 3:15)

"Be joyful always; pray continually; give thanks in all circumstances, for this is God's will for you in Christ Jesus." (1 Th 5:16-18)

"Let them give thanks to the LORD for his unfailing love and his wonderful deeds for men." (Psa 107:21)

COMMUNING WITH GOD: SUFFERING & TRAGEDY

Suffering is a part of the program, and you must expect it as a part of your natural existence. How we react to suffering, and our public attitude says volumes about our walk in Jesus.

Suffering and trials is what makes you long for heaven. When we see ourselves as spiritual creatures living a spiritual existence in the natural, we must remember that we live an eternal existence, which gives us a not only a great context on our suffering; it gives us great hope! It's ok to hurt and grieve and mourn and cry out to God - even in anger over your situation. God does not expect us to be robots! But when you do it, go to the throne of grace and vent and rant and rave to an almighty God. Seek your solace there. God wants us to

The Walk Applied

be real with him because it shows we're dependent on him. Above all, never forget that your suffering has a *purpose and a reason!* You may not be aware of the reason or see it readily, but your suffering is being used to somehow advance the kingdom. As Malachi 3:3 points out, we are like silver being refined – the impurities are being refined out of us.

"The apostles left the Sanhedrin, rejoicing because they had been counted worthy of suffering disgrace for the Name." (Acts 5:41)

"Now if we are children, then we are heirs - heirs of God and co-heirs with Christ, if indeed we share in his sufferings in order that we may also share in his glory. I consider that our present sufferings are not worth comparing with the glory that will be revealed in us." (Rom 8:17-18)

"By faith Moses, when he had grown up, refused to be known as the son of Pharaoh's daughter. He chose to be mistreated along with the people of God rather than to enjoy the pleasures of sin for a short time. He regarded disgrace for the sake of Christ as of greater value than the treasures of Egypt because he was looking ahead to his reward. By faith he left Egypt, not fearing the king's anger; he persevered because he saw him who is invisible." (Heb 11:24-27)

"They were stoned; they were sawed in two; they were put to death by the sword. They went about in sheepskins and goatskins, destitute, persecuted and mistreated-- the world was not worthy of them. They wandered in deserts and mountains, and in caves and holes in the ground. These were all commended for their faith, yet none of them received what had been promised. God had planned something better for us so that only together with us would they be made perfect. (Heb 11:37-40)

"Blessed are you when people insult you, persecute you and falsely say all kinds of evil against you because of me. Rejoice and be glad,

252

The Walk Applied

because great is your reward in heaven, for in the same way they persecuted the prophets who were before you". (Matt 5:11)

"But the Lord said to Ananias, "Go! This man is my chosen instrument to carry my name before the Gentiles and their kings and before the people of Israel. I will show him how much he must suffer for my name." (Acts 9:15-16)

" Then, he said to them all: "If anyone would come after me, he must deny himself and take up his cross daily and follow me." (Mat 5:11-12)

To re-iterate: When we see ourselves as spiritual creatures living a spiritual existence placed in the natural it puts our suffering in a spiritual context. Since we are eternal beings, that means our suffering is temporary compared to the immeasurable vastness of our eternal existence as spiritual creatures. If it's true that we are being trained here for our eventual use in heaven, and this natural existence is no more than a short temporary existence, that makes a great deal of difference that puts context on our suffering!

"Why, you do not even know what will happen tomorrow. What is your life? You are a mist that appears for a little while and then vanishes." (James 4:14)

"for we were born only yesterday and know nothing, and our days on earth are but a shadow." (Job 8:9)

"Show me, O LORD, my life's end and the number of my days; let me know how fleeting is my life. You have made my days a mere handbreadth; the span of my years is as nothing before you. Each man's life is but a breath. Selah." (Psa 39:4-5)

"Remember how fleeting is my life." (Psa 89:47)

253

The Walk Applied

CHAPTER 9
THE GODLY MARRIAGE

The Walk Applied

The Walk Applied

CHAPTER 9
THE GODLY MARRIAGE

Marriage is a God-ordained and God-oriented institution. God instituted marriage to be the model and the fundamental basis of how He wants us to organize ourselves in society. Genesis 2:20-25 lays out God's plan for the family: one man, one woman separating themselves unto themselves as a family unit within a covenantal union to conceive and raise children. There is only ONE option for a valid marriage: one man and one woman in lifetime commitment. Anything else is a perversion of God's law and plan.

"But for Adam no suitable helper was found. So the Lord God caused the man to fall into a deep sleep; and while he was sleeping, he took one of the man's ribs and then closed up the place with flesh. Then the Lord God made a woman from the rib he had taken out of the man, and he brought her to the man. The man said, "This is now bone of my bones and flesh of my flesh; she shall be called 'woman,' for she was taken out of man." That is why a man leaves his father and mother and is united to his wife, and they become one flesh. Adam and his wife were both naked, and they felt no shame." (Gen 2:20-25)

The Bible tells us that marriage is commended and is a good thing.

"He who finds a wife finds what is good and receives favor from the Lord." (Pro 18:22)

"Marry and have sons and daughters; find wives for your sons and give your daughters in marriage, so that they too may have sons and daughters. Increase in number; do not decrease." (Jer 29:6)

257

The Walk Applied

"So I counsel younger widows to marry, to have children, to manage their homes and to give the enemy no opportunity for slander." (1 Tim 5:14)

"Marriage should be honored by all," (Heb 13:4)

God's perfect plan for marriage is that it be an unconditional, lifetime commitment. The Bible tells us it is to be considered indissoluble during the lives of the parties. Jesus clearly emphasized God's intention that marriage be a lifetime commitment. He affirmed this as the principle of marriage inherent in divine creation.

"Haven't you read," he replied, "that at the beginning the Creator 'made them male and female,' and said, 'For this reason a man will leave his father and mother and be united to his wife, and the two will become one flesh'? So, they are no longer two, but one. Therefore, what God has joined together, let man not separate." (Mat 19:4-6)

"To the married I give this command (not I, but the Lord): A wife must not separate from her husband. But if she does, she must remain unmarried or else be reconciled to her husband. And a husband must not divorce his wife. To the rest I say this (I, not the Lord): If any brother has a wife who is not a believer and she is willing to live with him, he must not divorce her. And if a woman has a husband who is not a believer and he is willing to live with her, she must not divorce him. For the unbelieving husband has been sanctified through his wife, and the unbelieving wife has been sanctified through her believing husband. Otherwise your children would be unclean, but as it is, they are holy." (1 Cor 7:10-14)

"For example, by law a married woman is bound to her husband as long as he is alive, but if her husband dies, she is released from the law of marriage." (Rom 7:2)

The Walk Applied

"A woman is bound to her husband as long as he lives. But if her husband dies, she is free to marry anyone she wishes, but he must belong to the Lord. (1 Cor 7:39)

This does not mean that God will not allow separation and divorce. We will talk about divorce subsequently and the conditions under which God permits a divorce. God certainly understands that there will be divorces; we do live in a sinful world. We believe it saddens Him greatly when it occurs; the Bible says as much.
.

SOLEMN OBLIGATIONS:
A COVENANT RELATIONSHIP

In God's economy, marriage is meant to be a solemn obligation of the highest order. It is based on a covenant that God takes most seriously.

"Some Pharisees came to him to test him. They asked, "Is it lawful for a man to divorce his wife for any and every reason?" "Haven't you read," he replied, "that at the beginning the Creator 'made them male and female,' and said, 'For this reason a man will leave his father and mother and be united to his wife, and the two will become one flesh'? So, they are no longer two, but one. Therefore, what God has joined together, let man not separate." (Mat 19:3-6)

"You ask, "Why?" It is because the LORD is acting as the witness between you and the wife of your youth, because you have broken faith with her, though she is your partner, the wife of your marriage covenant. Has not the LORD made them one? In flesh and spirit they are his. And why one? Because he was seeking godly offspring. So, guard yourself in your spirit, and do not break faith with the wife of your youth. "I hate divorce," says the LORD God of Israel, "and I hate a man's covering himself with violence as well as with his garment," says the LORD Almighty. So, guard yourself in your spirit, and do not break faith. (Mal 2:14-16)

259

The Walk Applied

"For example, by law a married woman is bound to her husband as long as he is alive, but if her husband dies, she is released from the law of marriage. (Rom 7:2)

MARRIAGE:
A MONOGAMOUS RELATIONSHIP

"Do you not know that your bodies are members of Christ himself? Shall I then take the members of Christ and unite them with a prostitute? Never! Do you not know that he who unites himself with a prostitute is one with her in body? For it is said, "The two will become one flesh." But he who unites himself with the Lord is one with him in spirit. Flee from sexual immorality. All other sins a man commits are outside his body, but he who sins sexually sins against his own body. Do you not know that your body is a temple of the Holy Spirit, who is in you, whom you have received from God? You are not your own; you were bought at a price. Therefore, honor God with your body." (1 Cor 6:15-20)

The biblical standard for marriage is a monogamous relationship in which 1 man and 1 woman share a lifetime commitment to each other, second only to their commitment to God. Paul cited this key principle to show the sinfulness of sexual relations outside marriage.

MARRIAGE WAS DESIGNED
FOR THE HAPPINESS OF ALL MANKIND

"The LORD God said, "It is not good for the man to be alone. I will make a helper suitable for him." (Gen 2:18)

The Walk Applied

GOD WANTS US TO INCREASE
THE HUMAN POPULATION

"God blessed them and said to them, "Be fruitful and increase in number; fill the earth and subdue it." (Gen 1:28)

"Then God blessed Noah and his sons, saying to them, "Be fruitful and increase in number and fill the earth. (Gen 9:1)

MARRIAGE IS TO RAISE UP GODLY SEED

"Has not the LORD made them one? In flesh and spirit they are his. And why one? Because he was seeking godly offspring. So, guard yourself in your spirit, and do not break faith with the wife of your youth." (Mal 2:15)

MARRIAGE IS TO PREVENT IMMORALITY

"Now for the matters you wrote about: It is good for a man not to marry. But since there is so much immorality, each man should have his own wife, and each woman her own husband. The husband should fulfill his marital duty to his wife, and likewise the wife to her husband. The wife's body does not belong to her alone but also to her husband. In the same way, the husband's body does not belong to him alone but also to his wife. Do not deprive each other except by mutual consent and for a time, so that you may devote yourselves to prayer. Then come together again so that Satan will not tempt you because of your lack of self-control." (1 Cor 7:1-5)

MARRIAGE IS FOR COMPANIONSHIP

"The LORD God said, "It is not good for the man to be alone. I will make a helper suitable for him." (Gen 2:18)

The Walk Applied

MARRIAGE IS ABOUT AUTHORITY AND MUTUAL SUBMISSION.

"Submit to one another out of reverence for Christ. Wives, submit to your husbands as to the Lord. For the husband is the head of the wife as Christ is the head of the church, his body, of which he is the Savior. Now as the church submits to Christ, so also wives should submit to their husbands in everything. Husbands, love your wives, just as Christ loved the church and gave himself up for her to make her holy, cleansing her by the washing with water through the word, and to present her to himself as a radiant church, without stain or wrinkle or any other blemish, but holy and blameless. In this same way, husbands ought to love their wives as their own bodies. He who loves his wife loves himself. After all, no one ever hated his own body, but he feeds and cares for it, ... However, each one of you also must love his wife as he loves himself, and the wife must respect her husband." (Eph 5:21-33)

Paul described the kind of mutual submission that should characterize the marriage relationship. Although the husband is head of the home, his role is modeled after the role of Christ as head of the church, who "loved the church and gave himself up for it". Paul also emphasized the importance of self-giving love in marriage.

MARRIAGE REFLECTS CHRIST'S UNION WITH HIS CHURCH.

God uses the imagery of marriage to emphasize His union with the Jewish nation. He wants us to know how strong that unity should be.

"For your Maker is your husband - the LORD Almighty is his name - the Holy One of Israel is your Redeemer; he is called the God of all the earth. The LORD will call you back as if you were a wife

262

The Walk Applied

deserted and distressed in spirit-- a wife who married young, only to be rejected," says your God." (Isa 54:5-6)

*""Return, faithless people," declares the LORD, "for I am your husband. "(*Jer 3:14)

"I will betroth you to me forever; I will betroth you in righteousness and justice, in love and compassion. I will betroth you in faithfulness, and you will acknowledge the LORD " (Hosea 2:19-20)

"Husbands, love your wives, just as Christ loved the church and gave himself up for her to make her holy, cleansing her by the washing with water through the word, and to present her to himself as a radiant church, without stain or wrinkle or any other blemish, but holy and blameless. " (Eph 5:25-27)

"Let us rejoice and be glad and give him glory! For the wedding of the Lamb has come, and his bride has made herself ready. Fine linen, bright and clean, was given her to wear." (Fine linen stands for the righteous acts of the saints.) Then the angel said to me, "Write: 'Blessed are those who are invited to the wedding supper of the Lamb!'" And he added, "These are the true words of God." (Rev 19:7-9)

THE MARRIAGE COVENANT
A SPIRITUAL INSTITUTION

Marriage is a spiritual institution established by covenant. The symbolism of the wedding and the marriage is singularly important in helping us understand how God wants us to see marriage from a spiritual point of view.

The Walk Applied

THE "ECHAD": THE FIRST WEDDING

"The man said, "This is now bone of my bones and flesh of my flesh; she shall be called 'woman, ' for she was taken out of man." For this reason a man will leave his father and mother and be united to his wife, and they will become one flesh." (Gen 2:23-25)

The phrase "one flesh" comes from the Hebrew word "echad", which implies a oneness or unity that contains more than one entity. The implication is that the whole of the entity is greater than the mere sum of the parts. A good way to understand the term echad is to think of the difference between the word "house" and the word "home". We think of a "house" as a structure. "Home" implies something else altogether that is emotionally charged. "Echad" is the same word used in the following passage:

"Hear, O Israel: The LORD our God, the LORD is one."
(Deu 6:4)

This foundational scripture in the Hebrew heritage emphasizes the significance of "one flesh". It underscores in a most emphatic way of how the newly married couple is like God: they are far more than 2 people joined together: they are something entirely new. By implication, we can look at Genesis 1 and draw a startling conclusion:

So God created mankind in his own image; in the image of God he created them; male and female he created them. God blessed them and said to them, "Be fruitful and increase in number; fill the earth and subdue it. Rule over the fish in the sea and the birds in the sky and over every living creature that moves on the ground." (Gen 1:27)

The Walk Applied

A COPY OF THE TRINITY?

Given the physical differences between both men and women, God cannot be referring to both. Obviously, men and women have physical similarities, but they are physically dissimilar as well. It seems far too simplistic to examine this passage to opine that God is talking about mere physical similarities to God Himself. It appears much more likely that this passage is telling us that when a man and a woman come together in the marital covenant, we are witnessing the creation of a new spiritual image of the triune God – an amazing thought, indeed! This idea also communicates that God himself is an active participant in our marriage. He is not just an observer.

A way to look at this idea would be to compare marriage to a coin. A coin is merely a flat piece of metal until it is stamped with both the obverse and the reverse. Only after the coin has passed rigorous quality control checks will it be considered a valid medium of exchange. Paper money is the same: both sides of the paper must be properly imprinted and pass thorough inspections before a given bill is considered valid to make legitimate purchases. Even the humble penny or the lowly $1 bill must pass significant muster before they would be allowed into circulation.

COVENANT:
THE MARRIAGE FOUNDATION

Webster's dictionary tells us that a covenant is "a binding & solemn agreement by 2 or more parties to do or keep from doing certain specified things." In our society, the vast majority still see marriage as a very serious arrangement to enter into. The wedding ceremony is the celebration of the execution of the marriage covenant that typically is fraught with all kinds of symbolism.

The Walk Applied

The following was gleaned from Laurie Hall's well-researched book "An Affair of the Mind". Ms. Hall's reporting of the various customs that constitute our present-day ceremonies helps us to understand why we do what we do in most wedding ceremonies.

WEDDING SYMBOLISM

The groom enters first. He is the covenant initiator; therefore, he takes greater responsibility for enforcement of the covenant. The families are situated on either side of the aisle symbolizing either half of the sacrificed animal. This action is reminiscent of Abraham in Gen 15, where God passed His light through the pieces of the animals. The bride walks between them symbolizing God's holiness as she passes between. She is in white symbolizing her own purity, as well as God's. There are 3 tiers of witnesses, symbolizing:

- The Family is symbolized via the Best Man and the Maid of Honor. They are responsible for making sure the Bride and Groom are accountable.
- The local church body is symbolized by the wedding party.
- All of God's people are symbolized by the rest of the church.

This all fits with the following scriptural admonition:

"...every matter must be established by the testimony of two or three witnesses." (2 Cor 13:1)

The Officiant presides over the ceremony because he symbolizes God's authority. He is legally authorized to perform the ceremony; He oversees the creation of the covenant. The vast majority of wedding ceremonies feature this line: "...by the authority vested in me ..."

The Walk Applied

THE "SPIRITUAL CONTRACT"

The wedding covenant is a very special one. Another way of looking at a covenant is that it is fundamentally a contract that has been initiated by God. In that context, we can come to a new and profound appreciation for marriage.

Contracts require:

1) Ready, willing, and able buyer & seller
2) Consideration (something of value) must pass hands. The consideration must be of sufficient value as to justify the contract. A down payment of sufficient value is typically expected if the full contract price is not met.
3) Witnesses attest to the validity of the agreement.
4) The contract must be sealed or notarized.
5) There must be a legitimate offer and valid acceptance.
6) Trust is the fundamental basis of a contract: A fundamental belief that the participants will hold up their end of the bargain.

Two sellers and two buyers: The wedding uniquely brings together two sellers & two buyers because both the bride and groom are both a buyer and a seller. The marriage license indicates that they are ready, willing, and able buyers and sellers.

The down payment: The engagement is the promise and initiates the covenant. The engagement ring is the down payment. It symbolizes the seriousness of his intent and indicates sufficiency of value.

Consideration: The rings are the final payment to each other.

Witnesses: The vows are spoken in front of witnesses to profess that they are ready, willing, and able participants in the covenant.

267

The Walk Applied

THE WEDDING VOWS

*I, Nick, take you Kathy, to be my lawfully wedded wife, **to have and to hold,** to the exclusion of all others, from this day forward for better, for worse, for richer, for poorer, in sickness and in health, to love and cherish, till death do us part, according to God's holy ordinance, and therto I plight my troth... (an Old English phrase meaning I will keep my word).*

WHAT PASSES HANDS?

"The wife's body does not belong to her alone but also to her husband. In the same way, the husband's body does not belong to him alone but also to his wife." (1 Cor 7:4)

Note that each partner "takes title" to the other's body. They literally take out a lifetime, exclusive sexual use lease of each other's bodies.

GOD IS THE OWNER OF YOUR BODY:

"Do you not know that your bodies are members of Christ himself? ... Do you not know that your body is a temple of the Holy Spirit, who is in you, whom you have received from God? You are not your own; you were bought at a price. Therefore honor God with your body." (1 Cor 6:15-20)

The Seal: God provides the seal of approval thru his blessing.
Consummate: Webster's' dictionary: "To finish or perfect; to **make marriage actual by sexual intercourse**."

So, each partner agrees to "lease" their body out to the spouse for their exclusive sexual use. The owner of our bodies - God - has given His permission for each of us to "lease" their body out to their spouse. Thus, if we want to use our bodies in a sexual way, we have

The Walk Applied

to get permission from 2 sources: the owner – God and the "lessor" – their spouse. Thus, if we misuse our body sexually, the terms of the lease have been broken. Therefore, either has broken the grounds of spiritual authority and submission. They are still legally married, to be sure, but the terms of the lease have been violated. God's proper and good authority and submission structure have been violated – which will ultimately lead to the chaotic if not mitigated.

THE STRUCTURE OF MARRIAGE

"For the husband is the head of the wife as Christ is the head of the church, his body, of which he is the Savior. Now as the church submits to Christ, so also wives should submit to their husbands in everything. Husbands, love your wives, just as Christ loved the church and gave himself up for her to make her holy."
(Eph 5:23-26)

It is interesting to note that the wedding installs the husband as the spiritual leader in the household - immediately. Marriage is vitally important as it gives us the image of God's government for the family. Ephesians tells us of comparison of Christ and His church and a husband and his wife. There is the preservation of the purity of the seed. Order is maintained via God's rules of the authority and submission structure. From all this we can conclude that marriage is nothing less than the establishment of a spiritual stronghold!

THE WEDDING OF ADAM AND EVE

"The LORD God said, "It is not good for the man to be alone. I will make a helper suitable for him." (Gen 2:18)

The story in Genesis 2 of the marriage of Adam and Eve is most significant. Verse 18 above tells us that Adam is apparently unaware that he needs someone. In the text there's no indication that

269

The Walk Applied

he feels he's missing anything. However, God recognizes that Adam is incomplete. Eve is described in the Hebrew as the "help meet" in the passage. She is his "ezer". This powerful Hebrew term means much more than someone to complement Adam. The root word used here can be translated "defender". It can also be construed to mean someone who brings water to someone who is in the desert and very thirsty. In other words, this isn't just some nice favor, this is someone who provides for a vital life need. That's what is meant when we say that Eve "completed" Adam by providing something that he desperately needed.

THE IMAGE OF GOD: THE "IMAGO DEI"

Let us recall that we are made in God's image:

*"Then God said, "Let us make man in our image, in our likeness, and let them rule over the fish of the sea and the birds of the air, over the livestock, over all the earth, and over all the creatures that move along the ground." So God created man in his own image, in the image of God he created him; **male and female he created them.** (Gen 1:26-29)*

The phrase "male and female he created them" is crucial. Males and females are both an incomplete image of God. Only when we are united together under the marital covenant are we a complete image of God. Otherwise, why would He tell us that the two have become one? Now, we ponder the following extraordinary passage:

"A man ought not to cover his head, since he is the image and glory of God; but woman is the glory of man. For man did not come from woman, but woman from man; neither was man created for woman, but woman for man. ... Nevertheless, in the Lord woman is not independent of man, nor is man independent of woman. For as woman came from man, so also man is born of woman. But everything comes from God." (1 Cor 11:7-12)

The Walk Applied

The above passage is quite profound. The text reflects on the incredible spiritual significance of marriage and what it all entails. We conclude that a Godly blessed marriage not only reflects a complete image of God, but also reinforces and integrates that a Godly marriage is far more significant that what we might have dared to think. He is not a mere observer; He is an active participant in the marriage.

THE MAKING OF ADAM AND EVE

Adam and Eve were not created by speaking them into existence where nothing existed prior. Instead, they were both made from pre-existing materials - still something only God could do. Adam came from dust, and Eve was fashioned from Adam's rib. By making Adam and Eve from different substances no one could ever say that they were somehow different from the rest of humanity. Indeed, Adam and Eve were just like us: formed from pre-existing material under a miraculous process that only God could do.

"So the LORD God caused the man to fall into a deep sleep; and while he was sleeping, he took one of the man's ribs and closed up the place with flesh. Then the LORD God made a woman from the rib he had taken out of the man, and he brought her to the man. The man said, "This is now bone of my bones and flesh of my flesh; she shall be called 'woman, ' for she was taken out of man." For this reason, a man will leave his father and mother and be united to his wife, and they will become one flesh. The man and his wife were both naked, and they felt no shame. (Gen 2:21-25)

""Haven't you read," he replied, "that at the beginning the Creator 'made them male and female,' and said, 'For this reason a man will leave his father and mother and be united to his wife, and the two will become one flesh'? So, they are no longer two, but one. Therefore, what God has joined together, let man not separate." (Mat 19:4-6)

271

The Walk Applied

"But at the beginning of creation God 'made them male and female.'
'For this reason, a man will leave his father and mother and be
united to his wife, and the two will become one flesh.' So they are
no longer two, but one. Therefore, what God has joined together,
let man not separate." (Mark 10:6-9)

AGAIN, THE ECHAD:

We recall that "echad" refers to an entity that is greater than the sum
of the parts. We become "one flesh". We are not 2 entities that are
somehow tied together by some sort of "contractual or covenantal
rope" if you will. When we get married, we become a living,
breathing, spiritual unity that's greater than the sum of the 2 natural
entities that make it up.

Only God can create. God takes 2 natural creatures and thru His
blessing on the word of the agreed upon covenant He creates
something that is completely new in the spiritual realm. Indeed, He
creates a new living, breathing, spiritual unity: a new spiritual image
of God! In Mark 10 we see why God is so vehement about divorce
and how much He hates it.

Marriage is God's mechanism for bringing about a complete image
of Himself that is created thru a blessed covenant. It is also His
chosen and blessed instrument for being fruitful and multiplying
and subduing the earth.

ADAM AND EVE AND THE LINE OF AUTHORITY

"The man said, "This is now bone of my bones and flesh of my flesh,
she shall be called 'woman,' for she was taken out of man." For this
reason, a man will leave his father and mother and be united to his
wife, and they will become one flesh. (Gen 2:23-24)

The Walk Applied

It is curious that Adam would pose a thought regarding "his father and mother". Adam certainly has no "biological parents". Why would he even say it? We can surmise that Adam has been taught by God, certainly.

This passage is telling us something very profound about how the spiritual realm works. Once again, we note that Adam is seemingly unaware that he needs someone. Adam certainly may have "complained" to God, which upon reflection, seems to make sense. After all, no one likes to be alone for very long. Yet, God's word implies there's no indication that Adam feels he's missing anything. God, however, knows Adam needs someone. We do know that Adam needs "completion" because the Word says so.

It is thru the union of two natural beings that they are "completed" thru the covenant of marriage. We reiterate to emphasize that the marriage covenant, when executed and blessed by God, creates a new spiritual unity. Further, it's a unity that mimics God and bears blessed fruit that builds up His kingdom. Marriage is His spiritual logistic - A spiritual mechanism created by God thru His blessing via his covenant word to achieve his purposes for subduing the earth thru the bearing of fruit.

Marriage is also His mechanism for letting us know that God knows what we need. Marriage is a spiritual device that operates in the natural. We are natural creatures who don't truly understand the spiritual. We don't understand what makes it go and we don't understand what makes it work. We need the lawgiver - the rule maker who is the one who set it all up to tell us how it works and how it operates within the framework of what we can understand.

The Walk Applied

AUTHORITY & SUBMISSION IN MARRIAGE

At this stage, it is worthwhile to review in depth the notion of how true authority and submission are supposed to work as God desires. In our day and age, we tend to think of authority and submission as if we were discussing a master-servant relationship. We might tend to think of the husband wife mechanism in terms of the husband being "in charge" and the wife as the submissive servant who is there to do the husband's bidding. This belief surrounding the marital unit is quite wrong. indeed! We recall earlier discussion of a significantly different interpretation of what the marital structure is like when we understand the true meaning of Godly authority and submission.

Webster's dictionary gives us the etymology of the word authority. "Author" comes from the Latin "augere" which means to create the conditions for growth. "Author" refers to "one who produces or brings into being or creates". The suffix "ity" means "the state of". Thus, authority can be construed to mean the constant state of creating the conditions for growth.

"Submission" can be interpreted to mean "line up under to support". Concrete supports are positioned in a certain way and are of sufficient weight and strength to hold up a massive building. When we submit to the valid authority of a given individual, we are contributing to the overall mission of the organism, as well as fomenting an environment of peace and harmony. In our context, that organism is the family. God, in His word, makes it clear that the Husband is in authority in the family unit. The New Testament (Ephesians in particular), does make it clear that we are to submit to one another's needs. The Husband is not to run roughshod over the wife or the children.

To have authority, you must have willing submission to the authority figure. To have Godly authority, you must have Godly submission. Without Godly authority and submission, you cannot have the conditions for growth - you can only have chaos. Without the conditions for growth, you can only have stagnation and death, chaos, confusion, and depression. Under these conditions, there can be no hope. Without hope, you cannot bear fruit and multiply and subdue.

WHY HUSBANDS ARE IN AUTHORITY OVER WIVES

The line of spiritual authority in marriage is established in 3 ways:

There must be Agreement by the Submitter to Submit
    The Seed Receiver and the Name Receiver chooses to Submit
        Without a Submitter, you cannot have an Authority

The Authority tenders the Covenant offer
        The Submitter may choose to accept or reject the offer
Upon Free Acceptance of the Authority's offer
        The Authority and the Submitter jointly enter
            Into the Covenant

The Name Giver is how Authority is established and conferred
        The Name Receiver is the Submitter
The Husband is the Name Giver and the Authority
        The Wife is the Submitter

The Seed Sower initiates the process of life and growth
        The Husband is the Seed Sower
            Therefore, Husband is the Authority
        The Wife is the Seed Receiver and agrees to Submission

In Luke 2, we see how God operated with Mary. The name giver was the Holy Spirit; He named the baby Jesus. The seed giver was the Holy Spirit; there was the passage of the seed from the Holy

The Walk Applied

Spirit to Mary, who was the submitter. Mary freely chose to submit to the name giver and the seed giver.

THE SEED

What happens to the seed? Genesis 1 points out that all living things reproduce after their own kind. Thus, the seed reproduces after its own kind. It sacrifices itself so that there can be growth. If the seed does not sacrifice itself, there can be no growth – no fruit. The husband is the seed sower. There needs to be consummation so that the seed can be passed. Webster's tells us that consummate means to "make marriage actual". In other words, there must be a passing of the seed so that growth can occur.

THE NAMING PROCESS

Naming is what gives us an identity and individuality. It's what allows us to place ourselves in a societal context. I can be called "Man". But "Man" does not establish who I am. My name is Nicholas, which gives me an individuality, but it's not enough. My last name is Marica, which gives me an identity. Marica gives me a family context. Marica puts me in a context in relation to others.

Who named me? My spiritual authority: my parents. It is this authority structure that names children. It was an echad who named me - a spiritual unity. I was created and blessed by God thru a covenant word that bore fruit. That is why I must honor both my mother and father. Not just that, but the echad that bore me also gave me a bloodline that gave me an identity and a heritage. Your bloodline determines who your authority is. You are the product of your "echad" whom God has designated as your authority.

"...honor your father and your mother, so that you may live long in the land the Lord your God is giving you." (Ex 20:12)

The Walk Applied

"...children obey your parents in the lord, for this is right. "honor your father and mother"- which is the first commandment with a promise - "that it may go well with you and that you may enjoy long life on the earth." (Eph 6:1-3)

"...for God said, 'honor your father and mother' and 'anyone who curses his father or mother must be put to death.'". (Mat 15:4)

Without valid authority and submission, the creation and maintenance of the conditions for growth cannot happen. We can have no context; there can be no structure. The inevitable result will be chaos and confusion and stagnation. The conclusion? We have the conditions for death if the proper authority and submission structure is not present. If we have the conditions for death there cannot be the conditions for growth.

WHY DID SATAN WAIT TO ATTACK?

Why didn't Satan attack Adam to begin with and be done with it? Why wait for Eve to come along? Think about it: what is the first thing that Adam did after the fall? Consider Gen 3:20:

"Adam named his wife Eve, because she would become the mother of all the living."

This is the first time Adam named Eve. What If Gen 3:20 was "Gen 2:26"? (Of course, there is no Gen 2:26!) It is likely we would not have fallen. Gen 2:20 is the first time Adam is named. Why did Adam name the animals in Genesis 2? What was God trying to show us? Adam had been named individually, thus, Adam had covering. Adam did call her a woman in Genesis 2, but Adam did not name her individually at that point in time. She had not received her name from her spiritual authority. Spiritual authority had not been established, so she never had the protective covering. Thus, it's likely this is why Satan waited to attack Eve. This is why we are

The Walk Applied

told about Adam naming the animals. That action of naming the animals was how Adam was establishing his authority. In addition, as long as Adam was alone, there was no passing of the seed. Without the seed, there was no chance for growth.

CONSUMATION

"… the man and his wife were both naked, and they felt no shame." (Gen 2:25)

The passage implies that there was consummation. They did see one another naked and she is his wife at this point. We certainly don't get any idea that she refused submission. But Adam had been named individually by God thus covering and protection had been extended over him. But Adam did not name the woman individually. She had not yet submitted to Adam's naming her – she was spiritually uncovered and exposed.

Again, we consider: Adam, by himself, could not bear fruit. Adam, by himself alone, could never "multiply". We note that in Genesis 3 "the eyes of both of them were opened" only after Adam followed Eve's lead in taking a bite of the fruit.

The preceding line of thought should also tell us something further about the extraordinary significance of the marriage echad. From Satan's standpoint, it was not enough that we fall. It was very important that the authority structure established by the marriage covenant be shattered. Marriage is the fruit bearing "machine" if you will. That's why Satan waited for Eve to come about. The conditions for growth had not yet been established. The authority-submission structure was not yet in place. Adam, of course, was the guilty party. What exactly was Adam guilty of?

The Walk Applied

"...therefore, just as sin entered the world through one man, and death through sin, and in this way death came to all men, because all sinned..." (Rom 5:12)

Let's re-examine the pertinent scriptures. We recall Gen 2:23:

"The man said, "This is now bone of my bones and flesh of my flesh; she shall be called 'woman,' for she was taken out of man."

Now, Gen 3:20:

"Adam named his wife Eve, because she would become the mother of all the living."

Consider: As the Spiritual authority, Adam was guilty of his misuse (actually, defaulting) of spiritual authority: He did not give her a new name until after the Fall. In Adam's omission of the appropriate use of his spiritual authority, Adam did not protect Eve. It was his duty to protect and spiritually cover her. Adam's job was to subdue, and he failed. He allowed Eve to be deceived, and in so doing, he allowed himself to be deceived. Adam did not handle spiritual authority properly. There are a number of ways to invalidate the authority-submission structure:

- Misuse/Default of authority
- Judgement & Self-seeking
- Rejecting the covering (not submitting)
- Invoking a curse
- Lack of repentance
- Unforgiveness: a form of judgement
- Invalid covenants: Anything other than one man one woman
- They must be competent so as to truly understand
	the ramifications of what they are doing

The Walk Applied

WHY NOT HOMOSEXUAL "MARRIAGE"

This is the appropriate place to comment on Homosexual "marriages". Homosexual marriages cannot and will never be blessed by God. Who is the husband? Who is the wife? Who is the authority figure? Who is the submitter? Who is the name giver? Where is the seed sowing? We are not allowed to change the fundamental structure of how God intended it all to work.

ON BEING THE SPIRITUAL LEADER

Marriage makes the husband the spiritual leader. The husband does not have to be the most biblically knowledgeable in the family. He just has to be the leader and act like it. The most Godly person that people know should be their husband or father. Advertise your growth in your relationship with God. Let your family see your spiritual growth. The Husband is the *spiritual* leader in the family. He is to be the leader in a *spiritual* way, not just in a *natural* way.

"Husbands, in the same way be considerate as you live with your wives and treat them with respect as the weaker partner and as heirs with you of the gracious gift of life, so that nothing will hinder your prayers. (1 Pet 3:7)

"Wives, submit to your husbands as to the Lord. For the husband is the head of the wife as Christ is the head of the church, his body, of which he is the Savior. Now as the church submits to Christ, so also wives should submit to their husbands in everything. Husbands, love your wives, just as Christ loved the church and gave himself up for her to make her holy…In this same way, husbands ought to love their wives as their own bodies. He who loves his wife loves himself" (Eph 5:22-32)

280

The Walk Applied

SPIRITUAL ISSUES IN MARRIAGE

Spiritual issues will affect all marriages. Temptation is a very obvious implication. Another implication of how the spiritual issues will affect marriage is that of judgement and self-seeking. We will first review the topic of how judgement and self-seeking work, and then examine how they can wreak havoc in a marriage

IDOLATRY

We recall that James and Romans teach that idolatry has devastating practical, day-to-day effects. Romans 2 itemizes for us the two main symptoms of idolatry: judgment and self-seeking. Romans 2:1 tells us we are all guilty and that none of us have any excuse. Romans 2:2 declares we all pass judgement, and we recall that we are not to judge. To judge means we take spiritual authority over others in ways we are not authorized to do. One example of this is when we refuse to forgive others. Further, Romans 2:8 describes "self-seeking" whereby we do things out of selfish interest such that we foment chaos (Greek "eritheia"). Romans 2:8-9 states that self-seekers reject truth and follow evil, and the four things that await self-seekers are "wrath, anger, trouble & distress". The root of judgement and self-seeking lies in the attempt to exert power and control over others - including those we are closest to. At this juncture, we'll review the all-important difference between the Satanic power-control mechanism versus the Godly authority-submission logistic.

Authority asks for your submission. True authority never seeks to exert power and control. This is what God seeks. God is love, and He only wants to support us and have us grow in Him. God asks for our loving submission to Him; God never demands our submission to Him.

281

The Walk Applied

Power demands and enforces control. This is what Satan does. Satan and His minions try to manipulate, cajole, threaten, incite, intimidate to get us to come under Satanic control. Satan's methods were exposed in the story of the temptation of Jesus. Power is demonstrated by control. Control is imposed on one by another for the purposes of advancing the controller's agenda. Control limits and stunts growth and ultimately only can bring about death and stagnation. Control is characterized by aggression, manipulation, withholding, criticism, intimidation, and fear, among others.

IN THE HOME

Ephesians 5:21 tells us that we are to submit to one another out of respect for Christ. We are to occupy our places in a Godly authority-submission structure. This is how we can best meet one another's needs. The Husband is to occupy the position of spiritual leader with great love, sensitivity, respect, and wisdom for those who have been placed in his spiritual care. The wife is to occupy the submissive role with the same characteristics as the leader: love, sensitivity, respect, and wisdom. To properly observe the Godly authority-submission mechanism is to ensure peace and harmony in the home.

When the wife attempts to take control and exert power over her husband, she assumes an office she is not delegated to have. When the husband misuses or defaults in his God-assigned authority, he is exercising sinful and unbiblical power and control. In either case, there will be chaos and discord. The fundamental, practical result will be that home is not a safe place for any of the occupants.

WHAT WE BRING INTO MARRIAGE

In the beginning of this book, we talked about how we are idolatrous, grossly sinful creatures who are driven by a relentless sinful flesh. Of course, we are capable of performing good actions and living decent, reasonable lives. It's why we tend to think of

282

The Walk Applied

ourselves as basically good people who sin from time to time, as opposed to the spiritual reality that we are idolaters. We are to compare ourselves to the absolute perfection of Jesus Christ and not conveniently rate ourselves against some imaginary yardstick that only exists to make us feel better about ourselves. Paul, the author of over half of the New Testament, certainly viewed himself from an idolatrous perspective. He claimed that he was "the chief of all sinners" (1 Tim 1:15).

The sobering reality is that the we enter marriage as idolaters who seek our own agenda. Very few married couples do not experience serious and significant problems that threaten their union. The divorce rate is sad testimony to the difficulties that marriage can bring.

We want to refresh our understanding of the overwhelming sinful idolatry that drives us as we enter marriage. They may be the 2 nicest, most congenial people in the world, but they are still idolaters, regardless. We re-present the highlights of the sinful idolatry systems:

THE SINFUL FLESH: THE FOUNDATION

SINFUL NATURAL FLESH: The foundational layer of the natural belief system – has 4 roots:

GUILT: The innate, gnawing paranoia of the knowledge that we
   have offended God.
SHAME: Our deep-seated regret that we offended God; the deep
   root of why we know something "is wrong with us".
INSECURITY: Since we have been separated from God,
   who will take care of us?
IDOLATRY: FALSE WORSHIP: Our innate need to seek that
   which will bring us security.

The Walk Applied

REBELLION IDOLATRY
"THE DELUSION OF CONTROL":

PRIDE: I am the authority; I am above God.
FAÇADE: I can control what others think by how I present myself.
SECURITY: Human institutions protect me.
PERFORMANCE: I can control my "position" in the community.
PLEASURE: A temporary escape from the chaotic and my shame.
ENTITLEMENT: I should have what you have; I am above you.

NEED IDOLATRY "FALSE WORSHIP":
WE WORSHIP THE CREATION; NOT THE CREATOR

PURPOSE: We all need a purpose.
PROVISION: We have fundamental physical needs.
HOME: We need a place we deem our own.
ACCEPTANCE: We need relationships with others.
KNOWLEDGE: The innate drive to know what we don't know.
IDENTITY: We all need to know what sets us apart from others.

THE SYMPTOMS OF IDOLATRY:
JUDGEMENT
SELF-SEEKING
EXPECTATIONS

MARRIAGE EXPECTATIONS

Because we live in an idolatrous world, we enter marriage with various emotional wounds as well as our own idolatry. Expectations about what marriage is and how it will work never fully match what our spouse brings. Cultural differences, family differences, personal history, and a host of other influences ensure that we are not 100% compatible, despite the passionate insistence that "rose-colored glasses" bring.

284

The Walk Applied

We all have expectations about what our future spouse should or should not do. Expectations are judgements that we expect our spouse to conform to. Many of these expectations are not critical and we find we can easily adjust. However, there are differences of expectations that are not so easily dismissed. How chores are handled, foods we eat, holiday traditions etc., can quickly grow into major bones of contention. Sex, money, in-laws - these areas, among others, can become areas of great conflict quickly. Living with another human being is stressful in and of itself and presents its own unique challenges.

When expectations about our spouse are not met or is not arbitrated to the satisfaction of both, it can lead to resentment. Over the years resentment can fester into anger and bitterness, perhaps even leading to separation and/or divorce. Expectations are a valid part of life and in many cases they are quite legitimate. My wife had the proper expectation that I would hold a job and support us. She had expectations that I would act like a mature adult (it happens every so often…). We both had expectations regarding the other. We both expected that we would be faithful to one another. We both expected that the money would be "ours" and not "each other's". Other couples may decide otherwise, and that's certainly fine. The important thing to remember is that to hold onto invalid judgments is to attempt to exercise power and control.

MARRIAGE AS A SAFE PLACE

There is no such thing as the perfect marriage. Marriage is a wonderful institution that God has given to us, and there is no other arrangement that even comes close. That is because God blesses us when we obey Him and seek His perfect purpose plan and will. Now we will consider some ways to make our marriages a "safe place".

The Walk Applied

HOSPITALITY IN MARRIAGE:
CREATING THE SAFE PLACE

The old adage goes like this: "You don't really know someone until you live with them". When a couple gets married, they don't really know one another. They may *think* they know one another, and they will likely insist they know one another, but ask just about anyone who has been married for several years or more. Indeed, the vast majority of couples are essentially "familiar strangers" when they get married. We may *think* we know a lot about one another when we get married, but to live with one another and all that living together as a married couple brings as part of a permanent relationship is for the most part a different realm of inquiry altogether.

Marriage tends to create a subtle undercurrent of apprehension amidst the excitement of being "hitched". Most are certainly familiar with the divorce rate. Virtually all of us know someone who has been divorced or affected significantly by a divorce. Without question, the vast majority of those who get married certainly deal with the nagging question of how to "make it work".

We just noted how we are fundamentally strangers when we enter into the marriage. We also recall how we bring judgement and self-seeking into our marriages and that we are still sinful idolaters. If we enter the marriage with so much against us, how in the world does *ANY* marriage survive? Obviously, many marriages "go the distance", so we have compelling proof that many marriages DO work. The question is: How?

After 25+ years of ministry to hurting men and couples, I have come to the conclusion that the main cause of marital problems is that home is not a safe place because of the aforementioned issues of

286

The Walk Applied

idolatry, judgement and self-seeking. Marriage can be the safe place many seek if we understand some basic principles.

MARRIAGE AS A SAFE PLACE: HOSPITALITY

Nouwen's book, "Reaching Out", provides an excellent starting place. Nouwen's take on hospitality is instructive and well worth pursuing. Nouwen notes that when we think of hospitality, we tend to think of it in terms of having people over for a meal or allowing them to stay in our homes for a few days. These are healthy and meaningful activities, and most Christians express them. Nouwen looks at the concept of Hospitality and what it means from a different context than we are typically accustomed to, and the results are truly illuminating.

Nouwen defines Hospitality as: "…the friendly reception and treatment of guests or strangers; the quality of receiving and treating guests and strangers in a warm, friendly, generous way." Nouwen also tells us that the German word for hospitality "*gastfreundschaft*" means "friendship for the guest" and that the Dutch word for hospitality "*gastvrijheid*" means "freedom for the guest". Nouwen takes this further when he writes: "…hospitality wants to offer friendship without binding the guest and freedom without leaving him alone".

Nouwen offers a radical take on hospitality: "…The creation of a free space whereby the stranger enters and becomes a friend, not an enemy to change them as we want, but allow them to change as God wants. The free space is not an invite to adopt the life style we might want, but it's a gift of a chance to change as God sees fit."

Agai, the sobering reality is that we enter marriage as "familiar strangers" who have significant expectations of our spouses. This is normal. The main emphasis here is to provide a safe, protected environment for each mate to grow and prosper as God directs. The

287

The Walk Applied

covenant commitment that each makes to each other provides the comfortable freeing boundary that helps us become what God wants us to be – and the Godly people we should want to be.

MARRIAGE AS A SAFE PLACE:
CARRY EACH OTHER'S BURDEN'S

"Carry each other's burdens, and ... you will fulfill the law of Christ." (Gal 6:2)

In this verse from Galatians, Paul makes a startling statement: "…you will fulfill the law of Christ". Few apply this ponderous verse to marriage. The imagery evoked by the passage is similar to that of when someone is carrying several bags of groceries and they are just barely holding on to that one bag with their little finger. If you help them out by taking hold of that little bag, the rest becomes much more manageable. In other words, that seemingly small help has a far larger contribution than the act itself. What Paul is telling us is that many times we help others far more by doing something simple, as opposed to taking their entire burden over as our own.

MARRIAGE AS A SAFE PLACE:
ACCOUNTABILITY

Accountability serves to provide an outlet to share with someone of the same sex that we trust. Ideally, we should be able to share everything with our spouse. However, we all have our weak spots that we are sensitive to. In addition, very few individuals are totally open about absolutely everything. The vast majority of spouses also need someone trustworthy who they can turn to when things are not going exactly right. No marriage is perfect, so wise marriage partners cultivate close relationships with others (of the same sex please!) to pray with, vent, and seek solid advice. Advice that was given to me by a very wise former pastor was: "you don't have to tell each other *everything!*" Eph 4:29 tells us:

288

The Walk Applied

"Do not let any unwholesome talk come out of your mouths, but only what is helpful for building others up according to their needs, that it may benefit those who listen."

There will be those times we must face unpleasant discussions. But there will be those instances - hopefully quite rare - that spouses will want to confide in a trusted confidante.

MARRIAGE AS A SAFE PLACE: PRAY TOGETHER

The practice of praying together is invaluable when it comes to a married couple. We recall that Pastor Burr pointed out that his observation was that after some 25+ years of pastoring, he had never seen a couple who prays together on a regular basis get a divorce. Yet, surveys show that only 5% of married couples do. Consider:

"Again, I tell you that if two of you on earth agree about anything you ask for, it will be done for you by my Father in heaven. For where two or three come together in my name, there am I with them." (Mat 18:19-20)

"This is the confidence we have in approaching God: that if we ask anything according to his will, he hears us. And if we know that he hears us - whatever we ask - we know that we have what we asked of him. (1 John 5:14-15)

MARRIAGE AS A SAFE PLACE: THE LAW OF PRAYER

Recall that the passage above from 1 John 5 was referred to as the Law of Prayer. Matthew tells us that whatever we agree on, it will be granted according to His perfect purpose, plan and will. Thus, we can make the assertion that if the two mates pray blessing on

289

The Walk Applied

their marriage and that God make it a successful and Godly marriage, then it will happen. Thus, Burr's contention that couples who pray together regularly has a strong scriptural justification.

MARRIAGE AS A SAFE PLACE:
THE BLESSING

We talked about the blessing earlier, and how it means to bring others under Godly authority. We also recall that the blessing, once issued, could not be taken away. Words matter, especially when we understand that God's word does not return to Him void. Wise mates will bless their spouse, families, and their marriage regularly. We need to take caution that in our words, we never curse our mate or our children or our union.

MARRIAGE AS A SAFE PLACE:
THE 5 LOVE LANGUAGES

Gary Smalley has written one of the most successful books (series, actually - there's several "flavors" of the book) on relationships ever produced, and with good reason. *"The Five Love Languages"* is a simple, easy to understand, yet quite profound book. Smalley's advice should be mulled over by every person who is married. There are dozens of web sites regarding the 5 love languages, so we'll only list the "languages" here. I encourage you strongly to read what's out there, and to read at least one of the books. Briefly, Smalley points out that the vast majority of us seek to receive love, intimacy and affirmation in some combination of 5 "languages". Few will only "speak" one of the below - most will react to 2 or 3. To be sure we want to express our love to our mate and children in all 5, but we should know for each person in our family at least what their major one is, and their "second" as well. The Love Languages:

WORDS OF AFFIRMATION: We all like to be affirmed by those closest to us. Frequent "I love you" as well as words of praise and

The Walk Applied

compliments (sincere, remember) are always welcome and refresh and deepen our relationships in ways we cannot begin to imagine.

TOUCH: Sincere affection and appropriate touching communicates acceptance and intimacy to others. Holding hands, embracing, affectionate kissing, etc., all say to others: I accept you as you are. NEVER underestimate the amazing and extraordinary power of touch. On the other hand, people do have boundaries regarding how and why they are touched, and it is only common courtesy to observe them. For example, when it comes to men, my wife prefers to be hugged only by me and other close male relatives. Also, she doesn't like it when I hug other women who I am not related to, so I try to observe that boundary, as well. Since I'm a "touchy feely" type, she also is concerned that other women might be offended as well.

Now, I just spent more than twice as much space talking about how careful you have to be with touch as opposed to espousing how wonderful appropriate touching can be. This is a testimony to the extraordinary power of touch. Properly used in your family, it refreshes, encourages, and assures others. It says, "I love you" and "I accept you" and reinforces your words of affirmation. Appropriate, welcomed touch expresses these sentiments far more than mere words.

QUALITY TIME: Spending time with someone is another way of saying "I love you" and "I accept you". When we say quality, it means just that: no surfing on the smartphone allowed! It means to be occupied by and with them for them. Kathy loves to watch the Hallmark channel at Christmas time. From Thanksgiving to New Years, Hallmark gives us a 24x7 stream of sappy Christmas movies. She knows I don't care for them, but I watch them with her. I do it because I love her. When I watch them with her, it is quality time for her. Sometimes she just wants me to sit with her.

The Walk Applied

Quality time can be expressed in many ways. Walks together or simply conversing are but two examples of a myriad of ways that we can carve out time for each other. It goes without saying that this works for your kids, too. Need more ideas on how to spend quality time? That's what the 'net is for! There's dozens, if not hundreds of sites that have great suggestions! Look 'em up!

GIFTS: Everyone loves gifts - especially other than birthdays and Christmas! For many, gifts speak a language of acceptance and intimacy like no other. You just cannot replace the smile and the joy many people experience when they are surprised with a thoughtful gift. It says: "You are special, and I appreciate how special you are".

Of course, gifts should be used appropriately. Many people have boundaries - they may think you are being too "forward" or they may be suspicious of your motives.

ACTS OF SERVICE: Almost everyone enjoys a nice favor or the gift of having someone perform a gracious act "simply because". I'm retired, and Kathy is still working (she is 10 years younger than me). Our children are grown, and her act of service by continuing to work brings in needed income and provides wonderful benefits that we could not afford otherwise. In return, I'm up with her at 5:30 am. I bring her hot coffee when she's done with her shower. I make her breakfast and her lunch for her, and it save her lots of time in the morning. Dinner is usually ready when she gets home. I do the laundry and our youngest, Valerie, takes care of the house cleaning as her contribution. Acts of service speaks volumes – never underestimate them!

BRING ABOUT CHANGE:
BRINGING YOUR MARRIAGE UNDER GOD'S CONTROL

There is no such thing as the perfect marriage. Virtually all marriages experience some strife. Sometimes, professional or

The Walk Applied

pastoral help is certainly called for. However, The Bible gives us wise instruction as to how we can bring about needed change by going to the Fathers throne.

REPENT AND ASK FORGIVENESS

First, we need to ensure that we are truly under Godly authority. This means we must go through the formality of repenting before God. We want to be sure we declare our submission before Him. In addition, we want to be sure that we have been forgiven for our sins, which is the simple business of sincerely asking God for forgiveness. This can be accomplished in a session of prayer.

WE MUST FORGIVE OUR SPOUSE

The bible tells us that if we do not forgive others, He will not forgive our sins. (Matt 6:15) This action is pivotal if we want to experience change in our marriage.

SEEK GOD AND ASK HIM FOR WISDOM

James tells us that we can be certain if we ask for wisdom, He will grant it. We are to believe it and simply trust in what He wants us to do. He is pretty emphatic about it and minces no words, to say the least:

"... If any of you lacks wisdom, you should ask God, who gives generously to all without finding fault, and it will be given to you. But when you ask, you must believe and not doubt, because the one who doubts is like a wave of the sea, blown and tossed by the wind. That person should not expect to receive anything from the Lord. Such a person is double-minded and unstable in all they do." (James 1:5-8)

293

The Walk Applied

Many are understandably confused by how the passage works in our lives. Some Christians will tell you that they hear directly from God via a "mental voice". Others report that God will communicate wisdom thru teaching or a sermon. Still others will describe a vison or a dream. Some may say that a passage from a book they have read ministered to them. People may tell of a verse that was particularly profound for them at the time. He might put someone in your path who can impart wisdom to you. There's any number of ways that God may choose to communicate to you.

PRAY, PRAY, PRAY - THEN PRAY SOME MORE!

We thank God that He will do what is necessary to be done to change us, as well as our spouse. Remember the law of prayer: Anything you pray according to His purpose plan and will be answered. The same thing goes when you and your spouse pray together.

The preceding thoughts outline the Biblical way you can bring about change in your spouse. God will change your spouse as they open their heart to change. Bringing about change in your spouse is accomplished by praying them under the authority of God. Be patient, sit back and watch them change as God works. They may even get worse at first as God works out idols and sin in them. Oh, and by the way: He will likely change you, too!

CHILDREN &
THE INTENTIONAL INVESTMENT

We recall at this point our discussion of the "Intentional Investment". We as parents are to "Intentionally Invest" in our children. Indeed, your offspring are the most important disciples you will ever have! You get the opportunity to deal with someone who is a virtually a "blank slate".

294

The Walk Applied

Our purpose in raising children is to Intentionally Invest in your children so as to raise up Godly submitters to prepare them be Godly authority figures who will bear lasting fruit for the kingdom.

Saying this is a whole lot easier than doing it, of course, as any parent will attest to. Kids mimic their parents, so it's vital that parents model Biblical principles. Teaching your kids to pray, having home Bible studies and devotion times play a substantial role in training them as a Godly submitter. Going to church and participating in church activities are critical towards laying the foundation of turning your young Godly submitter into a Godly authority figure as they reach adulthood. The doing is important, of course, but even more important is the why of the doing. Making sure they understand the why will be hyper-critical as they enter the adult world. The secular world eagerly awaits the opportunity to destroy in your child what you took years to build.

Many children go thru a rebellious phase, and unfortunately walk away from their parents teaching. All kids are different, and the stories of how kids can turn out differently from what they are taught are legion. Proverbs 22:6 will hold true the vast majority of the time: *"Start children off on the way they should go, and even when they are old they will not turn from it."* Thus, it is up to US as parents to start them off right.

THE INTENTIONAL INVESTMENT PLANNING FOR YOUR CHILDREN

"...bring them up in the training and instruction of the Lord." (Eph 6:4):

...Applies to far more than just bringing up your children in a Godly home. We need to plan what we want to teach to our children. We simply can't expect that our kids will just absorb what we want them

295

The Walk Applied

to know or practice. Developing and executing a plan is one of the best things you can do for your children. What values do we want to implant in our children? What kinds of behaviors do we want to instill? Do we somehow just expect them to know how to do the things we want? Following this thought will allow you to be proactive instead of merely being reactive.

The prior paragraph implies that we actually sit down and come up with a plan. Yes, that is exactly what it means. It means to discuss with your spouse how you should proceed when it comes to raising your children. The plan does not have to be overly formal or intricately planned to the last detail. It's intuitive that these approaches won't work. There has to be wide latitude in how the plan is laid out. As we ponder how we want to guide and teach our kids, we may think of things such as:

Know Jesus	Read the Bible	Go to Church
Handle Money	Be Honest	Do Chores
Be Thankful	Develop work habits	Pray regularly
Be Polite	Develop patience	

Next to each topic, you might want to jot down how you will approach each one. Again, it shouldn't be overly ambitious or detailed. It's meant to be a general guide to allow you to be proactive in training your children. Great flexibility is key, and you'll need to re-evaluate the how as you go.

OF KIDS AND MARSHMALLOWS

A good test to try with your children around the age of 4 is the infamous and brilliant marshmallow experiment. Developed by Walter Mischell of Stanford, this simple yet profound exercise will give you great insight into your child's ability to defer gratification - a vitally important skill in our modern society.

296

The Walk Applied

You can read in far greater detail the ins and outs of the experiment, but here's the gist: Put your toddler in a non-descript room that has little to occupy their attention. The less to distract them, the better. Have a table and a chair ready. On the table, put a marshmallow or an equally inviting treat (a pretzel or a cookie or a piece of chocolate, etc.). Explain that you need to leave, but that you will be back very soon. Tell your child that they can have the treat in front of them, but if they wait to eat the treat until you get back, they'll get another treat, and they can then have both - but they can have both only if they wait. Stress that they will only get one if they consume the treat while you are gone. You can see some hilarious videos on the 'net of kids who have great difficulty as they "sweat it out" while deciding if waiting is worth it or not.

Mischell later found that children who "waited" in the original experiment seemed to have an almost innate sense of delayed gratification, or that it had already been communicated to them somehow. Follow up efforts over the years indicated a congruence between the kids who exhibited the ability to delay gratification and greater "life success".

297

The Walk Applied

If you administer the test and your kid doesn't show that they can exhibit delayed gratification, certainly don't fret or worry. It's your signal that perhaps it's time to teach your child that it's ok to be patient, and that waiting can be a good thing.

SEXUALITY IN MARRIAGE

It is indeed unfortunate that our society has turned sexuality into a mass, open-air market display for all - regardless of age - to see. The problems in our society vis-à-vis being awash in pornography and immorality are well documented, and do not need to be re-hashed here.

Per what you and your spouse agreed to in your marriage vows at the altar, marriage gives you that safe space to express your sexuality. Marriage reserves you and your spouse exclusively for one another for a lifetime. Many in our immoral, secular society proclaim that remaining faithful to one another ranges anywhere from "stupid" to "impossible". Yet, there is little doubt that those couples who stay together and remain faithful are the happiest and most content. Divorce and infidelity are life-changing propositions - not just for the couple, but for their children and extended families as well.

The Song of Solomon is that terrific book of the bible that is often associated with sexuality. The prose of the book celebrates marital fidelity and encourages reveling in one another in a "garden of delights". In the New Testament, Paul encourages us to "come together often". The advice from here is to seek to satisfy one another in many ways and often. There are numerous valuable resources on sexuality and intimacy, and married couples should investigate them. There are also many good Christian resources that approach marital intimacy frankly and openly.

CHAPTER 10
RESTORATION

The Walk Applied

CHAPTER 10
RESTORATION

HEALING, RENEWAL, & RESTORATION:

"Brothers and sisters, if someone is caught in a sin, you who live by the Spirit should restore that person gently. But watch yourselves, or you also may be tempted. Carry each other's burdens, and in this way you will fulfill the law of Christ." (Gal 6:1-2)

"And the prayer offered in faith will make the sick person well; the Lord will raise them up. If they have sinned, they will be forgiven. Therefore, confess your sins to each other and pray for each other so that you may be healed. The prayer of a righteous person is powerful and effective." (James 5:15-16)

HEALING: TO MAKE WHOLE AGAIN

To heal means to take what is broken and make it whole again. The large majority of Christians come to Jesus because they are hurting in one way or another and want to be healed. Indeed, you can ask most Christians to give their testimony and invariably you will hear a story of significant personal pain and perhaps tragedy. Many of these testimonies are incredibly heartbreaking.

HEALING:
TO BE AT A RELATIVE LEVEL OF PEACE

We define a healed Christian as one who is at a *relative* level of peace. Because we are all idolatrous sinners who live in a driven flesh, it is rare to run across a Christian who is perfectly at peace. That said, there are numerous Christians who have come to terms with their personal hurts and tragedies that may have occurred in

301

The Walk Applied

their lives. How do we reach that "relative" level of internal peace? Many Christians who deal with significant anxiety or pronounced depression cannot imagine a life of peace.

True healing involves being in a faithful, trusting, and right relationship with Christ and being at peace and rest with God's will for your life. It also involves full loving submission to God as the one true living God of the Universe. The Bible discusses peace numerous times and lets us know in no uncertain terms that as we walk with God over our lifetime, it is the day to day relationship with God that counts. It is through this incredible and awesome intimacy with God that we achieve peace and rest. Jesus told us:

"Come to me, all you who are weary and burdened, and I will give you rest. Take my yoke upon you and learn from me, for I am gentle and humble in heart, and you will find rest for your souls. For my yoke is easy and my burden is light." (Matt 11:28-30)

Please note that healing does not mean that your life will be easy and luxurious. Healing does not mean that you must lead a life that is ascetic - a life that means rigid denial of any and all comforts (although some do!). What is important to realize is that we are called to walk a path in full submission to His purpose plan and will. Truly, it is when we are on that path that we will have rest and peace.

Crises therapists will tell you that the object of therapy is to return the victim to a relative state of peace, so they can integrate and deal with their misfortune in a reasonably healthy way. Obviously, people who are victims of maladies will vary widely in how and how long it can take them to heal.

Ministering to Christians can be much the same. We are not necessarily here to fully heal those who are hurting, but to come alongside and assist them in spiritual ways as well as Biblical modes of healing and restoration. We maintain that there will be

302

The Walk Applied

individuals who will indeed be healed and restored by our sincere and heartfelt "intentional investment" in them. Of course, the praise and the honor and the glory goes to God for putting us in position to assist those who are hurting.

WHAT IS FUNDAMENTALLY WRONG WITH US:
A BRIEF REVIEW
IDOLATRY – THE 12 IDOLS.

We recall our discussion of the Sin nature (the Flesh) and the twelve belief idols that comprise our belief system.

THE SINFUL FLESH: THE FOUNDATION

SINFUL NATURAL FLESH: The foundational layer of the natural belief system – has 4 roots:

GUILT: The innate paranoia that we know we offended God.
SHAME: Our deep-seated regret that we offended God; the deep root of why we feel that something "is wrong with us".
INSECURITY: We have been separated from God, who will take care of us?
IDOLATRY: False worship: Our innate need to seek that which will bring us security.

REBELLION IDOLATRY:
"THE DELUSION OF CONTROL"

PRIDE: I am the authority; I am above God.
FAÇADE: I can control how others perceive me.
SECURITY: Human institutions protect me.
PERFORMANCE: I can control my "position" in the community.
PLEASURE: Temporary escape from the sinful chaotic.
ENTITLEMENT: I should have what you have; I am above you.

The Walk Applied

PURPOSE: We all need a purpose.
PROVISION: We all require provision.
HOME: We all need a place to call our own.
ACCEPTANCE & INTIMACY: We all need others in our lives.
KNOWLEDGE: The innate drive to know what we don't know.
IDENTITY: We all require a way to distinguish ourselves.

THE SYMPTOMS OF IDOLATRY(Rom 2:1-10)

JUDGEMENT: To the fullest extent possible, we must not allow ourselves to be judged by others.
SELF-SEEKING: Self-seeking come from the Greek word, "eritheia", which means "chaos". Self-seeking results in "wrath, anger, trouble, and despair", according to Romans 2:8-9.
EXPECTATIONS: Expectations is a form of judgement. In general, we expect (read: judge) people to act and treat us in a given way when all we can realistically expect is sinful behavior.

DR. DAVID STOOP:
"YOU ARE WHAT YOU THINK"
ATTITUDE IS EVERYTHING

Stoop begins his terrific book "You Are What You Think" with this phrase: "Attitude is everything!" It is no exaggeration to say that our attitude determines if we will be successful this life or not. Attitude describes how we choose to approach others and how we assess and react to situations in our lives. We can either see situations or problems as opportunities to excel and succeed, or we can view the same situations or problems as too daunting and too fearful. Even times when it seems everything on the planet is stacked against us there will surely be alternatives. God is always there!

304

The Walk Applied

God is surely not about the business of seeing us fail. He has a purpose plan and will for us that He expects us to seek and follow. We must remember that our earthly "success" is not the object. Being faithful in our day to day walk is the object; it is the definition of success. It is no exaggeration to say that the definition of success in God's eyes is: Did we follow the path He set out for us?

Joseph is perhaps the ultimate example of someone who despite all odds, followed the path. Joseph was a spoiled braggart that his brothers despised – so much so that Joseph's brothers sold him into slavery and lied to their father. Joseph persevered despite horrendous circumstances over a prolonged period of time and learned how to be humble under the most severe conditions. Joseph's attitude was: There's a way, despite everything that confronted him.

In God's economy, there is always a way. Even under the worst of circumstances, what God asks of us is to trust and believe and be faithful. Thus, our attitude should be: What does God want? What is His purpose plan and will for us in the worst of circumstances?

This logistic applies to our past as well. You may have been a victim of abuse by one of your close relatives. Any number of tragic things may have happened in your life. Yet, our attitude determines virtually everything. If your attitude is rooted in Jesus and His ecstatic love for you, you will be able to overcome. If your attitude is rooted in resentment and bitterness, your life can be a living hell. Attitude play a foundational and pivotal role in healing.

The Walk Applied

UNDERSTANDING OUR EMOTIONS
AND OUR ATTITUDE IN CONTEXT

Stoop's basic premise postulates that our attitude is largely governed by how our foundational belief system has been formed. Stoop presents an excellent discussion and summary of the "Fight/Flight/Freeze" logistic of human behavior. Stoop points out that most commentators on the science of human behavior see essentially 3 forms of human emotions: Love, Anger, and Fear. For convenience, we repeat this graphically using four foundational attitude types. We expand on them here to include subtle but significant distinctions to make the dynamic more complete. The arrow symbols in the parenthesis indicate if we are drawn towards or away from a relationship.

ACCEPTANCE (DRAWCLOSE/CREATE BOND) (--->|<----)
AVOIDANCE: DISLIKE (FLIGHT): (<---|<---->)
AVOIDANCE: FEAR (FLIGHT): (<---|<---->)
CONTROL: ANGER (FIGHT): (--->|<--->)
FREEZE (IGNORE) (<---|---->)

ACCEPTANCE
(DRAW CLOSE / CREATE BOND): LOVE / LIKE
Belief: See the possibilities; manifests as loving.
(--->|<----)

Love and Acceptance indicates drawing closer to one another. We all want to be liked and loved. We want to have strong bonds of love with family. Most yearn for an exceptionally strong bond of love and intimacy with one other that they deem exclusive. Indeed, marriage continues to be highly desired in our society.

Acceptance: This attitude type should be what we ultimately experience as Christians. It is an attitude of love, forgiveness, giving, and service. We are salt and light, and we see our

The Walk Applied

circumstances and situations in terms of Christ. Paul talks about what our attitude should be:

"In your relationships with one another, have the same mindset as Christ Jesus: Who, being in very nature God, did not consider equality with God something to be used to his own advantage; rather, he made himself nothing by taking the very nature of a servant, being made in human likeness. And being found in appearance as a man, he humbled himself by becoming obedient to death— even death on a cross! ...Do everything without grumbling or arguing, so that you may become blameless and pure, "children of God without fault in a warped and crooked generation." Then you will shine among them like stars in the sky as you hold firmly to the word of life. And then I will be able to boast on the day of Christ that I did not run or labor in vain. (Phil 2:4-16)

As we have discussed, many will need healing from our Orphaned Spirit. Various influences of idolatrous, sinful people and living in a sinful world - along with our own idolatry in our sinful nature - will lead many to have a foundational attitude of fear or anger. It seems intuitive that we will surely have vestiges of both, but it is also highly likely that one or the other will be dominant.

AVOIDANCE: FLIGHT RESPONSE
DISLIKE (AVOID)
Belief: Avoid situations/people; manifests as avoidance.
(<---|<---->)

Dislike is essentially a type of avoidance. It manifests when we are neither angry nor fearful of a given person, but we simply prefer to avoid an individual because of personality differences. To dislike means we are not experiencing pronounced negative emotions; we are simply expressing a preference to not be in that person's presence. While it would be nice that everyone would like everyone

The Walk Applied

else, it is reality that many people simply do not get along with certain others.

AVOIDANCE: FLIGHT RESPONSE
FEAR (FLIGHT); ANGER (AVOID)
Belief: Push away or confront; manifests as control.
(<---|<----)

Avoidance is exhibited in stronger terms when fear or anger are involved. When we perceive danger, we can exhibit fear or anger (or both), which can cause us to avoid. In most cases involving fear, we likely want to extricate ourselves from the situation in hopes that withdrawal or retreat mitigates the situation.

FEAR: Those who operate out of fear are usually seen in those who are reticent to develop relationships and avoid new situations. They build emotional walls and typically seek security by avoiding others. They tend to be overwhelmed by life. There can be a pronounced tendency to see their security in their job. Setbacks can crush them emotionally. The New Testament addresses the topic of our fear directly:

"For God has not given us a spirit of fear and timidity, but of power, love, and self-discipline." (2 Tim 1:7 NLT)

FEAR (FREEZE)
Belief: manifest as avoidance
(<---|--->)

Fear can trigger the "freeze" response, leading to indecision or worse. A person can literally be "stuck" for weeks, months or ever years. Quite often, an individual will be looking for the "perfect" alternative to a given problem or troubling situation. People who live fearfully will find that they simply cannot reconcile various alternatives, even though there is almost never a "perfect" solution

308

The Walk Applied

Some even bypass obvious beneficial situations simply because they are too afraid to take the first step.

CONTROL FIGHT RESPONSE
ANGER(CONFLICT)
(--->|<--->)

Anger and Fear can trigger the fight response, bringing on or exacerbating conflict. Unfortunately, there are times when conflict may be the only way to resolve an ongoing clash.

ANGER: Those who operate out of anger typically exhibit pronounced controlling tendencies. They are very likely quick tempered and can be confrontational. They may be manipulative and will usually go to significant efforts to present an elaborate façade of themselves so as to intimidate. They tend to be mistrusting of others. Once again, the Bible instructs us:

"Get rid of all bitterness, rage and anger, brawling and slander, along with every form of malice." (Eph 4:31)

Those who operate out of attitudes of fear and anger are people who will have great difficulty achieving peace in their lives. Healing can and often is a long and arduous road for people like this. They very rarely trust others (much less God) and can harbor great resentment. They can exhibit great anger at God for their circumstances. Their lives are typically very stressful. Since trust is at a minimum, they often regard attempts to befriend them with great suspicion.

The Walk Applied

"SELF-TALK": WHAT WE
REALLY BELIEVE ABOUT OURSELVES

Stoop asserts that, by and large, we are circumstance driven.:

"If good things happen to us, we are happy and satisfied. If bad things happen to us, we feel sad or mad.... we spend all kinds of effort trying to rearrange our circumstances of our lives to insure our happiness.... We have been taught to believe that our feelings and emotions are determined by the events in our lives."

Put differently, we may interpret events in our lives with reactions that are way out of line with what actually happened. If I typically operate out of anger, I might jump to the conclusion that you did not return my phone call because you are rude and insensitive. You're such a jerk! I can get angry with no justification whatsoever. If I tend to operate out of fear, I might think that you don't like me because I am stupid and ugly. These examples tend to the extreme, but the critical factor that influence how we respond is what we believe about ourselves: i.e., what and how we think. Hopefully, both you and I are more mature than the examples given! (Don't ask my wife…)

Stoop advocates that our belief system governs how we will interpret events that happen in our lives. He calls these events "Activating events". So, when you fail to return my phone call that might be an "activating event" for me. My belief system might be fear driven, so when I "filter" your non-action thru my "fear" belief system, my conclusion will probably be that you don't like me. I might feel that there's "something wrong with me" such that you have chosen to ignore me. This thinking can send a fearful person off into a maelstrom of negative thinking that can affect them for days!

The Walk Applied

OUR THOUGHT LIFE
CREATES OUR EMOTIONS

Stoop points to Proverbs 23:7 which says: *"As a man thinks in his heart so he is"*. In other words, between our sinful nature and potential demonic influence (2 Cor 10: 3-7; Eph 6:12), we often think far worse of ourselves than we really are. Stoop notes we constantly compare ourselves to others instead of seeing ourselves as God sees us. The bible tells us that God loves us extravagantly! Psalm 139 reinforces the notion that God only thinks thousands of good thoughts about us.

OUR THOUGHT LIFE
AFFECTS/DICTATES OUR BEHAVIOR

Once again, Proverbs 23:7 is applicable *"As a man thinks in his heart so he is"*. If we have negative, ungodly emotions rooted in a negative thought life, then our actions will almost always be negative. What we believe about what is occurring is what will usually matter most to us. A good friend of mine likes to say: "perception creates reality". How we perceive a situation is often more important to us than what actually happened. We constantly filter events and situations through our biases rooted in our belief system. If we have a biased, faulty belief system, we will see events and situations through our faulty and biased system.

BECAUSE WE ARE IDOLATORS,
WE TEND TO THINK "IRRATIONALLY"

Stoop notes that we are sinful, self-seeking idolaters who quite often see what happens in our lives from a skewed and sinful point of view. Thus, we do not think "rationally" many times even though we may vigorously insist that we are thinking properly. Often, we can exhibit self-seeking while advocating our agenda so as to benefit our façade and other idols. We may choose to achieve our

The Walk Applied

earthly goals, wants, and desires as opposed to following the path that Jesus wants us to. Surely, many Christians have made more than their share of sinful choices knowing full that what they were doing was wrong but did it anyway.

ANXIETY: THE LACK OF PEACE

Anxiety is rooted in our idolatry as well as judgement and self-seeking. Anxiety is defined here as an overall and profound lack of peace, regardless of the cause. Anxiety is a good overarching term to sum up our "wrath, anger, trouble, and despair". Where our anxiety is coming from and the degree to which we have anxiety is a good indicator of the source and "depth" of our idolatry. The depth of our anxiety indicates how "dedicated" we are to a given idol. It is axiomatic that our idolatry will run the spectrum of the 12 idols that the Walk Applied posits. That said, some idols will be stronger and more pronounced in us than others.

Worry, stress, grief, depression, anger, bitterness, resentment, etc., are but a few of the many conditions that will rob of us our peace to one degree or another. Fear and despair represents other kinds of anxiety as well.

We live in a sinful fallen world that is beset with innumerable sin issues. It's virtually impossible to live without experiencing anxiety over SOMETHING. Yet, the Bible teaches us that we are to be at peace *in Jesus*. The significance of the distinction that our peace is to be in Jesus is of paramount importance:

"I have told you these things, so that in me you may have peace. In this world you will have trouble. But take heart! I have overcome the world." (John 16:33)

So, we will have trials, problems and issues. We will not go thru this life somehow "unscathed". But when we view our issues

312

The Walk Applied

through the "lens" of Jesus, it brings vital context to our trials and tribulations. Seeing life thru the "Jesus lens" means there is a purpose to our suffering – even when we don't see it or understand it. Indeed, we are asked to walk in faith regardless of our circumstances:

"Who among you fears the LORD and obeys the word of his servant? Let the one who walks in the dark, who has no light, trust in the name of the LORD and rely on their God. But now, all you who light fires and provide yourselves with flaming torches, go, walk in the light of your fires and of the torches you have set ablaze. This is what you shall receive from my hand: You will lie down in torment." (Isa 50:10-11)

None of us are so stoic as to assume that we will never experience deep levels of various types of anxiety. We are human, after all. Death of a loved one, serious illness, tragedy, injury, assault, emotional trauma, and financial setbacks as well as any number of other maladies all serve to remind us of how very fragile we are and can indeed bring on extraordinary levels of loss and grief. These are normal, and they should be expected over a person's lifetime. We need to learn how to manage anxiety as it occurs in our life. In cases where anxiety become unmanageable, we may need professional help.

THE ORPHANED SPIRIT &
PTSD: (POST-TRAUMATIC STRESS DISORDER)
(The Orphaned Spirit is reproduced here for convenience.)

The Orphaned Spirit phenomena most often occurs when you believe that you were abandoned, betrayed, rejected or deeply hurt by your spiritual authority (usually your biological parents). Primarily, those who have an orphaned spirit will describe their experience as a profound deprivation of acceptance & intimacy. There is almost always a feeling of helplessness; there is an

The Walk Applied

overwhelming sense of a lack of security. Paranoia is common because there is the sense that security is for all intent and purposes totally and completely absent. In the vast majority of cases, there is a pronounced and tragic sense of violation. It goes without saying many feel horribly victimized - helpless and powerless playthings who were objects of some gross malevolent evil. There is no denying that the vast majority of these sad cases do have good reason for their hurt, anger and bitterness. They did not ask to be born; yet they were subjected to an environment that was outrageous sinful and unspeakable things may have been foisted on them.

Of course, the Orphaned Sprit does not just occur in a family setting. Trauma that precipitates the Orphaned Spirit can come from any number of sources: tragedy, attack, and war are but a few. Any number of emotional abuses that may bring on the Orphaned Sprit include bullying, humiliation, criticism, being demeaned or dismissed, being belittled, contempt by others – just to name a few. The same symptoms enumerated in the prior paragraph certainly apply here as well.

Those who deal with an Orphaned Spirit tend to hold on to their overwhelming anger and hurt for years and even decades. Tragically, many go to their grave after holding on to the enormous bitterness that made life a living hell. People who choose to live this way typically experience massive depression; many finally commit suicide to escape the overwhelming anguish.

There is no escaping that we live in a sinful, depraved world whereby there is virtually no limit to the evil and depravity. The Bible tells us as much. We are all sinners. Jeremiah has stunning news for us: ""The human heart is _the_ most deceitful of all things and desperately wicked." Unfortunately, our families, our relatives and our friends and acquaintances - all of our "people circles" - are not excluded. Jeremiah's statement tells us that all of us are dark

314

The Walk Applied

hearted sinners who are capable of anything we can think of despite our fervent pleas and fantasies that insist that we are surrounded by good and decent people. And many times we are involved with people who truly loving and treat us well.

But let us recall our discussion of expectations. As we discussed earlier, the only thing we can realistically expect out of anyone is sinful behavior. We can hope and pray that things turn out nicely, but the stark truth is very often the opposite. The people closest to us - the ones who we expect will treat us lovingly and honorably - simply do not, and deeply hurt and violate the ones they are supposed to love.

When we are young, often we believe parents and adults are "perfect". Since we perceive that they are perfect, if they hurt us, the problem must somehow be us. We must have done something to have this done to us. Therefore, we can tend believe that something must be wrong with us! We see this lots of times when parents are divorced. The kids are perfectly innocent, but many children feel they are the problem. This kind of unneeded guilt and shame can persist for years and even decades.

Yet, that does not mesh with another fundamental belief that we should not be mistreated. We have a natural belief: they shouldn't do that! They are supposed to be our security! We want protection and love from those who are supposed to protect us. The innate fight or flight response also kicks in. Many times, we simply can't escape; we are trapped.

Again, our discussion should not be construed to be limited to the immediate family. The extended family can certainly be complicit as well as the community at large. Unmitigated, all of these influences breed ever growing anger, resentment and bitterness over the years and decades. The heart, over time, turns to emotional stone, and the notion of forgiveness becomes virtually impossible.

315

The Walk Applied

Yet, we are not only called to forgive, we are called to forgive the unforgivable. God tells us that we must forgive, or He will not forgive us. Despite how difficult it may be, true forgiveness is something we must bring ourselves to do. If we do not forgive, we will likely never achieve a state of true peace.

Many who deal with an Orphaned Spirit will find that they are contributing to their suffering, as hard as that might be to accept. Many recoil at that statement and understandably so. After all, "How dare they do that?!?!" Romans Chapter 2:8-9 tells us that because of our unmet expectations - a form of judgment - we "are self-seeking and [we] reject the truth and follow evil... [The result is] wrath and anger... trouble and distress for every human being who does evil.

The Orphaned Spirit is a complex topic and a few paragraphs here and there do not give the proper respect to its importance. However, we can comment here on a couple of topics where the notion of the Orphaned Spirit is applicable.

PTSD has been typically associated with the military and those who have been in combat. The horrific violence, the sights, sounds and smells of action are unimaginable by those who have never experienced the horrors of war. The terrible memories are without question unforgettable and nightmarish. The litany of symptoms and behaviors for veterans who suffer from PTSD is lengthy and heart-breaking.

But PTSD is certainly not limited to veterans of combat. The list of those who might display symptoms of PTSD is lengthy: Victims of abuse. Crime victims. Accident victims. Incest victims. Those who have experienced tragedy of almost any kind can certainly expect to exhibit symptoms of PTSD to one degree or another. The heartbreak is brutal and palpable in many cases.

The Walk Applied

A common trait that's often observed with PTSD is the absence of feeling safe and feeling extremely vulnerable. The violation, the fear, the betrayal, the devastation, the enormous emotional pain and anxiety, etc., all contribute to overwhelming feelings of helplessness, loneliness and fear. The result can be very traumatic instances of anger, self-harm and very violent behaviors, just to name a few. Nightmares are common. The contention from here what we are really observing here is that PTSD and the Orphaned Spirit are very much alike.

CAN CHRISTIANS BE DEPRESSED OR SUFFER FROM MENTAL ILLNESS?

Christians are susceptible to everything that non-Christians might experience. Christians can experience mental illness and suffer from deep depression. There are Christians who have committed suicide. As we talked about earlier, we are capable of drifting out of Godly authority such that we are capable of just about anything man can conceive of - including murder, suicide, or other hideous sins. Certainly, there are those who make a passionate profession of faith, yet ultimately drift into a lifelong lifestyle of witchcraft or homosexuality. Others might succumb to massive depression or significant mental illness. Yet, we believe that once you have truly accepted Christ as you savior, you are indeed saved. Only the Father knows for sure, of course. But it is also our position that the Father will never truly let you slip out of His hands:

"My sheep listen to my voice; I know them, and they follow me. I give them eternal life, and they shall never perish; no one will snatch them out of my hand. My Father, who has given them to me, is greater than all; no one can snatch them out of my Father's hand. I and the Father are one." (John 10:27-30)

317

The Walk Applied

God can and will provide ample opportunities for healing, but the Christian must take advantage of them. We are certainly free to walk away if we choose to. If we choose to walk away, then the very real question comes to the fore: were they really saved to begin with? There is no final conclusion here; decide for yourself. That said, we are certain of this: if you want to be healed, God will make the way. If you elect to walk away from Godly authority, then it seems highly doubtful you were ever saved in the first place.

REASONS WHY CHRISTIANS ARE NOT AT PEACE

Thoreau wrote: *"The mass of men lead lives of quiet desperation. What is called resignation is confirmed desperation."* As a pastoral therapist over the last 25 years, I have had the enormous and humbling privilege to mentor, disciple, minister and restore well over 100 hurting Christian men and couples. I will go so far as to say the number one problem that Christians experience is they are not at peace. Be it anxiety, depression, overwhelming despair or resignation, many Christians are not at peace, and they do not feel safe.

Indeed, after over 25 years of ministering to Christians, I have become convinced that many Christians simply believe many wrong things about a true relationship with Jesus. Christians are not at peace for many of the following reasons:

LACK OF UNDERSTANDING
OF THE TRUE IDENTITY IN CHRIST

Many Christians do not see themselves as new creations in Christ. Indeed, they do not see themselves according to their true spiritual identity. We teach that we are:

318

The Walk Applied

Spiritual creatures living a spiritual existence placed in the natural according to God's purpose plan and will to bear lasting fruit for the Kingdom"

Unfortunately, many Christians do not understand what it means to be a new creation. Without that understanding, it is virtually impossible to appreciate the "peace that passes all understanding".

A LACK OF AN UNDERSTANDING OF THE FOUR LINES OF AUTHORITY AND SUBMISSION

The New Testament gives 4 "lines" of authority and submission:

FAMILY – EMPLOYER – CHURCH - GOVERNMENT

A fundamental appreciation of how we are to participate in these institutions is vital to understanding how the new creation person operates in the natural realm. We are called to honor and submit to God given authority. We are also called to handle authority in a Godly fashion. We are to be lights in the darkness. We are also commanded to always bless and never curse – the Bible is very forthright about our speech. Either way, when we do not respond biblically, we can easily foment chaos.

FALSE EXPECTATIONS OF FAIR TREATMENT IN A SINFUL WORLD

We typically expect non-sinful behavior from sinners. By and large in our modern world we do get fair treatment from most people under most circumstances. No one doubts that fair treatment is certainly desirable. We take many precautions in our sinful world; it is a testimony that we do understand that we might be subject to harm or great difficulties. It is rightly maddening when we become the target of "evildoers". When we are harmed to one degree or another, there can be understandable violation, betrayal, trauma,

319

The Walk Applied

anger, disappointment, and sadness amidst our emotions. No one wants to be harmed, and few expect us to be stoic in the face of overwhelming adversity.

Jesus was clear in his admonition that we "will have trouble in this world". We live in a world where we read about harm being inflicted on those in our society every day. In spite of that, Jesus tells us to "take heart" because "He has overcome the world".

No one is saying we should be "heroically stoic" in the face of overwhelming adversity. We all need time to grieve and emotionally heal depending on the severity of the harm done.

The appropriate Biblical response is to repent, forgive, and bless. To refuse to take these 3 steps is to put yourself in judgement over those you are not allowed to judge. Another way to look at this notion is that we take "spiritual authority" over those we are not authorized to do so. Romans 2 cautions us severely against judgement and self-seeking. When we self-seek, we *"reject the truth and ... follow evil"* which brings on *"...wrath, anger ... trouble and distress"*. Romans 2 is a profoundly significant yet largely misunderstood passage that many Christians tend to gloss over. What judgement and self-seeking address is when we do not forgive those who hurt us we are sitting in judgement over them, and we become "self-seekers". Indeed, the Greek word for self-seeking is "eritheia" which actually means "chaos".

In the Walk Applied, we address the proper ways to repent and forgive and bless in a process we call "proactive forgiveness".

A FALSE PERSONAL THEOLOGY OF IDOLATRY

We love to think of ourselves as decent people who try and do the right thing the vast majority of the time. After all, we're "basically ok" because we don't do "really dreadful things". We don't like to

The Walk Applied

acknowledge the sobering truth that we are really rebellious, sinful idolaters who are only saved by God's majestic grace. The reality is that we are in rebellion against God's truth the vast majority of the time. Rip away the paper-thin façade that many of us maintain, and we'll almost certainly find a lack of peace.

A FALSE PERSONAL THEOLOGY OF PERFORMANCE

A common misconception among Christians is that the more we "avoid sin" or "do more good things", the "more Godly" we are. Galatians 5 tells us that if we keep in step with the Spirit (who leads us into all truth) then He will develop our character. Second Peter does teach that we are to "make every effort" - so there is intentionality, to be sure, but the passage tells us to add to our faith, primarily, and the "good stuff" will follow. The point is, your sins have been forgiven and taken care of. Jesus wants you to follow Him, and the rest will happen. Avoiding sin and sidestepping temptations are desirable, but they are not the object. A living, breathing, vibrant faith filled relationship with Jesus is the object. Trying to be as good as you can be a theology of works and can easily lead to anxiety and a general lack of peace.

A FALSE PERSONAL THEOLOGY OF SECURITY AND ENTITLEMENT

Many seem to believe that God should protect us from really "bad" things, despite Jesus himself telling us that we will have difficulties in this life. Grieving, anger and great emotional trauma are normal, but many Christians invite chaos and anxiety into their lives by blaming God and how dare He allow THAT to happen? While we are not saying that we should expect great tragedy any second, railing against God is certainly not the answer.

The Walk Applied

THE CHURCH HAS IN MANY CASES
NOT BEEN A SAFE PLACE

Tragically, many churches have not been the safest of places. When this happens - that you truly believe there is no one in your local church who you can confide in - shame and guilt easily become the emotional prison cell that enslaves many Christians. "They're all hypocrites!" or "I'm the only one!" or "I'll be humiliated" or "no one will understand" or any one of dozens of "fearsome" statements can easily lead to a significant lack of peace.

THEY HAVE NEVER TRULY RECONCILED
PAST EMOTIONAL TRAUMA

Many who have been traumatized or victimized carry the emotional devastation for years – sometimes even to their grave. These truly sad cases, for assorted reasons, simply cannot get past "it". Obviously, life can be truly chaotic.

THEY REFUSE TO MAKE A DECISION

There are those who either avoid or simply refuse to make a decision. Indeed, life brings on many troubling situations that are anything but easy. Should I take this job? What to do about "x"? If only so-and-so were out of my life! I really need to take a second job, but what about "y"? Anxiety and fear often set in. What to do? What if this? What if that? Suppose this? Suppose that? We can easily be frozen with indecision – which is really the fear of making a choice.

By definition, life itself is a risky proposition. Many situations that arise in life are not clear cut as to what to do. It is a very rare decision that will 100 % upside with no downside – and that's not a decision at all. Get advice and seek wisdom. Analyze it on paper. Above all

The Walk Applied

seek the Lord, pray and pray with others. Then, make your decision and don't look back.

THEY LIVE IN FEAR OF MAKING A MISTAKE

In many cases, the fear of "doing the wrong thing" or "making a bad choice" looms like a dark cloud as we ponder what to do. We all want to make the right choice – but many times we look back and say "I should have done the other. The fear of doing the "wrong thing" can indeed haunt us. Scripture tells a different story, though.

Paul writes: *"...forgetting what is behind and straining toward what is ahead..."* (Phil 3:13) - excellent advice, that! We have all made mistakes and bad decisions. Dare I say it: We've all done really downright stupid things that we look back on and shudder. But God says: *"Never will I leave you; Never will I forsake you"*. (Heb 13:5) John writes: *"I give them eternal life, and they shall never perish; no one will snatch them out of my hand."* (John 10:28) Consider the following passage that tells us that we are His no matter what:

"For I am convinced that neither death nor life, neither angels nor demons, neither the present nor the future, nor any powers, neither height nor depth, nor anything else in all creation, will be able to separate us from the love of God that is in Christ Jesus our Lord." (Rom 8:38-39)

THEY DON'T KNOW HOW TO
SET PERSONAL BOUNDARIES

Another area where people can experience great anxiety is when they don't know how to set personal boundaries with toxic people. Often times, toxic people in our lives can be a close family member or an employer or another in our various "people circles". It's all too easy in that we believe that we have to let people take advantage of us under certain conditions. Be it a simple issue of inertia ("it's always been like this and I can't change it!) or circumstance (My boss is a bully boss and I can't change it…If I stand up to them, they will fire me!) or any number of other situations, we must remember that we can change our response to it such that our anxiety level is reduced or eliminated.

I once counseled a woman who believed that it was OK for her daughter to be outrageously verbally abusive. She was literally astounded when I advised her that it was perfectly permissible to set boundaries. I instructed her that she could tell her daughter: "Look, you can yell and stomp and cuss and scream all you want, but when you are ready to speak to me like an adult with dignity and respect, then I'm ready to talk!" Then turn away, leave, and don't give her a chance to respond. We did some "role plays", as well. In a couple of weeks, the situation had changed dramatically.

I once worked for a classic bully boss. Through a series of circumstances, I learned to change my response to him, which significantly reduced my anxiety. The situation improved somewhat, as I learned to change my attitude. I began to bless him as opposed to cursing him. God showed me how I needed to change, as opposed to constantly opposing him.

There are many good references on the 'net for setting good personal boundaries. Setting common sense boundaries for yourself is a sign of maturity and good mental health. A good listing of personal boundries was found in a post on SoulCare's Facebook page:

1) It's not your job to fix others.
2) It's ok if others get angry or upset.
3) It's ok to say no.
4) It's not your job to take responsibility for others.
5) I don't have to anticipate the needs of others.

The Walk Applied

6) It's my job to make me happy.
7) Nobody has to agree with me.
8) I have a right to my own feelings.

THEY DO NOT UNDERSTAND THEIR CALLING

Heb 12:1 tells us that *"... let us run with perseverance the race marked out for us..."*

This topic is well worth re-visiting. We contend that this ponderous passage is telling us that God has a particular path he wants us to walk. In other words, each and every one of us has a specific call on their life. In the sanctification process, we believe that God wants us to seek Him and via the Holy Spirit, He will guide us into the calling he has set aside for us. Your individual call may be as simple as to be a prayer warrior – much like Anna at the Temple in the New Testament. Or perhaps you have been called to be a mighty evangelist – ala Billy Graham. There are many types of callings in God's economy. A friend expresses it this way: "My call: that's easy - I have been called to be the Godliest husband and father I possibly can! How do I know this? God has clued me in that He has set aside one of our children for something out of the ordinary, and it's my responsibility to make sure they are discipled properly!" Whatever your personal call, God assures us that He will give us rest and peace for our soul. We revisit Jer 6:16:

"This is what the LORD says: stand at the crossroads and look; ask for the ancient[eternal] paths, ask where the good way is, and walk in it, and you will find rest for your souls."

Virtually all translations use the word "ancient" in this passage, but the Hebrew *"owlam"* is more properly translated "eternal". By finding and following your call you will have your life purpose and as well as rest for your soul.

The Walk Applied

A FUNDAMENTAL MISUNDERSTANDING OF REPENTANCE AND FORGVINESS.

We revisit this important topic. Many Christians are confused when it comes to repentance and forgiveness. Some think they are essentially the same. Others are not quite sure which is which or what either really mean. In any case, a clear understanding of both concepts is required for a Christian to have peace. The difference is fairly straightforward.

Forgiveness applies to a person's sin or a sinful action. We ask or seek forgiveness regarding something we did or how we may have offended someone. We forgive those who have wronged us. We seek God's forgiveness for our sin.

Repentance means to cast off a wrongful belief. Thus, I might repent of my pride belief or my façade belief. To repent means to turn the other way, but it does not mean that we will necessarily cease doing what we have been doing. Repentance means to cast away an idolatrous belief and ask God to work in us to grow a Godly belief to replace the idolatry. It is most unfortunate when we hear admonitions like this: "You didn't repent properly!" or "You must not have meant it, or you would not have done it again". Statements like this - and others that are similar - indicate a very flawed and judgmental view of repentance. That said, repentance does imply intentional action on your part to replace the flawed belief system that may underlie the external sin issue. 2nd Peter tells us that we are to "make every effort" to increase our faith. In other words, we are to be intentional.

32€

The Walk Applied

HEALING APPROACHES

What follows should not be interpreted as a "step-by-step" recipe. We will present and discuss various approaches to the healing and restoration process. There are no hard and fast rules when you step into the role of walking alongside someone. When you enter the arena of being used by God to walk with someone, consider it a high honor to help restore a hurting person. Symptoms of the lack of peace and the overwhelming need for healing typically include the following:

Anxiety	Fear	Guilt
Shame	Worry	Anger
Confusion	Temptation	Health
Job problems	Money concerns	Relationships
Family issues	Spouse concerns	Parent problems
Terror concerns	Depression	Secret sin
Regrets	Unforgiveness	Envy
Lust	Sexual problems	Loneliness
And many more…		

All the unanswered questions that lead to paranoia and confusion! The list can go on and on: I'm scared! Who do I talk to? What do I say? What will they make me do? Do I need counseling? I can't afford counseling! What will people think? What will people say? What will my spouse say? What will my spouse think? What will my kids say? I'll lose all my friends! I'll lose my job!

YOU DON'T HAVE TO BE A PROFESSIONALLY TRAINED THERAPIST

It's vitally important to remember that you are not a professional counselor or legally licensed therapist. The good news is that you don't need to be one to simply come along side someone and be a Godly agent in someone's healing. The truth is that most of the time,

327

The Walk Applied

you don't need to be a counselor. The Walk Applied is deeply rooted in what the Bible has to teach us about healing.

MINISTERING TO HURTING CHRISTIANS

The passages quoted opening this chapter from James and Galatians are clear calls that God can use us to heal and restore others. Ministry to the hurting runs the full spectrum of just about anything that you can think of, as we listed above. This morning's quarrel with their spouse. The parents of the kid who just said their first four letter word. The person who just found out they are getting laid off. The Christian who is having a terrible time financially and cannot meet their obligations. The husband who discovers his wife is having an affair. The guy who is dealing with a porn addiction. The woman whose mother died in a horrible car accident. The person who just got diagnosed with cancer. And just about anything else you can think of.

HEALING OTHERS:
THE INTENTIONAL INVESTMENT

Without question, the single most important factor is your willingness to invest in another individual. Restoring and healing another individual requires that you be willing to invest yourself sincerely in another individual. This is NOT about you; it is about God working thru you to establish a "safe place" for another individual to move from a state of anxiety to a place of peace.

More to the point, we want to always be aware that bringing a person into a closer walk with Jesus is the top priority. Never lose sight of that. Helping someone with "behavior modification is desirable and important, to be sure. But it's not the main thing.

The Walk Applied

WHEN IT JUST "AIN'T HAPPENIN"

Unfortunately, there will be those times, when, despite your best efforts, people who claim to want help will simply not respond. They will profess that they want help but will refuse to do what is necessary. Sometimes they will just not respond to you as a person. Other times they won't "buy into" the approach. There can be a myriad of reasons why "nothing seems to work!". To be sure, we want to examine ourselves at these times. Is it me? Is it them? Is there another approach I can use? Self-evaluation is a good thing, and we need to pursue it. However, it's important to remember, and I can't emphasize this enough: It's probably not you that's the issue; it's likely them. Richard Renner, in his book "Spiritual Gems" discusses the passage "don't feed pearls to swine". Our traditional understanding of that passage is that we can only witness so many times to an individual. We may keep trying to throw scriptures or testimonies at someone, but to no avail. That said, Renner interprets a deeper, better meaning to the verse. Renner points out that many times we can try to work with someone for months or even years, but they just don't seem to "get it". No matter what you do, there's always an excuse. There's always a reason why this God thing just doesn't work "for them". The complaints are always the same. For them, certain obstacles just cannot be overcome. These people seem to be frozen in time. The truth is that they have hard hearts, and much like swine, they simply want your attention. Like Renner says, they almost literally "suck the life out of you". They are consuming the valuable resource of your time – while you could be investing with someone else.

I've had individuals who had every excuse in the book and every objection you can think of. Quite honestly, they were simply wasting my time – and theirs. Far better to simply let them go and hopefully find someone else who can reach them, then to fuss and fume endlessly over "why isn't this working?!"

The Walk Applied

The solution to this problem is to evaluate once a month your progress with a given individual. If there seems to be no progress, think it through and then pray about it. By and large, if you find that there is a three-month period where there is no progress, then it's time to diplomatically and tactfully confront the individual. Be willing to accept criticism openly as well.

INITIATE CHANGE IN OUR LIVES
BY CHANGING WHAT WE THINK

"Do not conform to the pattern of this world, but be transformed by the renewing of your mind. Then you will be able to test and approve what God's will is—his good, pleasing and perfect will." (Rom 12:2)

Our "stinkin-thinkin" changes via God's Word. The theme of this book is to learn how to function in a spiritual way in the natural – in other words, change what we believe about how we operate as a spiritual creature placed in this natural realm. Preaching, teaching, and prayer contribute to how Romans 12:2 operates in our lives.

THEIR STORY

Everybody has a "story". There is no such thing as a "simple life" or a "simple person". Every person on this planet brings an extraordinarily complex conglomeration of events, history, emotions, and beliefs. Every life story has high points and low points. We live in a broken and sinful world, and we all will have encountered evil and sin at various points in our lifetime. Because of this, virtually all of us have the Orphaned Spirit to one extent or another. A sympathetic, empathetic, compassionate, non-judgmental healer will listen to the sufferer and determine the extent and causes of the Orphaned Spirit. For some, the story will only be what is germane to the situation at hand. For a few, their story may be a catharsis of their entire life as they "dump" all the venom

330

The Walk Applied

anger, and hurt from their entire life. For others, it will be something in between.

For many who are hurting, the place to start is to tell their life "story". I have had the honor of listening to numerous people who trusted me enough to share their "story". There have been many times I have been the first to hear emotionally tortured people pour out their story of how they have been deeply hurt in in their lives.

As you listen to someone's story, your job is to simply listen quietly and non-judgmentally. What you may hear may shock your sensibilities, to be sure. What happens behind closed doors in people's lives can be truly beyond belief. But shameful things do happen, and there a quite a few who have never felt secure enough to share. While they tell you their story, pray silently for them. Pray for yourself as well for wisdom and discernment as well as to be God's servant. Few will share their entire story in one or two sittings. Often, over the days and weeks ahead, they will share much of their story. Very few will share the most intimate or shameful things. No matter: be the safe place they need.

GET TO KNOW THEM!

Remember that your primary reasons for intentionally investing in a hurting individual is to allow Jesus to use you to help bring them to a state of peace as well as make them more like Jesus. Be yourself, take a *sincere* interest in them, and get to *know* them. Listen and don't judge. Emphasize confidentiality. Below are some questions and topics to help get you started.

What is their "story"?
> Are there defined emotional or traumatic "breaks"?
> Where/when/how did the Orphaned Spirit occur?
> What happened?

The Walk Applied

What is their real battle?
What idol(s) is/are being entertained?
What is their chief complaint? "Tell me about it"
　　What kinds of problems does it cause?
History of the problem(s)?
　　How long?
　　When did it start?
　　Why did it start?
Antecedents/roots of the problem:
　　What was life like growing up?
　　Tell me about your family?
What is their calling?
　　Do they know their call?
　　What have they done to pursue their call?
Miracle question:
　　If you woke up tomorrow and things were as you wanted
　　them, what would that look like to you?
What kind of a plan can we draw up for you to get there?
　　What goals & objectives can we set?
　　What obstacles do you foresee?
　　How will you plan to overcome them?
How do they see their problem?
　　Anyone else in the family have the problem?
　　What areas of your life does it affect?
What difficulties do we foresee in healing?
What emotions are being expressed?
　　Listen closely to what they are saying
What do their words express?

Happiness	Sadness	Fear	Uncertainty
Anger	Rage	Betrayal	Violation
Strength	Bitterness	Weakness	Shame
Guilt	Bitterness	etc.	

The Walk Applied

CREATING THE SAFE PLACE

Are we a sanctuary? Are we an agent of healing and restoration? Are we that safe place that people seek? Can we help people to resolve their anxiety? Are we the place where they can come without fear, guilt and shame? Many need someone who will just listen. Others want advice. There will be those who need the raw, unmitigated truth spoken over their lives. What people want and need in their lives will vary enormously. The bottom line is that virtually all Christians need other Christians to be a safe place at various times in their lives. The "Safe Place" describes the basis for a connection between the healer and the sufferer. It is a place where the sufferer feels completely safe to express themselves without fear of judgement or shame or guilt.

A critical part of healing involves you as a Christian providing that "safe place" for those who are hurting and not at peace to share their story. Henri Nouwen's take on Hospitality is instructive here: "a place where people are free to roam, yet with enough of boundaries so as to provide that "safe place". It's that place whereby the hurting person feels completely free while sharing their FULL story – no matter how shameful or guilt ridden without one iota of judgement.

RESTORATION & HEALING INTERVENTIONS

Interventions are "life changers" that moves the sufferer towards a more Godly life. We strive for positive, Godly change that brings peace as opposed to chaos. Again, the object of restoration and healing is to gravitate to peace.

333

The Walk Applied

SALVATION

The Walk Applied presumes one to be saved with an unwavering belief in God's word. The ultimate answer for healing lies in accepting and sincerely pursuing Jesus Christ. Jesus transforms people by changing what we believe.

REPENTANCE

Repentance is most assuredly the first step in healing and gravitating towards peace. If the relationship between God and the person is not a sound authority submissive relationship, then there can be little peace.

Repentance is "belief oriented" i.e., the rejection of false beliefs. Forgiveness is understood to be person oriented - that is to say, we forgive people of what they did or did not do. We ask God to forgive us when we commit sin, but we repent of our false beliefs - we repent of our idolatry.

True repentance has 2 phases. First, a heartfelt, sincere verbal rejection of all idolatry. The true repentance prayer should explicitly mention each idol of the 12. The second phase is a profound and deep emotional pledge to turn to the Lord's way. True repentance DOES NOT mean that you will never fall again, nor does it mean you will receive immediate deliverance. What it means is that you pledge to enter into a true submissive relationship with Jesus Christ. It means that you will do whatever it takes to resolve your issues through the love and power of Jesus Christ:

"Come to me, all you who are weary and burdened, and I will give you rest. Take my yoke upon you and learn from me, for I am gentle and humble in heart, and you will find rest for your souls. For my yoke is easy and my burden is light." (Matt 11:28-30)

334

The Walk Applied

FORGIVENESS

It is virtually axiomatic that if you do not forgive, you will never have peace. To not forgive is to judge, which means you are assuming spiritual authority over others that God has not delegated to you. As Romans 2 explains when we judge we are self-seeking which results in "...wrath, anger, trouble and distress". Thus, forgiveness of those in the sufferer's life of those who have hurt them is a necessity.

Recall our earlier discussion that we tend to assume or expect that others should act in a given way. Yet, there is really precious little justification for believing that. The only true expectation you can really have is sinful behavior. Obviously, there are many nice people who do act in ways that are civil and pleasing. We encounter people like this all the time. Because we like it when people are nice to us, we gravitate to that. But when people do not treat us in a way we expect, we typically respond with various levels of offense or anger. When someone has wronged you, their insensitivity can propagate the notion that "they owe me". In essence, to not forgive means you have assigned an "emotional debt" to them. We expect to somehow be "paid back" as in an apology, at a minimum. In truth, there is no such thing as an emotional debt. What's done is done. We cannot undo what has happened. I may be able to pay to have my friend's car fixed if I damaged it (an appropriate remedy, of course) but it does not change what happened. In all likelihood, my friend would consider it a "debt" that I must repay until I ensure the car is fixed. They quite reasonably expect that I will apologize for what I did, not to mention paying at least the deductible.

TRUE FORGIVENESS: ONE AND DONE

First and foremost, forgiveness is a one-time legal action and declaration that you are no longer judging that person for what they did or did not do. True forgiveness occurs when you sincerely and

The Walk Applied

completely release someone (living or dead) from any real or imagined emotional debt or liability towards you. It's also conscious, ongoing choice and a refusal on your part to entertain any further angry or hurtful thoughts about the person(s). This is no way implies that you completely forget the situation or what happened, or that you proceed as if it never happened, although that is hopefully a true consequence of forgiveness. True forgiveness should mean expressed or implied release of all anger or animosity, however justified, towards them. Obviously, that is not going to be the case in many instances. The hurt and the anger are simply too much and too overwhelming; the grief and the negative emotions rule the day. After all, we're only human and reality and common sense tell us we will experience this.

FORGIVENESS AND JUDGEMENT

We repeat: To not forgive someone is to judge them. Only God and those he appoints are to judge. To not forgive and judge is to place yourself in spiritual authority over them. Since we are all sinners, we occupy the same place before Jesus.

"You, then, why do you judge your brother? Or why do you look down on your brother? For we will all stand before God's judgment seat. It is written: "'As surely as I live,' says the Lord, 'every knee will bow before me; every tongue will confess to God.'" So then, each of us will give an account of himself to God. Therefore let us stop passing judgment on one another. Instead, make up your mind not to put any stumbling block or obstacle in your brother's way.' (Rom 14:10-13)

"You, therefore, have no excuse, you who pass judgment on someone else, for at whatever point you judge the other, you are condemning yourself, because you who pass judgment do the same things." (Rom 2:1)

336

The Walk Applied

"For if you forgive men when they sin against you, your heavenly Father will also forgive you. But if you do not forgive men their sins, your Father will not forgive your sins." (Mat 6:14-15)

"PROACTIVE FORGIVENESS"

"Do not let any unwholesome talk come out of your mouths, but only what is helpful for building others up according to their needs, that it may benefit those who listen. Get rid of all bitterness, rage and anger, brawling and slander, along with every form of malice. Be kind and compassionate to one another, forgiving each other, just as in Christ God forgave you." (Eph 4:29-32)

We advocate a process called "proactive forgiveness" when called on to forgive. Forgiveness simply means to declare that you legally release them from any sort of an emotional debt – real or implied; deserved or not. By doing so, you take yourself out of unlawful spiritual authority over them, and you quit judging them. The process is straightforward; practicing it is another thing entirely.

- Praying in the name of Jesus, pronounce that you release and forgive them from any expressed or implied emotional debt.
- Bless them by name in the name of Jesus.
- Never talk badly about them again. (i.e., do not curse them)
- Never talk badly about the situation again.

When you think about the situation, praise God that He got you through it and that He is healing you. Feel free to cry out about how badly you were hurt and how hard it is to work through the healing and restoration and recovery. Express your grief and sadness to Him. The point here is not to deny what has happened but to try and focus on your healing and not the incident or situation itself.

The Walk Applied

Whenever you think about the person in relation to the same situation again, pray that God will bless that individual. No doubt, you'll have to do this many times!

DEALING WITH THE
HURT AND THE ANGER

TRY TO DE-PERSONALIZE THE SITUATION:
Without question the most difficult task is to dispense with the hurt and the anger. Many times, the hardest thing to do is to take the first step. In a lot of cases, you, the offended, may be downright inconsolable. The hurt and anger can be absolutely overwhelming. This is by no means unusual. It is perfectly normal to express your deep anger and overwhelming pain that you feel. However, try (if you can) to resist the temptation to personalize it. Obviously, this can take some time. It goes without saying that calling them names is something to try and avoid.

SUBSTITUTION: If at all possible, try to begin substituting pronouns like "he", "she", or "them" for their name. Again, try to avoid the name calling. Depending on the level of hurt and betrayal, this may take several days to a few weeks – perhaps even months - to reach this stage.

FIND SOMEONE TO TALK TO: Many times, you need a sympathetic individual who you can trust to just listen to you. Job's 3 buddies were great until they opened up their mouths! You may need a professional, or a pastor or an elder. Maybe it's that very spiritual person you know.

WINDSHIELD THERAPY/THE EMPTY CHAIR/THE PILLOW: No question about it, there's those times you just have to "let 'er rip" and get it off your chest! That's where your car windshield comes in handy. It won't yell back at you; it won't judge it won't criticize you for using four letter words; and it won't take

The Walk Applied

offense. You car windshield may be the best counseling tool ever. Take a drive and find a nice quiet spot where no one can hear you and have at it. It is very effective at letting your anger out – at least temporarily. Expect to do this several times. The Empty Chair is a similar approach - just use a chair instead of going for a drive. If you can get a trusted friend to occupy the chair, that may prove beneficial as well. Another highly effective counseling tool is a pillow. You can throw a pillow and kick it, too - lots of advantages, indeed!

WRITE A LETTER THAT YOU DON'T SEND: Many have found it very helpful to write a letter that you don't send. Write it all out - vent you anger and hurt! Once you're done; *RIP IT UP AND THROW IT AWAY*. Many find this approach very therapeutic, indeed!

CONFRONTATIONS are not recommended. The majority of the time, you simply will not get the response you want. I recall a memorable confrontation. It was a situation where they were clearly in the wrong, and they had hurt me deeply. Their response was not exactly what I expected. "We're so sorry that YOU took all that in the wrong way!" and "Gee, you should have talked out YOUR misunderstanding with someone well before this!" My protestations went nowhere - it was inconceivable to them that they had done ANYTHING wrong. I left, angrier than I had been to start with. I learned 2 very valuable lessons that day. Lesson #1: If I was going to heal, it would be up to me to change my perceptions. Lesson #2: In the end, it really didn't matter. Even if they got down on the floor and begged forgiveness, I would get that satisfaction, but in the end, it would have changed absolutely nothing - at all. The past would not have changed. The hurt would not have lessened at all. In the end, it was up to me to accept what had happened and deal with it. It was harsh, indeed. But it was reality. However, some choose to go the confrontation route. Should you consider a confrontation,

339

The Walk Applied

check your expectations at the door. Hopefully, you will get what you are looking for and you will be at peace.

"For if you forgive men when they sin against you, your heavenly Father will also forgive you. But if you do not forgive men their sins, your Father will not forgive your sins." (Mat 6:14-15)

"Lord, how many times shall I forgive my brother when he sins against me? Up to seven times?" Jesus answered, "I tell you, not seven times, but seventy-seven times." (Mat 18:21-22)

"Do not let any unwholesome talk come out of your mouths, but <u>only what is helpful for building others up according to their needs, that it may benefit those who listen.</u> Get rid of all bitterness, rage and anger, brawling and slander, along with every form of malice. Be kind and compassionate to one another, forgiving each other, just as in Christ God forgave you." (Eph 4:29-32)

FORGIVENESS MYTHS

Forgiveness is certainly a major issue in the church. Millions of words have been written on the subject, yet many Christians still find themselves in great internal turmoil because forgiveness is so largely misunderstood. Indeed, the great doctrine of forgiveness remains largely misapplied. To be sure, in my own ministry with men and married couples who are hurting, I have yet to find a situation where forgiveness issues (to one degree or another) does not rear its ugly head. The result? Christians who can go on for years being miserable and nowhere near a state of peace simply because they have an incorrect interpretation of forgiveness.

MYTH: You forgave them, but you're still so angry and hurt OBVIOUSLY, you're doing it wrong, or you didn't really mean it. **TRUTH:** True forgiveness has absolutely nothing to do with how you feel. Forgiveness has nothing to do with emotions whatsoever

The Walk Applied

Forgiveness is "one and done": it is a one-time legal declaration whereby you declare that you no longer sit in judgement over another individual. Once you declare that you forgive and release them from any emotional debt - real or implied - the simple act of forgiveness is over and done; you have forgiven them. Obviously, there are almost always significant emotional and psychological considerations that need to be dealt with, but that act of forgiveness has been accomplished once and for all for that particular person and that particular episode.

MYTH: You simply can't face them after what they did. There is no way you can go to them and tell them you forgive them.
TRUTH: Nothing, absolutely nothing, obligates you go to them and face them. True forgiveness is indeed great when it's done face to face. Sometimes, it's physically impossible to face them. In the ministry, we've had many people who forgive people who have long since passed on. Many times, what you sincerely believe is a noble gesture on your part by forgiving them face to face cancan backfire badly. Also, no one should think that they have to put themselves back into a situation whereby their physical safety or mental health is threatened: that is simply not realistic. There is simply no call to confront your offender face to face.

MYTH: Forgiving means it's all forgotten, as if it never happened.
TRUTH: To believe that one can simply forget traumatic events in their lives is to suspend reality. To somehow think that the fear, terror, humiliation or that feeling of being grossly violated will somehow disappear is irrational. Forgiveness has nothing to do with any of those. Forgiveness is all about refuting your judgment of individuals.

MYTH: What they did was beyond HORRIBLE and AWFUL I was TRAUMATIZED! No one understands what they did to me! THEY DON'T DESERVE to be forgiven.

341

The Walk Applied

TRUTH: Forgiveness is nothing more than a simple legal declaration that is devoid of any emotional consideration. Forgiveness has nothing to do with the severity of the "crime". Forgiveness simply declares that you are no longer judging them. Indeed, forgiveness is a biblical command that must be observed. Many may think that this is simply a trite biblical observation, but the truth is that you will very likely condemn yourself to a life of shattered emotions until you do forgive.

MYTH: Forgiveness means I have to re-establish the relationship and I don't want to.
TRUTH: In some cases you may not have much of choice. But there is no biblical injunctive that says you must re-establish the relationship. Forgiveness merely means that you no longer judge them for what they did. You certainly may not feel anything even approaching love for them (as the Bible instructs us), but you are never commanded to re-establish the relationship.

MYTH: Forgiveness means doing something I should not have to. I didn't do this; they did this to me!
TRUTH: Again, you may think it trite or unwarranted, but Jesus forgave all of us and died a horrible death for us when He didn't have to. Jesus - your Lord and Savior – did it for you and he expects us to do the same. This is not negotiable. You don't have to do it right away, and in your flesh, you won't like it. But the Bible is very explicit on this point; there are no exceptions.

MYTH: Forgiveness is all about the relationship.
TRUTH: Forgiveness has nothing to do the relationship. It's all about how you perceive your standing in a relationship – a subtle but major distinction. When you choose not to forgive, you are continuing to put yourself in spiritual authority over someone else in a relationship. You are making yourself the judge - something Romans 2 says that we are never to do. In fact, Paul further stresses in the passage that at whatever point we judge them, we are really

342

The Walk Applied

judging ourselves. Romans 2:8 tells us we are then self-seekers. The Greek word there is "eritheia", which means to follow our own agenda regardless of what others think or do such that we cause chaos. We become self-seekers. The result, according to scripture, is trouble, distress, wrath and anger. In other words, anxiety and peace.

MYTH: Once I forgive, I'll be at peace.
TRUTH: Many times, anger and hurt can actually be increased by forgiveness. Most legitimately need time to get to the point whereby they can forgive sincerely. Getting to a point of peace can be quite lengthy. Depending on the severity of the "crime", the circumstances, and the individuals involved as well as the offended person(s) personality and psyche, it can take many weeks - even months or years to come to a place of peace. It is truly tragic that some never overcome a severe personal betrayal or violation. Some even go to their graves after many years of holding on to the anger and hurt.

PRAYER: ASKING GOD FOR HEALING

Many times, we forget that the simplest approach is to simply ask God to heal us. God's word is quite simple and clear: He wants us to live joyfully and peacefully. We point out that to live joyfully does not mean to live some sort of exuberant celebratory existence every single instant of every day. No, to live peacefully and joyfully means to acquire a lifestyle of relative peace. Your joy comes from the great hope that we have in Jesus in that there is coming a day when we will rejoice forever Christ's bride.

"The LORD gives strength to his people; the LORD blesses his people with peace." (Ps 29:11)

"Grace and peace be yours in abundance through the knowledge of God and of Jesus our Lord." (2 Pet 1:2)

The Walk Applied

"Let the peace of Christ rule in your hearts, since as members of one body you were called to peace. And be thankful." (Col 3:15)

"Now may the Lord of peace himself give you peace at all times and in every way. The Lord be with all of you." (2 Th 3:16)

PRAY TOGETHER

Never doubt the healing possibilities of praying together. When two or more go before God in true submissive worship, God will indeed answer prayer. However, we will likely be called to walk in faith. God will always answer according to His purpose plan and will. This means that God may want the person needing healing to walk a different road than we would like to see.

"Again, truly I tell you that if two of you on earth agree about anything they ask for, it will be done for them by my Father in heaven." (Matt 18:19)

THE WORD HEALS

The author of Hebrews tells us that His Word lives and it changes us. As we engage the word in our lives, it changes what we believe and our attitude. Never doubt the role the Word plays in our healing!

"For the word of God is alive and active. Sharper than any double-edged sword, it penetrates even to dividing soul and spirit, joints and marrow; it judges the thoughts and attitudes of the heart." (Heb 4:12)

"He sent forth his word and healed them; he rescued them from the grave." (Psa 107:20)

The Walk Applied

HEALING CAN BE SPOKEN OVER YOU

Encouragement, love, wisdom and counsel spoken over us often play a huge role in our healing.

"Reckless words pierce like a sword, but the tongue of the wise brings healing." (Prov 12:18)

"A wicked messenger falls into trouble, but a trustworthy envoy brings healing." (Prov 13:17)

"The tongue that brings healing is a tree of life..." (Prov 15:4)

APPROPRIATE GOD'S PEACE

Jesus tells us we can have His peace; but we must accept it! We teach the first law of prayer: If you say/ask it; and believe it; and truly trust God to do it and it is His will then He will do it in His way in His time

"And I will do whatever you ask in my name, so that the Son may bring glory to the Father. You may ask me for anything in my name, and I will do it." (John 14:13-14)

"Peace I leave with you; my peace I give you. I do not give to you as the world gives. Do not let your hearts be troubled and do not be afraid." (John 14:27)

"I have told you these things, so that in me you may have peace. In this world you will have trouble. But take heart! I have overcome the world." (John 16:33)

The Walk Applied

FAITH HEALS

The role that our faith plays as we gravitate towards peace is vital to healing. Faith is what allows us to trust God intimately in the direction and the progression of our healing. In the passage given below, it was the woman's faith in God that merited a miraculous physical healing when all else failed.

"And a woman was there who had been subject to bleeding for twelve years. She had suffered a great deal under the care of many doctors and had spent all she had, yet instead of getting better she grew worse. When she heard about Jesus, she came up behind him in the crowd and touched his cloak, because she thought, "If I just touch his clothes, I will be healed." Immediately her bleeding stopped and she felt in her body that she was freed from her suffering. At once Jesus realized that power had gone out from him. He turned around in the crowd and asked, "Who touched my clothes?" "You see the people crowding against you," his disciples answered, "and yet you can ask, 'Who touched me?'" But Jesus kept looking around to see who had done it. Then the woman, knowing what had happened to her, came and fell at his feet and, trembling with fear, told him the whole truth. He said to her, "Daughter, your faith has healed you. Go in peace and be freed from your suffering.' (Mark 5:25-34)

The passage above describes a physical healing. It's important to understand that physical healings are still a common place occurrence in God's kingdom here on earth. I am personally aware of numerous miraculous physical healings, including watching my daughter's leg lengthen. I am also aware of several documented instances of where people have been raised from the dead. None of these could have happened without faith.

True faith logically implies trust that God is real and will do what He says He will do. Without faith, you cannot be saved. It is a gift

The Walk Applied

from God. We trust implicitly that God wants to change us into more Godly people. As we pursue God over time, our faith and trust in Him increases. What that increase over time means is that we gravitate towards peace as we see Him working in our lives. We begin to understand more fully how He works and to trust Him regardless of the circumstances. As we progress, we gravitate towards greater peace because we see Him work.

ENTERING INTO GOD'S REST

"Come to me, all you who are weary and burdened, and I will give you rest. Take my yoke upon you and learn from me, for I am gentle and humble in heart, and you will find rest for your souls. For my yoke is easy and my burden is light." (Matt 11:28-30)

"Therefore, since the promise of entering his rest still stands, let us be careful that none of you be found to have fallen short of it. For we also have had the good news proclaimed to us, just as they did; but the message they heard was of no value to them, because they did not share the faith of those who obeyed. Now we who have believed enter that rest..." (Heb 4:1-3)

The concept of entering into God's rest – and thus appropriate peace – is nicely explained by www.gotquestions.org:

"Using the Israelites as an example of those who were not resting in God's promises, the writer of Hebrews goes on in chapter 4 to make the application personal, both to the Hebrew Christians and to us: "Therefore, since the promise of entering his rest still stands, let us be careful that none of you be found to have fallen short of it" (Heb 4:1). The promise that still stands is the promise of salvation through God's provision—Jesus Christ. He alone can provide the eternal rest of salvation through His blood shed on the cross for the remission of sins. God's rest, then, is in the spiritual realm, the rest of salvation. Faith, the author goes on to assert, is the key to

347

The Walk Applied

entering God's rest. The Hebrews had had the gospel preached to them, just as the Israelites knew the truth about God, but the messages were of "no value to them, because those who heard did not combine it with faith" (Heb 4:2)*. Some had heard the good news of Christ, but they rejected it for lack of faith."*

RELIEVING ANXIETY VIA PRAISE

The powerful notion of how praise heals is not typically appreciated. Read carefully through the next few paragraphs to help you understand how this extraordinary Godly mechanism works. When you begin to see how the overwhelming power of praise works, it is truly transformational. As you catch on to this idea, you will never look at your walk with Jesus in the same way again.

The passage below from Ephesians teaches us that we are to be very careful about what we say. Our speech should build one another up, and in doing so, there should be a corresponding reduction in many negative emotions. It seems intuitive that "unwholesome talk" aids and abets negative emotions and the negative ways we might see ourselves. Typically, we don't just "get rid" of bitterness, et al, as the passage describes. Certainly, we need to change our thought patterns and our self-talk. As we master new Godly thought patterns, we start to rid ourselves of the unwanted emotions that Paul describes:

" Do not let any unwholesome talk come out of your mouths, but only what is helpful for building others up according to their needs, that it may benefit those who listen. And do not grieve the Holy Spirit of God, with whom you were sealed for the day of redemption. Get rid of all bitterness, rage and anger, brawling and slander, along with every form of malice. Be kind and compassionate to one another, forgiving each other, just as in Christ God forgave you. " (Eph 4:29-32)

The Walk Applied

We note that the following passages tell us that we are to resist the Devil and he will flee. We are also to pray continually and give thanks always. In addition, we are told we are to take captive every thought! These passages present difficult challenges to say the least! How does anyone do that? Is it really even possible?

"Resist the devil, and he will flee from you." (James 4:7).

"Rejoice always, pray continually, give thanks in all circumstances; for this is God's will for you in Christ Jesus." (1 Thess 5:17)

"...we take captive every thought to make it obedient to Christ." (2 Cor 10:5)

The good news is that it is possible to comply with these Biblical commands. The further upside is that it is a lot easier than we might think - we just need to exercise faith and have an open mind. However, it's just not in the way we might think. Consider a rather strange passage in Revelation:

"Each of the four living creatures had six wings and was covered with eyes all around, even under its wings. <u>Day and night they never stop saying:" Holy, holy, holy is the Lord God Almighty, who was, and is, and is to come."</u> (Rev 4:8).

You read that correctly. Four unusual creatures all saying the same thing - repeating it over and over and over - apparently for eternity. If God provides for it in heaven, then surely, we can do it here. We conclude that if God wants us to know about this practice in His word, there surely is a lesson for us. God did not have to tell us about this practice or these unique creatures, but He does. We can infer that their purpose of praising God constantly thru eternity has a solid biblical foundation! If it is a desirable thing to mimic what God has provided for in Heaven, then the following passages take

349

on enormous significance. Without question, the thrust of verse after verse after verse is that we need to be praising God virtually continually:

"...I will extol the LORD at all times; his praise will always be on my lips." (Ps 34:1)

"My tongue will speak of your righteousness and of your praises all day long." (Ps 35:28)

"My mouth is filled with your praise, declaring your splendor all day long." (Ps 71:8)

"I will praise you more and more. My mouth will tell of your righteousness, of your salvation all day long" (Ps 71:14-15)

"My lips will shout for joy when I sing praise to you...My tongue will tell of your righteous acts all day long...." (Ps 71:23-24)

"Blessed are those who dwell in your house; they are ever praising you." (Ps 84:4)

"Blessed are those who have learned to acclaim you, who walk in the light of your presence, O LORD. They rejoice in your name all day long; they exult in your righteousness." (Ps 89:15-16)

"It is good to praise the LORD and make music to your name, O Most High, to proclaim your love in the morning and your faithfulness at night," (Ps 92:1-2)

"I will sing to the LORD all my life; I will sing praise to my God as long as I live." (Ps 104:33)

"Every day I will praise you and extol your name for ever and ever." (Ps 145:2)

The Walk Applied

"All you have made will praise you, O LORD; your saints will extol you." (Ps 145:10)

Psalm 22:3 says that God himself actually inhabits our praises!

"... O thou that inhabitest the praises of Israel." (Ps 22:3 KJV)

As Paul Billheimer points out in *"Destined for the Throne"*:

"Surely that which occupies the total time and energies of heaven must be a fitting pattern for earth. For some reason the Church at large has underestimated the importance of praise. Many have had the idea that praise is a beautiful aesthetic exercise but has little practical value. But if praise is the highest occupation of angels, there must be some valid reason for it. If heaven considers it important to maintain a chorus of praise unceasingly day and night around the throne, it must be supremely efficacious. Would God tolerate an activity and exercise in heaven that is futile and irrational?"

We recall the important notion that we are also priests:

"...you also, like living stones, are being built into a spiritual house to be a holy priesthood, offering spiritual sacrifices acceptable to God through Jesus Christ." (1 Pet 2:5)

"...But you are a chosen people, a royal priesthood, ..., that you may declare the praises of him who called you out of darkness into his wonderful light." (1 Pet 2:9)

As we recall that we are priests, we ask: What exactly did the Old Testament Priests do? One of their duties was to meditate on the word. "Meditate" appears in the OT some 18 times. It means to murmur or mutter or to speak lowly to yourself - as in under your breath. The import is that when you murmur or mutter the word or

351

The Walk Applied

praises, it forces you to concentrate on what you are saying...and significantly distracts or replaces the "stinkin thinkin". This must be done out loud - either lowly or under your breath or in usual conversational tones. This is how you counteract what's going on in your head. This technique is an Old Testament method that the priests used to use to memorize scripture. We can utilize it not only to memorize scripture, but to help us pray continually as well as pray on all occasions as the New Testament commands.

There are 2 types of "murmuring": We can praise Him continually by uttering praises to God or we can repeat a passage over and over and over. This practice of whispering and speaking repeatedly serves to reinforce God's word within you.

Never underestimate the power of this Godly mechanism and how it can change you. As we learn to continually praise God, we will find that our mind is being renewed. The Word of God changes us as we continually repeat it to ourselves. Continual praise ushers in God's presence, which will also bring peace and change.

THANKFULLNESS

"Do not be anxious about anything, but in everything by prayer and supplication with thanksgiving let your requests be made known to God." (Phil 4:6)

This famous passage is one of several that tell us to be thankful under virtually every circumstance. This "attitude of gratitude" is a state we need to gravitate to as part of our walk with Jesus. Deaths of family members, tragedy, illness, etc. will test severely our ability to be thankful under all circumstances.

Our attitude of thankfulness should be similar to that of consistent praise. We should be constantly "murmuring" and whispering praise and adoration and thankfulness to ourselves on a continual

The Walk Applied

basis. Much like we discussed constant, consistent praise a moment ago, the constant taking in of our own speech of God's word and our praise and adoration of God helps us to modify our thinking and belief system over time. Also, as we "practice" integrating thankfulness and praise, we will find that we will be able to praise and worship even during the most difficult of times, when we really need it.

THE BLESSING

"Out of the same mouth come praise and cursing. My brothers and sisters, this should not be." (James 3:10)

Blessing and cursing have been discussed several times in this book. Blessings and cursing are critical biblical topics and should never be taken lightly. When we understand that this idea is expressed more than 700 times in the Old Testament, it should be obvious we need to take the notion seriously. When we bless someone, the Old Testament accounts tell us that we are bringing them under Godly authority - with all the good things that go with it.

"Always bless, never curse" is a good way to remember this biblical injunctive. Jesus even cautioned us to bless our enemies. Consistent blessing is yet another way of renewing our minds and helping us gravitate us towards peace and healing.

SIN: "STOP TRYING TO STOP"

Quite often, sin is merely the symptom of the churning internal chaos that leads to the lack of self-control and the consequent lack of peace. If you're not at peace, you need healing. This may not be intuitive, but many times, we need to learn to "stop trying to stop" sinning. No one learns how to do anything by avoiding the wrong things. A skilled carpenter learns how to be skilled by learning correct techniques – not by learning how to avoid mistakes. Learn

353

The Walk Applied

how to do the right things right and you'll stop doing the wrong things.

There are times when "behavior modification" is called for, and counseling can be an excellent approach. The crucial distinction here is that effective behavior modification does not teach you to "stop doing the wrong thing". Behavior modification techniques are designed to teach you that you can live without whatever you are dealing with. Behavior Modification, when implemented properly, allows you "reframe" your belief. This isn't about "stopping", it's all about learning to live a more healthy way.

FORGET WHAT LIES BEHIND:
LEAVE BEHIND THE GUILT AND THE SHAME

Jesus action on that cross paid the price for our sins - past, present, and future. As we wrestle with our own guilt and shame and our idolatry, it's easy to forget that Jesus did it all. While we do not ever want to minimize the horror of our own idolatry and sin, we can rest in the peace and joy that God chooses to forget our sin and cover it with the blood of Jesus. We express our regret and resolve our guilt and shame via seeking God's forgiveness, and then worshipping Him in spirit and truth. Via the blood of Jesus, we are washed white as snow thru Jesus blood:

"Therefore, there is now no condemnation for those who are in Christ Jesus" (Rom 8:1)

"But one thing I do: Forgetting what is behind and straining toward what is ahead (Phil 3:13)

"He will not always accuse, nor will he harbor his anger forever, he does not treat us as our sins deserve or repay us according to our iniquities. For as high as the heavens are above the earth, so great is his love for those who fear him; as far as the east is from

354

The Walk Applied

the west, so far has he removed our transgressions from us. As a father has compassion on his children, so the LORD has compassion on those who fear him; for he knows how we are formed, he remembers that we are dust. As for man, his days are like grass, he flourishes like a flower of the field; the wind blows over it and it is gone, and its place remembers it no more. But from everlasting to everlasting the Lord's love is with those who fear him, and his righteousness with their children's children" (Psa 103:9-17)

GOD HAS FORGIVEN YOU, WHY CAN'T YOU?

One of the greatest impediments to healing and peace is our own guilt and shame. Paul reminds us to forget what lies behind:

"But one thing I do: Forgetting what is behind and straining toward what is ahead." (Phil 3:13)

DON'T TAKE RESPONSIBILITY
FOR OTHER'S CHOICES

We are idolaters who make sinful choices. Many worry to the nth degree over bad choices that others make. To be sure, we don't want those close to us to make harmful choices in their lives. It's normal to be very concerned about them. But it is also a great sign of spiritual maturity when we don't obsess over what others do, and properly segment that concern in our lives. Quite honestly, our worrying accomplishes very little most of the time except to give us heartburn. Like the Prodigal son, letting them go is often the solution. Those who deliberately and intentionally pursue lifestyles that are not what we would desire can actually reflect our own attempt to control someone else. In many cases, what seems like horrid choices to us may turn out well for the individual. Other times, where the lifestyle choices are clearly sinful, our own attempts to "reform" may actually push them further into trouble.

355

The Walk Applied

In any case, we are not responsible for their choices. It is unfortunately true that letting someone pursue their poor choices may be the only reasonable solution. Obviously, we need to pray for others and we may even be allowed to advise from time to time. But don't expect that the individual you are concerned about will make the choices you want. In the end it is their life, and they have the right to live it as they desire.

ACCOUNTABILITY:
REMOVE THE GUILT AND SHAME

Howard Hendricks once gave this stern warning about accountability: "A man who is not accountable is moral accident waiting to happen." Hendrick's advice could include both male and female, without question.

CONFESS TO ONE ANOTHER

"Confession is good for the soul" is an old admonition, and it remains just as true today. We will discuss accountability subsequently and how it frees us from the guilt and shame of our sins and mistakes. James gives the appropriate biblical statement:

"Therefore, confess your sins to each other and pray for each other so that you may be healed. The prayer of a righteous man is powerful and effective." (James 5:16)
Accountability, when properly done, can be a profound tool that frees one of guilt and shame. Accountability means to create that safe place where we can open up about our issues and problems. We are commanded to confess to another, so we can be healed:

"For you were once darkness, but now you are light in the Lord. Live as children of light (for the fruit of the light consists in all goodness, righteousness and truth) and find out what pleases the Lord. Have nothing to do with the fruitless deeds of darkness, bu

The Walk Applied

rather expose them. For it is shameful even to mention what the disobedient do in secret. But everything exposed by the light becomes visible, for it is light that makes everything visible. This is why it is said: "Wake up, O sleeper, rise from the dead, and Christ will shine on you." (Eph 5:8-14)

"Brothers, if someone is caught in a sin, you who are spiritual should restore him gently...Carry each other's burdens, and in this way you will fulfill the law of Christ." (Gal 6:1-2)

James points out that we need to understand the sin is a process:

"... but each one is tempted when, by his own evil desire, he is dragged away and enticed. Then, after desire has conceived, it gives birth to sin; and sin, when it is full-grown, gives birth to death." (James 1:13-15)

True accountability means it's not enough to confess the actual act of rebellion. Although that is necessary and good it also means we share what's going on in our lives - how and why were we being tempted, and why do we think we succumbed. Accountability also makes you responsible for your actions and removes guilt and shame. True accountability should mean you open up your life to a trusted, non-judgmental individual(s) of the same sex.

Accountability is really more about sharing your successes as well as your failures, concerns, and worries. A question that typically arises is that some feel that this kind of relationship should be limited to the spouse. Obviously, that's ideal. Spouses should be able to share everything. However, time and time again it has been shown that when you have a huge emotional investment in another person, it's virtually impossible to be objective. In my own experience, an offended spouse tends to turn into the "traffic cop". Usually, what they want is the offending spouse to stop the behavior that's hurting them, which is perfectly understandable. Yet, this

357

The Walk Applied

attitude tends to makes the issue all about the one who was offended, rather than healing the person who is dealing with a sin issue. Often, an offended spouse is beyond devastated and angry when the hidden, sinful behavior surfaces. Needless to say, this does contribute to a healing environment. Both may need help to heal.

TRUE ACCOUNTABILITY:
- Does not embarrass or humiliate you or "expose" you.
- Brings sin to light so you won't be saddled with guilt and shame.
- Revealing your issues means they usually lose power over you.
- Is done gently; we never berate or condemn.
- You do not need to go into great detail; just tell "jist".

ACCOUNTABILITY BASICS:
- Communicate on a regular basis: weekly is ideal.
- One on one is good; 3-4 is best.
- Pray that God will bring Godly accountability partners.
- Ask an elder or an experienced Christian that you trust.

BOUNDARIES: LEARNING HOW TO LIVE WITHOUT "IT"

"...do not give the devil a foothold." (Eph 4:27)
"...make no provision for the flesh, to fulfill the lusts thereof."
(Rom 13:14 KJV)
"...You cannot stand against your enemies until you remove it."
(Josh 7:13)

Boundaries are a _**Godly commitment**_ to resolve a weak area in your walk with God. You define a boundary so as to show that you recognize it as a weak area, and you want to honor God by no longer sinning in that area. Boundaries are an invaluable tool in that they teach you how to live without "it" or learn to moderate problematic areas in our lives. The above passage from Ephesians 4 alludes to the spiritual battle we all find ourselves enmeshed in.

358

The Walk Applied

Boundaries are nothing more than applied common sense. They really shouldn't be thought of as punishment as in how you might think of how we punish a child who gets caught being "naughty". Boundaries should be looked at as how we teach self-discipline. Boundaries are very useful when it comes to addiction. The addict has "trained" themselves over time, they have to be shown that they can live without a given behavior.

Sometimes, very strict boundaries are the only way to get addictive personalities to stop a given activity, especially at the beginning. In many cases, the only thing stopping them all is the fear of getting caught. Boundaries help to establish structure for the addict. Properly applied, they prove to the individual that they can live without the behavior. They need to *experience* that the sinful outlets are not the only way to live. Because they have almost always trained themselves in a given way they usually need to experience that they can indeed live life differently and in a more healthy way.

A very real danger with effective boundaries is in thinking that boundaries by themselves are the answer! Boundaries can delude us into thinking that we've resolved the issue, by handling the external, obvious manifestations of the sin. They can HELP to stop certain behaviors, but that's all. Boundaries can be especially inappropriate and ineffective when we start thinking that all we have to do is erect walls, and the problem is over and done with. Boundaries are only a temporary stopgap to assist the resolution of the problem. To think that you can construct boundaries that will make the problem disappear, you're fooling yourself. It's just not reality. Ultimately, however, boundaries are really only a stop gap method.

"...let us throw off everything that hinders and the sin that so easily entangles." (Heb 12:1)

359

The Walk Applied

"Nothing in all creation is hidden from God's sight. Everything is uncovered and laid bare before the eyes of him to whom we must give account" (Heb 4:13)

"For there is nothing hidden that will not be disclosed, and nothing concealed that will not be known or brought out into the open." (Luke 8:17)

ISAIAH 58 AND HEALING

We have covered Isaiah 58 before, but it bears repeating here in the healing context. Isaiah 58 has much to say about healing in how we are to serve in conjunction with our service. Note how strong God's language is as we work our way through the passage. God's emphasis could not be stronger. Verses 6 – 9a instruct us that a vital part of healing occurs when we meet others at their point of need:

"Is not this the kind of fasting I have chosen: to lose the chains of injustice and untie the cords of the yoke, to set the oppressed free and break every yoke? Is it not to share your food with the hungry and to provide the poor wanderer with shelter — when you see the naked, to clothe them, and not to turn away from your own flesh and blood? Then your light will break forth like the dawn, and your healing will quickly appear; then your righteousness will go before you, and the glory of the LORD will be your rear guard. Then you will call, and the LORD will answer; you will cry for help, and he will say: Here am I."

Verses 9b - 14 tell us that an integral part of our healing occurs when we do not judge one another:

"If you do away with the yoke of oppression, with the pointing finger and malicious talk, and if you spend yourselves in behalf of the hungry and satisfy the needs of the oppressed then your light will rise in the darkness, and your night will become

The Walk Applied

like the noonday. The LORD *will guide you always; he will satisfy your needs in a sun-scorched land and will strengthen your frame. You will be like a well-watered garden, like a spring whose waters never fail. Your people will rebuild the ancient ruins and will raise up the age-old foundations; you will be called Repairer of Broken Walls, Restorer of Streets with Dwellings."*

That we are to observe the Sabbath highlights a most critical idea. When we gather with others, we are observing God's call to corporate worship and prayer. In other words, we need to put ourselves in position to serve.

"If you keep your feet from breaking the Sabbath and from doing as you please on my holy day, if you call the Sabbath a delight and the LORD*'s holy day honorable, and if you honor it by not going your own way and not doing as you please or speaking idle words, then you will find your joy in the* LORD*, and I will cause you to ride in triumph on the heights of the land and to feast on the inheritance of your father Jacob. For the mouth of the* LORD *has spoken.*

The moral of Isaiah 58: Make a personal investment in someone. Don't judge people. Honor the sabbath.

ANNOINTING WITH OIL

Mark 6:13 and James 5:14 advocate the use of oil for healing. The use of oil for various ceremonial purposes is mentioned often in the Old Testament. The point is that the application of oil can and should be used for many different types of healing. At our church, we apply oil accompanied by prayer, blessing, as well as laying on of hands for anyone who feels the need - be it physical or emotional healing.

The Walk Applied

CHAPTER 11
THE SPIRITUAL REALM

The Walk Applied

The Walk Applied

The Bible emphasizes that we fight a conceptual, spiritual war that is unlike anything we face in the natural realm. Paul, in Ephesians 6, makes it abundantly clear:

"Finally, be strong in the Lord and in his mighty power. Put on the full armor of God, so that you can take your stand against the devil's schemes. For our struggle is not against flesh and blood, but against the rulers, against the authorities, against the powers of this dark world and against the spiritual forces of evil in the heavenly realms..." (Eph 6:10-12)

Paul further elaborates how we are to fight this war. Don't miss the idea that Paul is really emphasizing that a Biblical belief system is what it takes to fight this war. God's armor includes Truth, Righteousness, the Gospel, Faith, Salvation and the Sword of the Spirit - the Word of God.

"Therefore, put on the full armor of God, so that when the day of evil comes, you may be able to stand your ground, and after you have done everything, to stand. Stand firm then, with the belt of truth buckled around your waist, with the breastplate of righteousness in place, and with your feet fitted with the readiness that comes from the gospel of peace. In addition to all this, take up the shield of faith, with which you can extinguish all the flaming arrows of the evil one. Take the helmet of salvation and the sword of the Spirit, which is the word of God. And pray in the Spirit on all occasions with all kinds of prayers and requests. With this in mind, be alert and always keep on praying for all the Lord's people." (Eph 6:13-18)

365

The Walk Applied

Paul continues this theme in his second letter to the Corinthians. Paul hammers home how different this war really is:

"For though we live in the world, we do not wage war as the world does. The weapons we fight with are not the weapons of the world. On the contrary, they have divine power to demolish strongholds. We demolish arguments and every pretension that sets itself up against the knowledge of God, and we take captive every thought to make it obedient to Christ." (2 Cor 10:4-7)

We infer from the text that the strongholds we must demolish consist of "arguments and every pretension". We will examine these 2 terms from Thayer's Greek Lexicon. The word "arguments" comes from the Greek "logismos", which essentially means "thought" or "imagination" or "reasoning" or "judgement". More precisely, it refers to any thought that "is hostile to the Christian faith". Pretention actually reads in the text "lofty thing raised up", which comes from the Greek "hypsoma epairo", which basically means "to exalt oneself higher". In other words - raise yourself above God. So, we are to demolish prideful thoughts that are ungodly.

In this war, we observe that we do have responsibilities. We don't have the luxury of merely saying "The devil made me do it!". We have several specific marching orders

-We are to put on the full armor of God, so we can stand firm.
-We have weapons we can fight with.

Of course, there's much more that we have to be aware of:

"...sin is crouching at your door; it desires to have you, but you must rule over it." (Gen 4:7)

The Walk Applied

"...Be alert and of sober mind. Your enemy the devil prowls around like a roaring lion looking for someone to devour." (1 Peter 5:8)

A good example of how the bible teaches that the battle is spiritual is found in Matthew:

"From that time on Jesus began to explain to his disciples that he must go to Jerusalem and suffer many things at the hands of the elders, the chief priests and the teachers of the law, and that he must be killed and on the third day be raised to life. Peter took him aside and began to rebuke him. "Never, Lord!" he said. "This shall never happen to you!" Jesus turned and said to Peter, "Get behind me, Satan! You are a stumbling block to me; you do not have in mind the concerns of God, but merely human concerns." (Matt 16:21-23)

We do not believe in the context of this passage that Peter is somehow possessed by Satan. What the verse seems to be communicating is that Satan (or a powerful demon) is somehow manipulating Peter. The tone of the passage implies that Jesus is referring to Peter as Satan in a rather generic way. The lesson here is that Jesus wants us to see that it is a spiritual warfare aspect that is driving Peter, as opposed to Peter somehow acting ion some malevolent way. After all, Peter, by any measure, is indicating that he wants to save Jesus from any harm – hardly a vicious or attacking maneuver! Another example of how we are instructed that we need to see the spiritual battle is found in Mark:

"Some people are like seed along the path, where the word is sown. As soon as they hear it, Satan comes and takes away the word that was sown in them." (Mark 4:15)

Here, we see that Satan has been active in a person's belief system. Once again, we are talking about the belief system. The tone of the verse is that the individual has heard the word, but demonic forces have come against that person and caused him to disbelieve what

367

The Walk Applied

was sown in him. An astonishing example of the spiritual realm interacting with our natural realm is seen in Daniel 10:12-14 and 20-21

"Then he continued, "Do not be afraid, Daniel. Since the first day that you set your mind to gain understanding and to humble yourself before your God, your words were heard, and I have come in response to them. But the prince of the Persian kingdom resisted me twenty-one days. Then Michael, one of the chief princes, came to help me, because I was detained there with the king of Persia. Now I have come to explain to you what will happen to your people in the future, for the vision concerns a time yet to come.... So, he said, "Do you know why I have come to you? Soon I will return to fight against the prince of Persia, and when I go, the prince of Greece will come; but first I will tell you what is written in the Book of Truth. (No one supports me against them except Michael, your prince.")

We find out here is a major global spiritual conflict that we are totally unaware of. Even though Daniel's prayer was heard when he prayed and fasted, this heavenly creature (most likely an angel?) was detained because of the actions of other spiritual beings. We learn there are rulers of various earthly geographic locales. In addition, there are various ranks: "princes" and "chief princes". There are more scriptures that press home the notion of the spiritual warfare:

"... Satan has asked to sift all of you as wheat." (Luke 22:31)

"As soon as Judas took the bread, Satan entered into him. So Jesus told him, "What you are about to do, do quickly." (John 13:27)

"...to open their eyes and turn them from darkness to light, and from the power of Satan to God, so that they may receive

The Walk Applied

forgiveness of sins and a place among those who are sanctified by faith in me." (Acts 26:18)

"...hand this man over to Satan for the destruction of the flesh, so that his spirit may be saved on the day of the Lord." (1 Cor 5:5)

"Do not deprive each other except perhaps by mutual consent and for a time, so that you may devote yourselves to prayer. Then come together again so that Satan will not tempt you because of your lack of self-control." (1 Cor 7:5)

"...in order that Satan might not outwit us. For we are not unaware of his schemes." (2 Cor 2:11)

"... Satan himself masquerades as an angel of light. For we wanted to come to you—certainly I, Paul, did, again and again— but Satan blocked our way." (2 Cor 11:14)

Finally, Paul flatly states how we are to see ourselves and others:

"So, from now on we regard no one from a worldly point of view." (2 Cor 5:16)

In other words, Paul is telling us that we need to look behind the natural human behavior we might be observing. Our marked tendency is to attribute sinful behavior in ourselves and others to natural, human motivations. Scripture instructs us quite differently. Recall our earlier examination of our idolatry and our sinful flesh. Further, recall the discussion of judgement, self-seeking, and expectations that lead to "wrath, anger, trouble, and distress".

The teaching of scripture seems to be that we need to see the activities of demons (the servants of Satan) as influencing people's thoughts and provoking people into sinful actions. How this mechanism works in the way that spiritual entities are apparently

The Walk Applied

allowed to interact with us is unknown, but the Bible teaches that it occurs.

The above discussion will be unsettling for some, and that is most certainly understandable. The idea that people could infer that "well, the Devil made do it, so I'm not responsible!" The Bible is quite clear and forthright in that we bear personal responsibility for the choices we make. Implicit in the passages given above is that we each have the opportunity to choose to do the right thing. Indeed, scripture is firm in the notion that that we need to be aware that we can indeed be tempted, but it's up to us to do the right thing. From the Ten commandments to dozens of passages in scripture, we are continually commanded to make Godly moral choices. A temptation may be overwhelming at the time, but God, promises that there is always a way out.

EVE vs JESUS:
DEALING WITH TEMPTATION

We repeat this topic since it is pertinent to our present discussion.

It's an interesting exercise to compare and contrast how Jesus and Eve dealt with temptation. First, we will talk about how Jesus handled temptation, then we will discuss how Eve dealt with temptation (not very well...). Then we will finish with some general comments.

TEMPTATION: NOT EVEN JESUS WAS EXEMPT

Just to make sure we have all the bases covered, think about some general temptation considerations. First, God's Word is clear in that we will be allowed to be tempted. Even Jesus was not exempt. Most times, it will be at our weakest point. In a way, we can liken it to how pain works in our lives. Pain is, in fact, beneficial (as much as we don't like it!). If we did not have pain, how would your body know it was hurting? Pain is your body's way of communicating to you that something is wrong. Temptation in our lives tells us where we're weakest. Unfortunately, there are times we will have to work through temptation, Sometimes, it won't just "go away"; you may have to battle thru it! Temptation will occur over our lifetime, and the passages above illustrate how temptation is rooted in the spiritual battle that is going on all the time. The following passages also show how different strategies will be applied. The same tactics will be used until you change your response!

JESUS vs. SATAN (Matt 4:1-11)

"Then Jesus was led by the Spirit into the desert to be tempted by the devil. After fasting forty days and forty nights, he was hungry. The tempter came to him and said, "If you are the Son of God, tell these stones to become bread." Jesus answered, "It is written: 'Man does not live on bread alone, but on every word that comes from the mouth of God.'" Then the devil took him to the holy city and had him stand on the highest point of the temple. "If you are the Son of God," he said, "throw yourself down. For it is written: "'He will command his angels concerning you, and they will lift you up in their hands, so that you will not strike your foot against a stone.'" Jesus answered him, "It is also written: 'Do not put the Lord your God to the test.'" Again, the devil took him to a very high mountain and showed him all the kingdoms of the world and their splendor. "All this I will give you," he said, "if you will bow down and worship me." Jesus said to him, "Away from me, Satan! For it is written: 'Worship the Lord your God, and serve him only.'" Then the devil left him, and angels came and attended him.

WE WILL BE TEMPTED IN 3 GENERAL WAYS

The account given in Matthew 4 is virtually temptation 101. There is certainly no doubt that Jesus will pass this test. The purpose of

The Walk Applied

the passage is to illustrate the 3 general ways that we will be tempted.

TEMPTATION #1: TURN STONES INTO BREAD

The first temptation has to do with food. It shows us that Jesus is dealing with temptation tin his human state, while "the tempter" is apparently in a spiritual form. It's not made explicit in what form "the tempter came to him", but he does communicate with Jesus. Jesus is obviously hungry and weak after His 40 day fast. Note how the tempter prompts Jesus to mentally engage with his misleading question: "If you are the Son of God…" Jesus is propositioned to "prove" he is the Son of God by turning the stones into bread – something Jesus could easily do. This temptation is notable when we consider what Jesus tells us later in the New Testament in that He will only do what His Father tells him to do. Jesus obviously lived the credo that the Father would supply Jesus' every need. What this temptation illustrates is that we often want to fulfill our natural desires/needs on our own, rather than seeking God.

TEMPTATION #2: JUMP OFF THE TOP OF THE TEMPLE

Here, Jesus allows himself to be taken to the top of the temple. Now, it's "the devil" - presumably the same as "the tempter" - who transports Jesus to this very high place that evidently overlooks the "Holy City". The devil then quotes Psalm 91 to entice Jesus to "prove" He is the Son of God by jumping (again: "IF" you are the Son of God…). Given that it is not Jesus appointed time to die. Jesus could not and did not comply. Had Jesus accommodated the proposition, it would have falsified prophecy in the Old Testament The attempt here was to manipulate God by forcing His hand - in essence, to control God.

The Walk Applied

TEMPTATION #3: WORSHIP SATAN

Finally, Jesus allows "the devil" to take him to a very "high place". Jesus tells us it is Satan himself, and Satan is apparently quite exasperated at this point! Satan offers Jesus our world, if only Jesus will bow down before Satan. Our world already belongs to Jesus; He is a member of the Trinity, after all. This temptation illustrates the fundamental strategy of how we will be tempted to move away from the spiritual into the natural where Satan is in authority.

EVE vs. SATAN (Gen 3:1-7)

"Now the serpent was more crafty than any of the wild animals the LORD God had made. He said to the woman, <u>"Did God really say, 'You must not eat from any tree in the garden'?"</u> The woman said to the serpent, "We may eat fruit from the trees in the garden, but God did say, 'You must not eat fruit from the tree that is in the middle of the garden, and you must not touch it, or you will die.'" "You will not surely die," the serpent said to the woman. "For God knows that when you eat of it your eyes will be opened, and you will be like God, knowing good and evil." When the woman saw that the fruit of the tree was good for food and pleasing to the eye, and also desirable for gaining wisdom, she took some and ate it. She also gave some to her husband, who was with her, and he ate it. <u>Then the eyes of both of them were opened</u>, and they realized they were naked; so they sewed fig leaves together and made coverings for themselves. (Gen 3:1-7)

The first thing you might notice about the passage is that Eve let herself get involved in a conversation with "the serpent". He initiates the conversation and she allowed herself to engage. Eve focused on the object of the temptation, and we have paid the price ever since. Her thought processes as presented in the passage indicate that she rationalized and manufactured reasons why she should comply with the serpent's request. She clearly knew it was

373

The Walk Applied

forbidden to eat of the fruit; she had said so. The consequences of her rationalization were staggering and mind-boggling. We also note that Adam was either not paying attention or chose not to intervene. Some commentators contend that Adam was indeed very likely close by Indeed, the phrase "Then the eyes of both of them were opened..." is profound in that the Fall was not complete until Eve's husband - her spiritual leader - also fell.

SATAN'S STRATEGY: FOCUS ON THE OBJECT OF THE TEMPTATION

Note how both temptation scenarios begin: Both Jesus and Eve were prompted to draw their attention to the object of the temptation. In particular, note how the questions that were posed played on legitimate natural desires. The temptations were designed to draw the focus from the spiritual arena where God rules into the natural, where Satan is in temporary authority. Consider the following passages that show God has elected to allow Satan rule of the earth.

"... the prince of this world will be driven out." (John 12:31)
"... the prince of this world is coming." (John 14:30)
"... the prince of this world now stands condemned." (John 16:11)

THE RESPONSE: FIGHT TEMPTATION WITH SUPERNATURAL WEAPONS, NOT NATURAL

Jesus is the great example of how to approach the supernatural. Note how Jesus handled the situation in His weakened state:

- Jesus didn't acknowledge what was being asked of Him.
- Jesus didn't look at the object of the temptation.
- Jesus used the word of God.
- Jesus didn't "debate" the issue.
- Jesus didn't acknowledge Satan's name, except to rebuke him.
- Jesus used his God-given authority to rebuke Satan.

374

The Walk Applied

The objective is to get us to lose our focus by looking into the natural, where Satan is in authority. In doing so, we come out of peace into anxiety and chaos. We will be tempted to look at the object of the temptation, and it will usually be at our weakest point. To agree come into agreement with Satan is to be out of agreement with God and come under Satan's authority! Satan's aim is to modify what you believe at any cost and up to what he's been given permission to do. We emphasize that He wants to get you to agree with him - that brings you under his authority!

"IT IS WRITTEN"

We note that Jesus said "it is written" on all 3 temptations. The contention from here is that when you use the word in response to tempting thoughts, you must first identify it as God's word. This is what ushers in God's anointing on your speech. It's virtually the same thing as pulling the sword out of the scabbard: an allusion to Ephesians 6:17 where the Word is described as "the sword of the Spirit". The temptation here is to think that using the Word will bring about automatic relief to the potential anxiety that might be accompanying the temptation. The account in Matthew never indicates that Jesus used the word to avoid any anxiety he may have been experiencing. Certainly, we should not expect that result. The lesson to be garnered from this passage is that the use of God's word is something that we need to master over time. Remember, there are no pat solutions. God does not want us dependent on a technique! God wants us dependent on Him and Him alone!

ON ANGELS AND DEMONS

Both angels and demons are mentioned numerous times in the Bible. We see from scripture that there are virtually countless angels. Apparently, it's the same for demons although scripture implies there are significantly fewer demons. We might infer from scripture of the total number of these spiritual creatures, about 2/3 are angels. Demons appear to be the fallen angels. There are numerous resources on the 'net and in books and literally thousands of articles

Why does God allow angels and demons? God does not need angels, certainly. The contention from here is that angels and demons make our spiritual experience a very personal one. They make the battle personal to each and every one of us. If you didn't have angels or demons, the battle would never be "personalized".

ANGELS

Angels are thought to be "messengers" from God, and most scripture verses that mention angels certainly support that idea. Indeed, they are often portrayed as God's "servants". Numerous passages tell us of how they were dispatched from Heaven to carry out God's commands. Many times, we are told of how an angel is sent to assist someone. There are stories, especially in the Old Testament, whereby angels are sent on destructive missions. Certain passages that talk about angels, however, reveal interesting details about these wonderful and mysterious creatures of the spiritual realm. For example:

There is the possibility that they "eat", as Psalm 75 reports:

"Human beings ate the bread of angels; he sent them all the food they could eat." (Ps 78:25)

They can be sent on destructive missions:

"He unleashed against them his hot anger, his wrath, indignation and hostility— a band of destroying angels." (Ps 78:49)

The notion of having a "guardian angel(s)" is supported in Psalm 91 and Hebrews 11:

The Walk Applied

"For he will command his angels concerning you to guard you in all your ways" (Ps 91:11)

"Are not all angels ministering spirits sent to serve those who will inherit salvation?" (Heb 11:4)

They apparently will be very active when Jesus returns:

"The harvest is the end of the age, and the harvesters are angels." (Matt 13:39)

SELECTED "ANGEL" SCRIPTURES

"...and the enemy who sows them is the devil. The harvest is the end of the age, and the harvesters are angels." (Matt 13:39)

"At the resurrection people will neither marry nor be given in marriage; they will be like the angels in heaven." (Ps 22:30)

"For it seems to me that God has put us apostles on display at the end of the procession, like those condemned to die in the arena. We have been made a spectacle to the whole universe, to angels as well as to human beings.". (1 Cor 4:9)

"Do you not know that we will judge angels? How much more the things of this life! (1 Cor 6:3)

"A man ought not to cover his head, since he is the image and glory of God; but woman is the glory of man. For man did not come from woman, but woman from man; neither was man created for woman, but woman for man. It is for this reason that a woman ought to have authority over her own head, because of the angels. Nevertheless, in the Lord woman is not independent of man, nor is man

The Walk Applied

independent of woman. For as woman came from man, so also man is born of woman. But everything comes from God. (1 Cor 11:7-12)

"Are not all angels ministering spirits sent to serve those who will inherit salvation?" (Heb 11:4)

"For if God did not spare angels when they sinned, but sent them to hell, putting them in chains of darkness to be held for judgment..." (2 Pet 2:4)

SATAN (LUCIFER)

Satan is the King of the rebellion against God. He was originally created by God, many say, to be God's director of music. He leads and manipulates His army of demons. He is mentioned often in the scriptures, and He commands our respect. The following passage from Ezekiel 28:12-19 is widely interpreted to be about Satan:

"'You were the seal of perfection,
full of wisdom and perfect in beauty.
You were in Eden, the garden of God;
every precious stone adorned you:
  carnelian, chrysolite and emerald,
  topaz, onyx and jasper,
  lapis lazuli, turquoise and beryl.
Your settings and mountings were made of gold;
  on the day you were created they were prepared.
You were anointed as a guardian cherub, for so I ordained you.
You were on the holy mount of God;
  you walked among the fiery stones.
You were blameless in your ways from the day you were created
  till wickedness was found in you.
Through your widespread trade
  you were filled with violence, and you sinned.

The Walk Applied

So I drove you in disgrace from the mount of God,
and I expelled you, guardian cherub,
from among the fiery stones.
Your heart became proud on account of your beauty,
and you corrupted your wisdom because of your splendor.
So I threw you to the earth;
I made a spectacle of you before kings.
By your many sins and dishonest trade
you have desecrated your sanctuaries.
So I made a fire come out from you, and it consumed you,
and I reduced you to ashes on the ground
in the sight of all who were watching.
All the nations who knew you are appalled at you;
you have come to a horrible end and will be no more.'"

SELECTED "SATAN" SCRIPTURES

Even the great angel Michael, respected Satan:

"...even the archangel Michael, when he was disputing with the devil about the body of Moses, did not himself dare to condemn him for slander but said, "The Lord rebuke you!" (Jude 5)

"Satan rose up against Israel and incited David to take a census of Israel" (1 Chron 21:1)

"One day the angels came to present themselves before the LORD, and Satan also came with them. The LORD said to Satan, "Where have you come from"? Satan answered the LORD, "From roaming throughout the earth, going back and forth on it." Then the LORD said to Satan, "Have you considered my servant Job? There is no one on earth like him; he is blameless and upright, a man who fears God and shuns evil." "Does Job fear God for nothing?" Satan replied. "Have you not put a hedge around him and his household and everything he has? You have blessed the

379

work of his hands, so that his flocks and herds are spread throughout the land. But now stretch out your hand and strike everything he has, and he will surely curse you to your face." The LORD said to Satan, "Very well, then, everything he has is in your power, but on the man himself do not lay a finger." Then Satan went out from the presence of the LORD." (Job 1:6-12)

"On another day the angels came to present themselves before the LORD, and Satan also came with them to present himself before him. And the LORD said to Satan, "Where have you come from?"
Satan answered the LORD, "From roaming throughout the earth, going back and forth on it." Then the LORD said to Satan, "Have you considered my servant Job? There is no one on earth like him; he is blameless and upright, a man who fears God and shuns evil. And he still maintains his integrity, though you incited me against him to ruin him without any reason." "Skin for skin!" Satan replied. "A man will give all he has for his own life. But now stretch out your hand and strike his flesh and bones, and he will surely curse you to your face." The LORD said to Satan, "Very well, then, he is in your hands; but you must spare his life." So Satan went out from the presence of the LORD and afflicted Job with painful sores from the soles of his feet to the crown of his head. Then Job took a piece of broken pottery and scraped himself with it as he sat among the ashes." (Job 2: 1-7)

Satan is often shown to be the "Great Accuser:"

"Then he showed me Joshua the high priest standing before the angel of the LORD, and Satan standing at his right side to accuse him." (Zech 3:1)

"Jesus turned and said to Peter, "Get behind me, Satan! You are a stumbling block to me; you do not have in mind the concerns of God, but merely human concerns." (Matt 16:23)

The Walk Applied

"Some people are like seed along the path, where the word is sown. As soon as they hear it, Satan comes and takes away the word that was sown in them." (Mark 4:15)

"But when Jesus turned and looked at his disciples, he rebuked Peter. "Get behind me, Satan!" he said. "You do not have in mind the concerns of God, but merely human concerns." (Mark 8:33)

"Then should not this woman, a daughter of Abraham, whom Satan has kept bound for eighteen long years, be set free on the Sabbath day from what bound her?" (Luke 16:33)

"Then Satan entered Judas" (Luke 22:3)

"... Simon, Satan has asked to sift all of you as wheat." (Luke 22:31)

"Then Peter said, "Ananias, how is it that Satan has so filled your heart that you have lied to the Holy Spirit and have kept for yourself some of the money you received for the land?" (Acts 5:3)

"... hand this man over to Satan for the destruction of the flesh, so that his spirit may be saved on the day of the Lord." (1 Cor 5:5)

"Do not deprive each other except perhaps by mutual consent and for a time, so that you may devote yourselves to prayer. Then come together again so that Satan will not tempt you because of your lack of self-control." (1 Cor 7:5)

"...in order that Satan might not outwit us. For we are not unaware of his schemes." (2 Cor 2:11)

"...for Satan himself masquerades as an angel of light". (2 Cor 11:14)

The Walk Applied

"...because of these surpassingly great revelations. Therefore, in order to keep me from becoming conceited, I was given a thorn in my flesh, a messenger of Satan, to torment me." (2 Cor 12:7)

"For we wanted to come to you—certainly I, Paul, did, again and again—but Satan blocked our way.' (1 Thess 2:18)

"The coming of the lawless one will be in accordance with how Satan works. He will use all sorts of displays of power through signs and wonders that serve the lie," (2 Thess 2:9)

"Some have in fact already turned away to follow Satan." (1 Tim 5:15)

SELECTED "DEMONS" SCRIPTURES

Most contend that demons are thought to be the fallen angels. While some may contest this idea, what is important for us to remember is that demons do exist, and they we need to understand how they work and how we are to fight them. The following passages serve to remind us that demons are quite real, and they are apparently allowed to affect us in various ways if given permission. Some of the passages plainly claim that demons are responsible for inflicting physical ailments.

"News about him spread all over Syria, and people brought to him all who were ill with various diseases, those suffering severe pain, the demon-possessed, those having seizures, and the paralyzed; and he healed them". (Matt 4:24)

"When evening came, many who were demon-possessed were brought to him, and he drove out the spirits with a word and healed all the sick." (Matt 8:16)

The Walk Applied

"When he arrived at the other side in the region of the Gadarenes, two demon-possessed men coming from the tombs met him. They were so violent that no one could pass that way." (Matt 8:28)

"While they were going out, a man who was demon-possessed and could not talk was brought to Jesus." (Matt 9:32)

"Heal the sick, raise the dead, cleanse those who have leprosy, drive out demons. Freely you have received; freely give." (Matt11:18)

"Then they brought him a demon-possessed man who was blind and mute, and Jesus healed him, so that he could both talk and see." (Matt 12:22)

"Jesus rebuked the demon, and it came out of the boy, and he was healed at that moment." (Matt 17:18)

"... and Jesus healed many who had various diseases. He also drove out many demons, but he would not let the demons speak because they knew who he was." (Matt 1:34)

"So he traveled throughout Galilee, preaching in their synagogues and driving out demons." (Mark 1:39)

"Then he told her, "For such a reply, you may go; the demon has left your daughter." She went home and found her child lying on the bed, and the demon gone." (Mark 7:29-30)

"Jesus asked him, "What is your name?" "Legion," he replied, because many demons had gone into him." (Luke 8:30)

"Jesus had called the Twelve together, he gave them power and authority to drive out all demons and to cure diseases" (Luke 9:1)

The Walk Applied

CHAPTER 12
HEALING PASSAGES

The Walk Applied

The Walk Applied

CHAPTER 12
HEALING PASSAGES

"There was an estate nearby that belonged to Publius, the chief official of the island. He welcomed us to his home and for three days entertained us hospitably. His father was sick in bed, suffering from fever and dysentery. Paul went in to see him and, after prayer, placed his hands on him and healed him. When this had happened, the rest of the sick on the island came and were cured." (Acts 28:7-9)

GOD IS THE ONE WHO HEALS

(Psa 30:2) O LORD my God, I called to you for help and you healed me.

(Exo 15:26) He said, "If you listen carefully to the voice of the LORD your God and do what is right in his eyes, if you pay attention to his commands and keep all his decrees, I will not bring on you any of the diseases I brought on the Egyptians, for I am the LORD, who heals you."

(Deu 32:39) See now that I myself am He! There is no god besides me. I put to death and I bring to life, I have wounded and I will heal, and no one can deliver out of my hand.

(Psa 103:3) who forgives all your sins and heals all your diseases,

(Isa 53:5) But he was pierced for our transgressions, he was crushed for our iniquities; the punishment that brought us peace was upon him, and by his wounds we are healed.

(Hosea 11:3) It was I who taught Ephraim to walk, taking them by the arms; but they did not realize it was I who healed them.

The Walk Applied

THE NAME OF JESUS HEALS

(Acts 3:16) By faith in the name of Jesus, this man whom you see and know was made strong. It is Jesus' name and the faith that comes through him that has given this complete healing to him, as you can all see.

(Acts 4:9-10) If we are being called to account today for an act of kindness shown to a cripple and are asked how he was healed, then know this, you and all the people of Israel: It is by the name of Jesus Christ of Nazareth, whom you crucified but whom God raised from the dead, that this man stands before you healed.

(Acts 4:30) Stretch out your hand to heal and perform miraculous signs and wonders through the name of your holy servant Jesus.

(Acts 9:34) "Aeneas," Peter said to him, "Jesus Christ heals you. Get up and take care of your mat." Immediately Aeneas got up.

REPENTANCE

(1 Sam 6:3) They answered, "If you return the ark of the god of Israel, do not send it away empty, but by all means send a guilt offering to him. Then you will be healed, and you will know why his hand has not been lifted from you."

(Psa 6:2) Be merciful to me, LORD, for I am faint; O LORD, heal me, for my bones are in agony.

(Psa 41:4) I said, "O LORD, have mercy on me; heal me, for I have sinned against you."

(Isa 57:18-19) I have seen his ways, but I will heal him; I will guide him and restore comfort to him, creating praise on the lips of the mourners in Israel. Peace, peace, to those far and near," says the LORD. "And I will heal them."

(Jer 17:14) Heal me, O LORD, and I will be healed; save me and I will be saved, for you are the one I praise.

The Walk Applied

(Jer 33:6) Nevertheless, I will bring health and healing to it; I will heal my people and will let them enjoy abundant peace and security.
(Hosea 6:1) Come, let us return to the LORD. He has torn us to pieces but he will heal us; he has injured us but he will bind up our wounds.
(Mal 4:2) But for you who revere my name, the sun of righteousness will rise with healing in its wings. And you will go out and leap like calves released from the stall.

YOU MUST BELIEVE: FAITH

(Mat 9:21-22) She said to herself, "If I only touch his cloak, I will be healed." Jesus turned and saw her. "Take heart, daughter," he said, "your faith has healed you." And the woman was healed from that moment.
(Mat 15:28) Then Jesus answered, "Woman, you have great faith! Your request is granted." And her daughter was healed from that very hour.
(Mark 10:52) "Go," said Jesus, "your faith has healed you." Immediately he received his sight and followed Jesus along the road.
(Mark 5:28) because she thought, "If I just touch his clothes, I will be healed."
(Mark 5:34) He said to her, "Daughter, your faith has healed you. Go in peace and be freed from your suffering."
(Mark 6:5) He could not do any miracles there, except lay his hands on a few sick people and heal them.
(Luke 7:7) That is why I did not even consider myself worthy to come to you. But say the word, and my servant will be healed.
(Luke 8:47-48) Then the woman, seeing that she could not go unnoticed, came trembling and fell at his feet. In the presence of all the people, she told why she had touched him and how she had been instantly healed. Then he said to her, "Daughter, your faith has healed you. Go in peace."

The Walk Applied

(Luke 8:50) Hearing this, Jesus said to Jairus, "Don't be afraid; just believe, and she will be healed."

(Luke 18:42) Jesus said to him, "Receive your sight; your faith has healed you."

(John 4:47) When this man heard that Jesus had arrived in Galilee from Judea, he went to him and begged him to come and heal his son, who was close to death.

(John 12:40) "He has blinded their eyes and deadened their hearts, so they can neither see with their eyes, nor understand with their hearts, nor turn--and I would heal them."

(Acts 14:9) He listened to Paul as he was speaking. Paul looked directly at him, saw that he had faith to be healed

THE WORD

(Psa 107:20) He sent forth his word and healed them; he rescued them from the grave.

WISDOM

(Prov 12:18) Reckless words pierce like a sword, but the tongue of the wise brings healing.

(Prov 13:17) A wicked messenger falls into trouble, but a trustworthy envoy brings healing.

(Prov 3:17) Her ways are pleasant ways, and all her paths are peace.

BLESSING

(Prov 15:4) The tongue that brings healing is a tree of life, but a deceitful tongue crushes the spirit.

(Prov 16:24) Pleasant words are a honeycomb, sweet to the soul and healing to the bones.

The Walk Applied

HEALING (WHOLENESS) BRINGS ABOUT REPENTENCE

(Isa 19:22) The LORD will strike Egypt with a plague; he will strike them and heal them. They will turn to the LORD, and he will respond to their pleas and heal them.

(Isa 58:8) Then your light will break forth like the dawn, and your healing will quickly appear; then your righteousness will go before you, and the glory of the LORD will be your rear guard.

WE CAN HEAL THRU THE POWER OF GOD

(Jer 8:22) Is there no balm in Gilead? Is there no physician there? Why then is there no healing for the wound of my people?

(EEK 34:4) You have not strengthened the weak or healed the sick or bound up the injured. You have not brought back the strays or searched for the lost. You have ruled them harshly and brutally.

(Luke 5:17) One day as he was teaching, Pharisees and teachers of the law, who had come from every village of Galilee and from Judea and Jerusalem, were sitting there. And the power of the Lord was present for him to heal the sick.

(Acts 8:5-8) Philip went down to a city in Samaria and proclaimed the Christ there. When the crowds heard Philip and saw the miraculous signs he did, they all paid close attention to what he said. With shrieks, evil spirits came out of many, and many paralytics and cripples were healed. So there was great joy in that city.

JESUS CONFERS THE AUTHORITY ON THE 12

(Mat 10:1) He called his twelve disciples to him and gave them authority to drive out evil spirits and to heal every disease and sickness.

(Luke 10:9) Heal the sick who are there and tell them, 'The kingdom of God is near you.'

The Walk Applied

(Acts 5:15-16) As a result, people brought the sick into the streets and laid them on beds and mats so that at least Peter's shadow might fall on some of them as he passed by. Crowds gathered also from the towns around Jerusalem, bringing their sick and those tormented by evil spirits, and all of them were healed.

(Mat 10:8) Heal the sick, raise the dead, cleanse those who have leprosy, drive out demons. Freely you have received, freely give.

(Luke 9:2) and he sent them out to preach the kingdom of God and to heal the sick.

(Luke 9:6) So they set out and went from village to village, preaching the gospel and healing people everywhere.

JESUS HEALED

(Mat 4:23-24) Jesus went throughout Galilee, teaching in their synagogues, preaching the good news of the kingdom, and healing every disease and sickness among the people. News about him spread all over Syria, and people brought to him all who were ill with various diseases, those suffering severe pain, the demon-possessed, those having seizures, and the paralyzed, and he healed them.

(Mat 8:7-8) Jesus said to him, "I will go and heal him." The centurion replied, "Lord, I do not deserve to have you come under my roof. But just say the word, and my servant will be healed.

(Mat 8:13) Then Jesus said to the centurion, "Go! It will be done just as you believed it would." And his servant was healed at that very hour.

(Mat 8:16) When evening came, many who were demon-possessed were brought to him, and he drove out the spirits with a word and healed all the sick.

(Mat 9:35) Jesus went through all the towns and villages, teaching in their synagogues, preaching the good news of the kingdom and healing every disease and sickness.

The Walk Applied

(Mat 12:22) Then they brought him a demon-possessed man who was blind and mute, and Jesus healed him, so that he could both talk and see.

(Mat 14:14) When Jesus landed and saw a large crowd, he had compassion on them and healed their sick.

(Mat 14:36) and begged him to let the sick just touch the edge of his cloak, and all who touched him were healed.

(Mat 19:2) Large crowds followed him, and he healed them there.

(Mat 21:14) The blind and the lame came to him at the temple, and he healed them.

(Mark 1:34) and Jesus healed many who had various diseases. He also drove out many demons, but he would not let the demons speak because they knew who he was.

(Mark 3:10) For he had healed many, so that those with diseases were pushing forward to touch him.

(Mark 6:13) They drove out many demons and anointed many sick people with oil and healed them.

(Mark 6:56) And wherever he went - into villages, towns or countryside - they placed the sick in the marketplaces. They begged him to let them touch even the edge of his cloak, and all who touched him were healed.

(Luke 6:18-19) who had come to hear him and to be healed of their diseases. Those troubled by evil spirits were cured, and the people all tried to touch him, because power was coming from him and healing them all.

(Luke 9:42) Even while the boy was coming, the demon threw him to the ground in a convulsion. But Jesus rebuked the evil spirit, healed the boy and gave him back to his father.

(Acts 8:7) With shrieks, evil spirits came out of many, and many paralytics and cripples were healed.

The Walk Applied

NOT ALL HAVE THE GIFT OF HEALING

(1 Cor 12:9) to another faith by the same Spirit, to another gifts of healing by that one Spirit

(1 Cor 12:28) And in the church God has appointed first of all apostles, second prophets, third teachers, then workers of miracles, also those having gifts of healing, those able to help others, those with gifts of administration, and those speaking in different kinds of tongues.

(1 Cor 12:30) Do all have gifts of healing? Do all speak in tongues? Do all interpret?

(Heb 12:13) "Make level paths for your feet," so that the lame may not be disabled, but rather healed.

CONFESS TO ONE ANOTHER

(James 5:16) Therefore confess your sins to each other and pray for each other so that you may be healed. The prayer of a righteous man is powerful and effective.

GOD GRANTS PEACE

(Lev 26:6) I will grant peace in the land, and you will lie down, and no one will make you afraid. I will remove savage beasts from the land, and the sword will not pass through your country.

(Num 6:26) the LORD turns his face toward you and give you peace.

(1 Ki 2:33) May the guilt of their blood rest on the head of Joab and his descendants forever. But on David and his descendants, his house and his throne, may there be the Lord's peace forever.

(2 Ki 9:22) When Jorum saw Jehu he asked, "Have you come in peace, Jehu?" "How can there be peace," Jehu replied, "as long as all the idolatry and witchcraft of your mother Jezebel abound?"

(2 Chr 14:5-6) He removed the high places and incense altars in every town in Judah, and the kingdom was at peace under him.

The Walk Applied

(Job 22:21) Submit to God and be at peace with him; in this way prosperity will come to you.

(Psa 4:8) I will lie down and sleep in peace, for you alone, O LORD, make me dwell in safety.

(Psa 29:11) The LORD gives strength to his people; the LORD blesses his people with peace.

(Psa 34:14) Turn from evil and do good; seek peace and pursue it.

(Psa 37:11) But the meek will inherit the land and enjoy great peace.

(Psa 37:37) Consider the blameless, observe the upright; there is a future for the man of peace.

(Psa 85:8) I will listen to what God the LORD will say; he promises peace to his people, his saints-- but let them not return to folly.

(Psa 85:10) Love and faithfulness meet together; righteousness and peace kiss each other.

(Psa 119:165) Great peace have they who love your law, and nothing can make them stumble.

(Psa 122:6-8) Pray for the peace of Jerusalem: "May those who love you be secure. May there be peace within your walls and security within your citadels." For the sake of my brothers and friends, I will say, "Peace be within you."

(Psa 147:14) He grants peace to your borders and satisfies you with the finest of wheat.

(Prov 12:20) There is deceit in the hearts of those who plot evil, but joy for those who promote peace.

(Prov 14:30) A heart at peace gives life to the body, but envy rots the bones.

(Prov 16:7) When a man's ways are pleasing to the LORD, he makes even his enemies live at peace with him.

(Prov 29:9) If a wise man goes to court with a fool, the fool rages and scoffs, and there is no peace.

(Prov 29:17) Discipline your son, and he will give you peace; he will bring delight to your soul.

(Isa 26:3) You will keep in perfect peace him whose mind is steadfast, because he trusts in you.

The Walk Applied

(Isa 26:12) LORD, you establish peace for us; all that we have accomplished you have done for us.

(Isa 27:5) Or else let them come to me for refuge; let them make peace with me, yes, let them make peace with me.

(Isa 32:17) The fruit of righteousness will be peace; the effect of righteousness will be quietness and confidence forever.

(Isa 48:18) If only you had paid attention to my commands, your peace would have been like a river, your righteousness like the waves of the sea.

(Isa 48:22) "There is no peace," says the LORD, "for the wicked."

(Isa 52:7) How beautiful on the mountains are the feet of those who bring good news, who proclaim peace, who bring good tidings, who proclaim salvation, who say to Zion, "Your God reigns!"

(Isa 54:10) Though the mountains be shaken, and the hills be removed, yet my unfailing love for you will not be shaken nor my covenant of peace be removed," says the LORD, who has compassion on you.

(Isa 54:13) All your sons will be taught by the LORD, and great will be your children's peace.

(Isa 55:12) You will go out in joy and be led forth in peace; the mountains and hills will burst into song before you, and all the trees of the field will clap their hands.

(Isa 57:2) Those who walk uprightly enter into peace; they find rest as they lie in death.

(Isa 57:21) "There is no peace," says my God, "for the wicked."

(Isa 60:17) Instead of bronze I will bring you gold, and silver in place of iron. Instead of wood I will bring you bronze, and iron in place of stones. I will make peace your governor and righteousness your ruler.

(Isa 66:12) For this is what the LORD says: "I will extend peace to her like a river, and the wealth of nations like a flooding stream; you will nurse and be carried on her arm and dandled on her knees

(Jer 30:10) 'So do not fear, O Jacob my servant; do not be dismayed O Israel,' declares the LORD. 'I will surely save you out of a distant

The Walk Applied

place, your descendants from the land of their exile. Jacob will again have peace and security, and no one will make him afraid.

(Jer 33:6) Nevertheless, I will bring health and healing to it; I will heal my people and will let them enjoy abundant peace and security.

(Ezk 34:25) I will make a covenant of peace with them and rid the land of wild beasts so that they may live in the desert and sleep in the forests in safety.

(Ezk 37:26) I will make a covenant of peace with them; it will be an everlasting covenant. I will establish them and increase their numbers, and I will put my sanctuary among them forever.

(Micah 5:5) And He will be their peace. When the Assyrian invades our land and marches through our fortresses, we will raise against him seven shepherds, even eight leaders of men.

(Hag 2:9) "The glory of this present house will be greater than the glory of the former house,' says the LORD Almighty. 'And in this place I will grant peace,' declares the LORD Almighty."

(Mal 2:5-6) "My covenant was with him, a covenant of life and peace, and I gave them to him; this called for reverence and he revered me and stood in awe of my name. True instruction was in his mouth and nothing false was found on his lips. He walked with me in peace and uprightness, and turned many from sin.

NEW TESTAMENT

(Mat 10:13) If the home is deserving, let your peace rest on it; if it is not, let your peace return to you.

(Mat 10:34) Do not suppose that I have come to bring peace to the earth. I did not come to bring peace, but a sword.

(Mark 5:34) He said to her, "Daughter, your faith has healed you. Go in peace and be freed from your suffering."

(Luke 1:79) to shine on those living in darkness and in the shadow of death, to guide our feet into the path of peace.

(Luke 2:14) Glory to God in the highest, and on earth peace to men on whom his favor rests.

The Walk Applied

(Luke 7:50) Jesus said to the woman, "Your faith has saved you; go in peace."

(Luke 8:48) Then he said to her, "Daughter, your faith has healed you. Go in peace."

(Luke 10:5-6) "When you enter a house, first say, 'Peace to this house.' If a man of peace is there, your peace will rest on him; if not, it will return to you."

(Luke 12:51) Do you think I came to bring peace on earth? No, I tell you, but division.

(John 14:27) Peace I leave with you; my peace I give you. I do not give to you as the world gives. Do not let your hearts be troubled and do not be afraid.

(John 16:33) "I have told you these things, so that in me you may have peace. In this world you will have trouble. But take heart! I have overcome the world."

(Acts 10:36) You know the message God sent to the people of Israel, telling the good news of peace through Jesus Christ, who is Lord of all.

(Rom 2:10) glory, honor and peace for everyone who does good: first for the Jew, then for the Gentile.

(Rom 3:17) and the way of peace they do not know."

(Rom 8:6) The mind of sinful man is death, but the mind controlled by the Spirit is life and peace

(Rom 12:18) If it is possible, as far as it depends on you, live at peace with everyone.

(Rom 14:17) For the kingdom of God is not a matter of eating and drinking, but of righteousness, peace and joy in the Holy Spirit,

(Rom 14:19) Let us therefore make every effort to do what leads to peace and to mutual edification.

(1 Cor 7:15) But if the unbeliever leaves, let him do so. A believing man or woman is not bound in such circumstances; God has called us to live in peace.

(Gal 5:22) But the fruit of the Spirit is love, joy, peace, patience kindness, goodness, faithfulness,

The Walk Applied

(Eph 2:14-15) For he himself is our peace, who has made the two one and has destroyed the barrier, the dividing wall of hostility, by abolishing in his flesh the law with its commandments and regulations. His purpose was to create in himself one new man out of the two, thus making peace

(Eph 4:3) Make every effort to keep the unity of the Spirit through the bond of peace.

(Phil 4:7) And the peace of God, which transcends all understanding, will guard your hearts and your minds in Christ Jesus.

(Phil 4:9) Whatever you have learned or received or heard from me or seen in me - put it into practice. And the God of peace will be with you.

(Col 1:20) and through him to reconcile to himself all things, whether things on earth or things in heaven, by making peace through his blood, shed on the cross.

(Col 3:15) Let the peace of Christ rule in your hearts, since as members of one body you were called to peace. And be thankful.

(1 Th 5:23) May God himself, the God of peace, sanctify you through and through. May your whole spirit, soul and body be kept blameless at the coming of our Lord Jesus Christ.

(2 Th 3:16) Now may the Lord of peace himself give you peace at all times and in every way. The Lord be with all of you.

(2 Tim 2:22) Flee the evil desires of youth, and pursue righteousness, faith, love and peace, along with those who call on the Lord out of a pure heart.

(Heb 7:2) and Abraham gave him a tenth of everything. First, his name means "king of righteousness"; then also, "king of Salem" means "king of peace."

(Heb 12:11) No discipline seems pleasant at the time, but painful. Later on, however, it produces a harvest of righteousness and peace for those who have been trained by it.

(Heb 12:14) Make every effort to live in peace with all men and to be holy; without holiness no one will see the Lord.

The Walk Applied

(Heb 13:20) May the God of peace, who through the blood of the eternal covenant brought back from the dead our Lord Jesus, that great Shepherd of the sheep,

(James 3:17-18) But the wisdom that comes from heaven is first of all pure; then peace-loving, considerate, submissive, full of mercy and good fruit, impartial and sincere. Peacemakers who sow in peace raise a harvest of righteousness.

(1 Pet 1:2) who have been chosen according to the foreknowledge of God the Father, through the sanctifying work of the Spirit, for obedience to Jesus Christ and sprinkling by his blood: Grace and peace be yours in abundance.

(1 Pet 3:11) He must turn from evil and do good; he must seek peace and pursue it.

Made in the USA
Columbia, SC
22 June 2024

37139579R00248